Walead Beshty

33 TEXTS: 93,614 WORDS: 581,035 CHARACTERS SELECTED WRITINGS (2003–2015)

Edited by Lionel Bovier
Introduction by George Baker

JRP|Ringier, Zurich, & Les presses du réel, Dijon

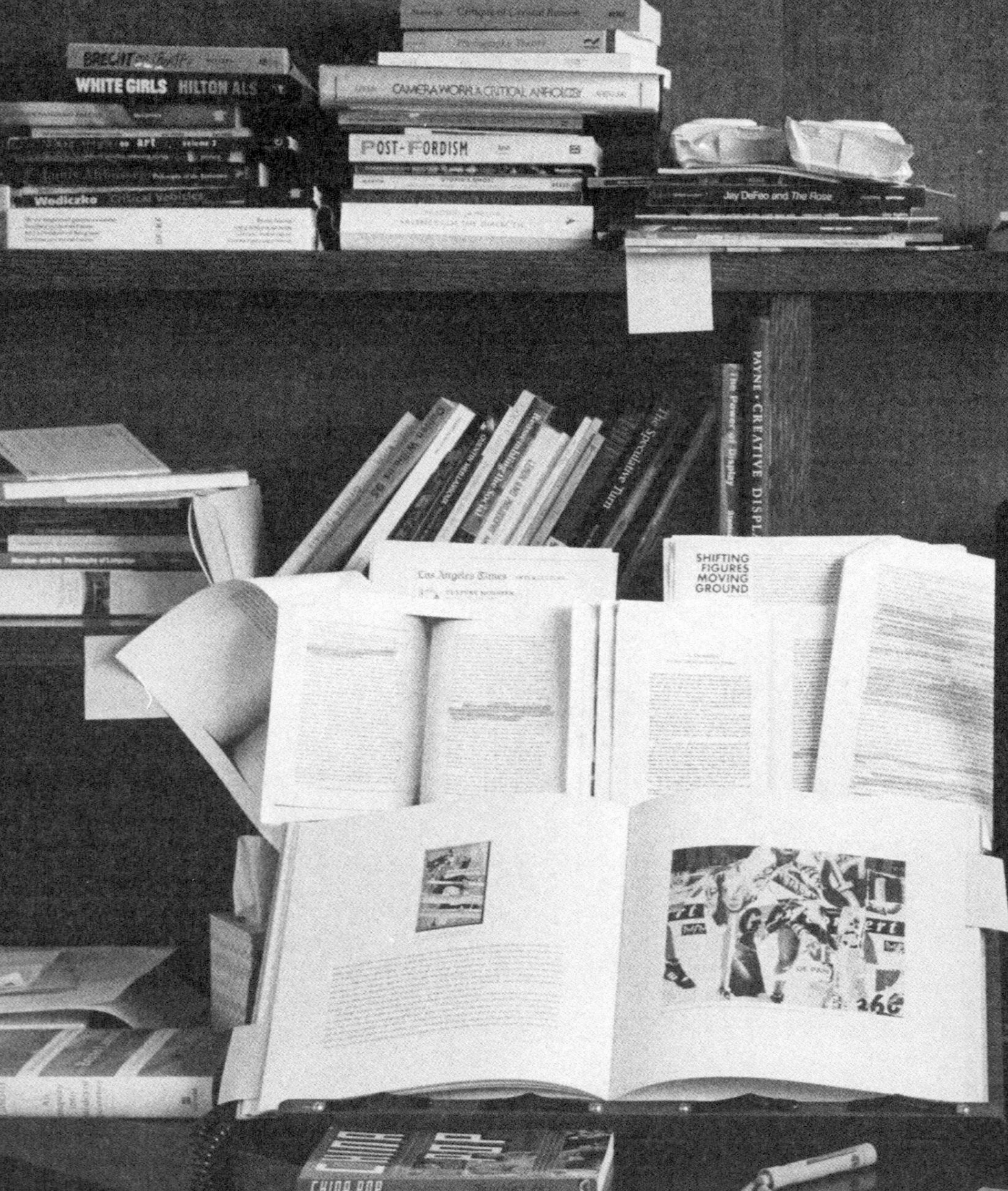

TABLE OF CONTENTS

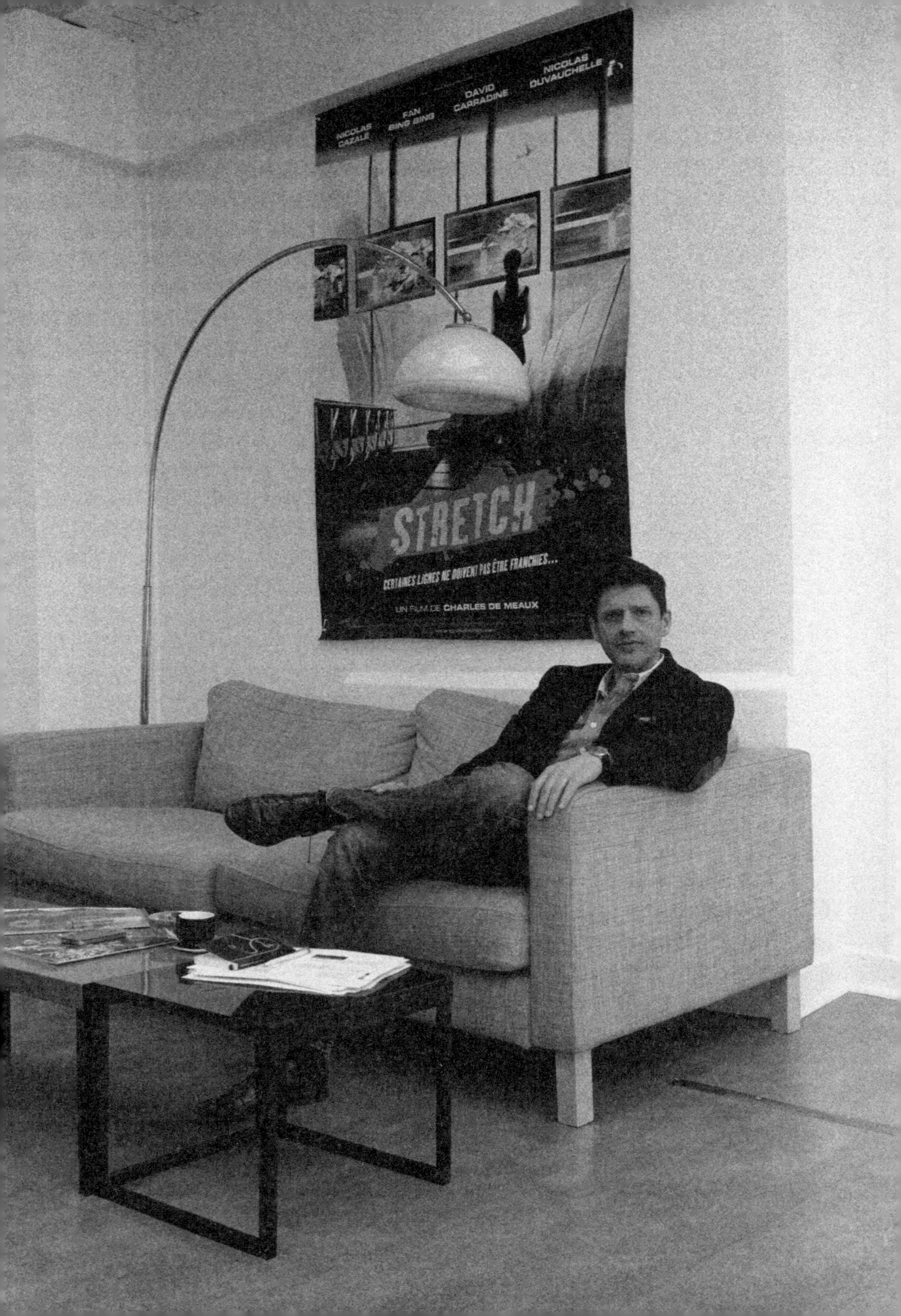

NICOLAS CAZALÉ
FAN BING BING
DAVID CARRADINE
NICOLAS DUVAUCHELLE
STRETCH
CERTAINES LIGNES NE DOIVENT PAS ÊTRE FRANCHIES...
UN FILM DE CHARLES DE MEAUX

Foreword
Lionel Bovier

Editing Walead Beshty's writings presents one, I would argue,
with the same level of complexity one would face curating a
retrospective of his work: the selection has to deal with the
quantitative importance of his production, a real diversity of
genres, a system of echoes and reappraisals, and the particular
type of analysis he performs. Part semiologist, par <u>Bricoleur</u>
(Claude Lévi-Strauss), Beshty demonstrates both a perfect
command of critical theory and an acute creativity juggling
its concepts. He likes to dismantle abstract constructs, break
them into pieces to recombine them within a formation I can
only describe as a drive to <u>operativity</u>. In fact, forms and
concepts are examined for what they can do, rather than what
they represent or the role they seem to play (in art history,
aesthetics, or art): the logic of their functioning is what
Beshty seeks, if only to draw another horizon of use to its various mechanisms. As his sculptures, photographs, and installations have demonstrated, there is a strong sense of history in
Beshty's practice, a talent to bring something to fore that wasn't
visible (or intellegible) before, and a balance between making
constructs more "transparent" and adding new layers of signif-
cation to them. The same can be said of his texts.

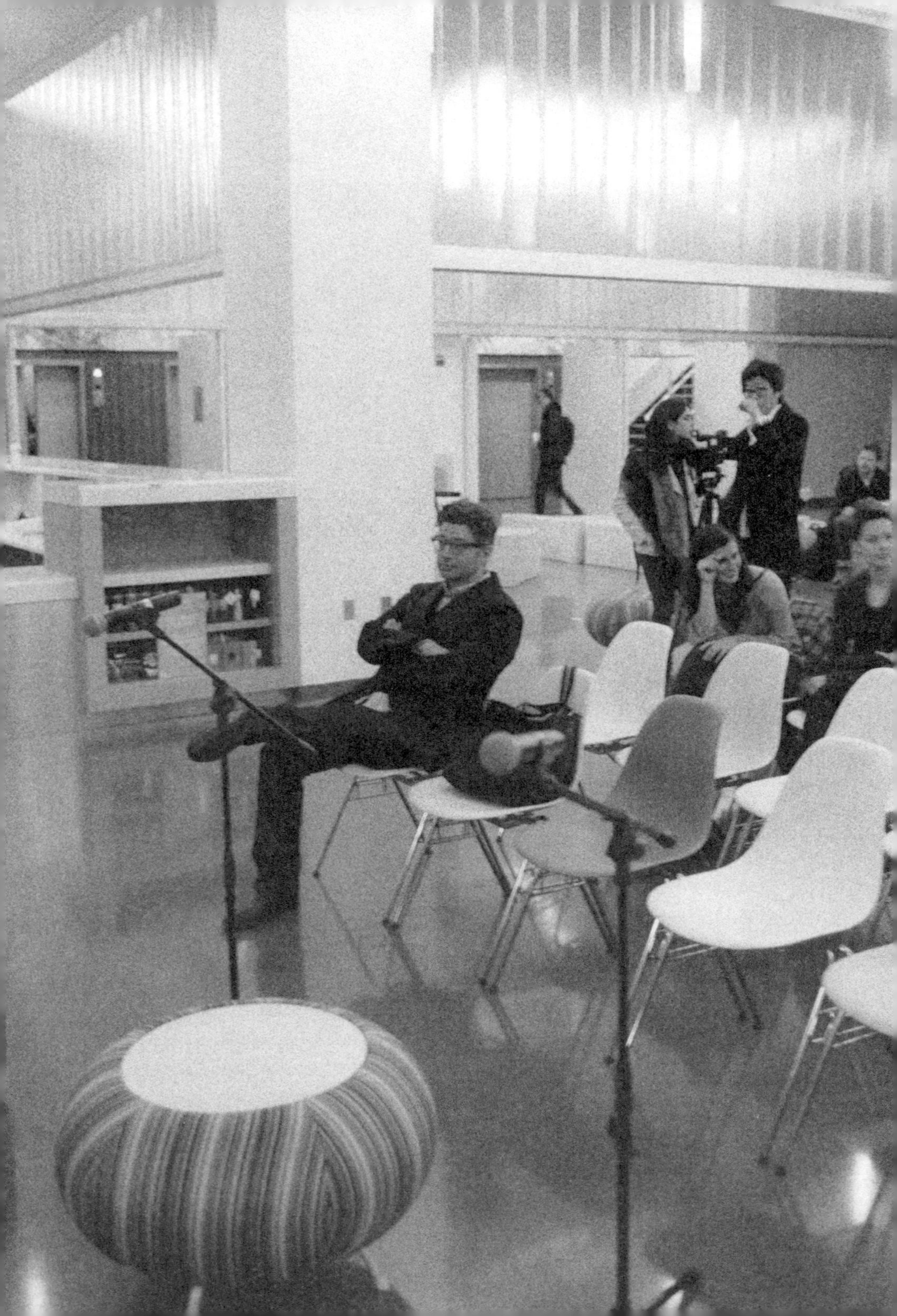

I Tiresias
George Baker

I think we are in rats' alley
Where the dead men lost their bones.

"What is that noise?"
             The wind under the door.
"What is that noise now? What is the wind doing?"
             Nothing again nothing.
                          "Do
"You know nothing? Do you see nothing? Do you remember
"Nothing?"

             I remember
Those are pearls that were his eyes.
"Are you alive, or not? Is there nothing in your head?"

—T.S. Eliot, "The Waste Land"

In an early series of photographs, the artist Walead Beshty
appears like an idiot Cindy Sherman, a more hapless Bas Jan Ader,
a postmodern photographer or performance artist gone awry.
Posing in some of the same shopping malls that I myself haunted
as a teenager in the 1980s—the Danbury Mall, the Dutchess
County Mall, sprawling architectural wastelands where one found
fried food, a new pair of parachute pants at the Chess King,

the manipulative smell of cinnamon buns, the inevitable Steven
Spielberg movie, momentary diversions in the consumerist crowd,
an after-school job—Beshty thrusts his head into the commodities on the floor and shelves, into a display case, or a pillow
case, or a miniature model of a camping tent, pressing his face
deep into a wall of party favors and fake flowers so that his
features completely disappear. Entitled The Phenomenology of
Shopping, 2002, the series depicts a kind of repeated "undeath"
of the author, who seems not only infinitely unthinking—all
body and no head—but also unable to support himself, sometimes
splayed out across the floor, sometimes stumbling forward as if
about to crawl, or leaning against the commodity displays that
provide the only armature for his otherwise lifeless, inanimate
body. The piece reads as somewhat disturbing, pathological,
but also darkly comical, as we witness the imperatives of greedy
"materialism" diverted, taken too literally, producing a pure
material thing. It is a serial photographic portrait of the artist as undead, the artist as brainless zombie.

Other early photographs exacerbated this zombie effect,
whether in the exploration of undead nature, trapped in the
interstitial zones created by the design of freeways (Island
Flora, 2005), or undead architectures, such as the failed housing
projects represented anachronistically in the stereoscopic
Excursionist Views, 2001/2005; whether in the mapping of stran-
ded political ruins like the old Iraqi Embassy to the defunct
GDR (un)recorded in the Travel Pictures, 2006/2008, or the
ongoing photographic typology dedicated to the now-disappearing
and seemingly abandoned spaces of the shopping malls that provided the sites for The Phenomenology of Shopping themselves
(American Passages, 2001-present).

"Twentieth-century debates over the politics of representation, the autonomy of art, and art's capacity for critique
still linger like disgruntled spirits on the hunt for living
bodies to inhabit." This is Beshty in his recent essay "The
Whiteness of the Whale," on fellow artist Kelley Walker. But the
trope of the undead, of the zombie, of reanimation and possession—all of this was already present in two of the first major

essays that Beshty penned, a pair of extraordinary texts, "The City Without Qualities" and "Notes on the Subject Without Qualities," that reconsidered the recent history of street photography in both its conceptualist and documentary modes. In a spirit similar to Allan Sekula's quip that the <u>New Topographics</u> photographers were the "neutron bomb school of photography," Beshty compared the emptied out spaces and melancholic architectures represented by artists as diverse as Ed Ruscha, Stephen Shore, Bernd and Hilla Becher, or Robert Adams to the simultaneous developments of the horror genre of the zombie film, the sci-fi fantasies of the apocalypse film.[1] For in these photographic projects, we confront a "vernacular" suddenly "devoid of life, the images appearing as though they were taken just after some cataclysmic event that vaporized the population ... while leaving the architecture untouched."

I underline the omnipresence of this undead metaphor in Beshty's art and writings—indeed, the crucial place of the figure of the zombie for the artist's very entrance into the practice of art criticism—not only for the importance of any individual statements or readings, but for the self-reflexive gesture that it seems to embody, a zombie paradigm coloring Beshty's understanding of the act of writing and criticism themselves.[2]

Emerging as a writer in the years after 2002 or 2003, Beshty in retrospect seemed self-consciously to step into a double critical void. First, the undead metaphor, which Beshty also names the "revolutionary undead," articulates a position on the general evacuation of art criticism and its recent confident positions—modernist or postmodernist—on critical art practices, a field that suddenly appeared as depopulated and moribund as the emptied-out cities described in Beshty's early photographic histories.[3] And so we hear the artist mourn, still lingering on the fate of contemporary photography, in an unexpected essay on the artist Boris Mikhailov:

> The art world's photographic taste for ... faux-naive
> diaries, the revivalist formalism of monolithic

transcriptions of evacuated postmodern geographies, and the glazed stares of alienated figures indicates its almost unanimous hesitance to reopen socio-political questions of representation. It suggests we are trapped in a prolonged lamentation over the defeat of liberal humanism, and the subsequent erosion of its core terms—'liberty,' 'freedom,' and 'democracy'—in a jingoist hijacking by neoconservative elements. The photographic repertoire of strategies appears reduced to the symbolic insinuation of external conditions, and an abandonment of direct intervention and contestation. In contradistinction to other practices, photography seems to have embraced a role as the conservator of a rarified aesthetic tradition, one that will likely, in time, be spoken of with the same derision that the early avant-gardes reserved for salon painting.

More specifically, we can now point to another void, sensing the manner in which Beshty's writing emerged ultimately in the face of the recent passing of the two greatest artist-critics in the specific cultural milieu that he occupies in Los Angeles. Of course the city was a focal point for the artist's apocalyptic or zombie-filled speculations. For example, Beshty cites Don DeLillo in an epigraph to a text extolling the writerly position of the visual artist Raymond Pettibon: "California deserves whatever it gets. Californians invented the concept of lifestyle. This alone warrants their doom." Or, in the "Subject Without Qualities" essay: "Los Angeles has been the backdrop for a multiplicity of destructions, easily molded to the worst we can imagine." Given the close focus on a renewed politics of photography history in Beshty's earliest major essays, given their uncanny turn to mass cultural histories of the horror film or of sci-fi, one inevitably thinks of the importance to Beshty's critical voice of the otherwise incompatible writings of Allan Sekula and Mike Kelley—both however sharing the vocation of artist-critics and artist-teachers simultaneously, two of the primary roles that Beshty now appears to extend. But he

extends the incommensurate writerly positions that these artists occupied in the massive void left by their recent passing,
with no more dialog or conversation possible.

Asked to comment on the difference of his essays from
Jeff Wall, another photographer invested in the project of critical writing, Sekula once insisted on the instability and contradictions of the artist-critic position: "If you are vain and
stupid enough to style yourself as both an artist and a critical
historian of art, as both Wall and I apparently are, you had
best follow each path to its own separate conclusions and not
expect the one enterprise to justify the other. In fact, you
best anticipate the likelihood that one role might well assassi-
nate the other."[4] The essays by Beshty gathered in this volume
are too various, their origins and tasks too multiplicitous,
to describe a singular project. This may be part of their project. But clearly, the essays that follow here are not the kind
we normally associate with the position of the "artist-critic."
There is little engagement with texts about how Beshty has made
his own projects, the kind of essay where an artist writes like
a critic, but in relation to his or her own work, explanatory
parameters, project descriptions, though Beshty has written
and published many such texts.[5] We are also not given a series
of extrinsic histories of under-known cultural phenomena, Mike
Kelley's notion of "minor histories," engaged for they are the
ideas responded to in the artist's work alone.[6] While there are
relationships of course between Beshty's practice and the writing collected here, the latter seems to have a semi-autonomy from
that "artist-critic" function of buttressing and filling out primarily one's own artistic practice. And surely, the essays that
follow distance themselves from any of the evidently false prom-
ises for critical renewal that the "creative" or paraliterary
position of the "artist-writer"—from Robert Smithson to Gregg
Bordowitz—has periodically provided. That hope is not theirs.

Beshty has written "literary" and experimental texts,
even poetic ones, though they are excluded for the most part
here. Often such texts produced art works in their wake, rather
than following and serving them, instrumentally, with, in a

specific case, the writing simultaneously constructed from the digestion of the non-literary functional writing of other art critics, from the larger field of art criticism itself. This is a description of Beshty's <u>Press Release</u>, 2008-, which seemed to inspire the series of artworks then entitled <u>Selected Works</u>, 1998/2008-, where rejected older photographs were recycled and reused, shredded and mulched, to be subsequently transformed into a solid, wall-bound mass. In an interview with Bob Nickas, Beshty explains:

> If parts of past ideas were playing into the work, why not allow the failed pieces, the false starts, the dead ends, to materially comprise the recent works? I often do this with texts, repurposing old fragments in new essays. I published a text that started out as "White Cow in a Snowstorm" under several different titles and in different configurations. Each version becomes an index of what was happening at the time—the editor or editors I'm working with, and the particular restrictions on the text. I've done this with interviews also, pasting in previous answers, previous ideas, snippets. That was the idea behind the <u>Press Release</u> (2008-) I've been using, which is simply made up of quotes from reviews of my previous shows arranged in rhyming couplets. It's actually a form of poetry from antiquity called "cento," which means "patchwork" in Latin. I'm drawn to the anonymity of forms like this. I think this is what I'm always left to do, piece things together, find some logic to connect things, and then excrete that logic, to do my part and then send it off, give it away to be digested again.[7]

As the workaday, desiccated art criticism was translated into rhyme and into collective poetry, so too the destroyed, dead-end photographs metamorphosed into other forms, appearing like excised architectural fragments or relief sculptures, or some new form of abstract, materialist painting. If such mobility can be linked to the citation by Sekula above, to what I have described as the inherent "instability" of the artist-critic position, its embrace by Beshty could also be called a work not just of intense internal contradiction, but of possible transformation. And so we witness almost half the essays here circling around a critical historicization and theorization of photography, from an artist who resists the label "photographer," and has simultaneously dedicated most of these essays to dismantling the notion of "photography" as a medium category. And so we follow a series of almost traditional art critical essays—monographic explications, catalog texts, reviews of exhibitions, examinations of the rhetoric of contemporary projects like so-called "relational aesthetics"—from a writer who at times seems to have declared war on art criticism itself, on a rebuttal and annihilation of the claims of almost all of its major recent practitioners (from populist critics like Dave Hickey to figures like Miwon Kwon, Benjamin Buchloh, and myself).[8]

Indeed, it was through Beshty's attempt at a complete dismantling of my critical essay "Photography's Expanded Field" that I first came to know the artist, after having participated in a panel discussion with him here or there, after seeing him around the Los Angeles scene, at this show or that bar. Beshty's essay "Abstracting Photography" amounts to the most serious critical engagement that my text has ever received. I also believe it to comprise a major misreading of that text, one that forced me as a critic to respond, but in a way I hope was more productive than defensive—perhaps as he intended—opening up new insights and shared terrain.[9] For in fact, the artist's critique opened my eyes to the specific aesthetic and philosophical concerns he was developing, and the shared concerns of our pair of essays has led to a crucial dialog—crucial for me, and one deepened immensely by the gathering of the ideas explored now in these collected texts. I want to bring this introduction to a conclusion by outlining very schematically some of the major productive tropes that have characterized Beshty's criticism as it has developed so far.

There are diatribes in what follows against crucial modernist and postmodernist notions alike, outgrowths of Beshty's

undead critical paradigm, his repeated evisceration of the
modernist value of medium-specificity, for example, or postmodernism's central "impulse," as Craig Owens called it, of allegory. And yet other marginalized practices from both critical
epistemes find themselves embraced, extended, and re-used. From
the discourse of postmodernism, Beshty returns repeatedly in
the essays that follow to the idea of a "minor" aesthetic, Mike
Kelley's key notion as inherited from Gilles Deleuze and Félix
Guattari, the adaptation, as Beshty puts it in his essay on
photographer Annette Kelm, of a "dominant tongue" to "provisional ends." Linked to this desire, but more surprising for
its throwback effect, would be Beshty's critical rehabilitation
of the postmodernist figure of the "Bricoleur," an entity chased
from the artist's essays on Boris Mikhailov to Gabriel Kuri,
described there as "an agent who refuses the iconicity of products for the brute fact of their material existence." An idea
inherited by postmodern criticism from anthropology, from
Claude Levi-Strauss, Beshty's re-imagination of the Bricoleur
invokes a figure who speaks "with" things, not through them,
less a disaffected, passive "voyeur" or "flâneur" than a "scavenger of everyday life," one that "tinkers with established meanings, investigating cultural symbols whose meanings are locked
up tight, and [then] pries them open, reimagining the place of
the object, and in turn, our place among objects." Beshty names
such labor a kind of "ethics of production."

From modernism, meanwhile, Beshty has been closely associated with both a re-imagination of abstraction, and a rede-
scription of its parallel concept of aesthetic autonomy (which
for Beshty, in his essay "Absolu Avec Vache," can instead be seen
as historically emerging from contingent, "marginal zones"—
"pirates and radicals hide like rats in the walls, housewives
stage mini-revolutions in their kitchens, office workers in
their cubicles"). Even more important would be Beshty's rethinking of the central avant-gardist tactic of the readymade—here
opening onto not just the Bricoleur's language of material,
obdurate things, but onto the "expression of a silent agreement"
in the social field, a thrusting of art into the fraught social

space of negotiations and mediations, of institutional but also
more broadly social and materialist contextualization.

From these ideas develop the major, and perhaps surprising, subset of essays collected here devoted to contemporary
forms of painting—Kelley Walker and Laura Owens, the extremely
beautiful meditation on Jay DeFeo and the short but crucial
text devoted to Allan McCollum—a medium that Beshty approaches
for its recent turn to its outside (mapped most thoroughly in
his introduction to a collection of essays published on "the aesthetics of ethics"), its immersion in contingent social networks
that surround the painterly object, "autonomy" inverted or
recast in an almost mystifying and vast "expanded field." Such
descriptions of painting run parallel to the extreme materialist
contingency of Beshty's own recent work, seemingly intensifying
a "photographic" concept through a literal and fraught embrace
of indexicality and physical receptivity, in works like his
Copper Surrogates (2009-) that receive all manner of marks from
the world that surrounds them, from their functional use or
institutional dissemination—from Beshty's dealers, or art han-
dlers, from gallery employees and also from viewers. Or we could
think of his many sculptural objects made in clear or mirrored
glass, completely beholden to and echoing the sizes and shapes
determined by a corporate or social agent, taking on the parameters of the common sizes of a FedEx box—and then shipped in
that box to arrive at their destinations most often shattered
and cracked, formed and then worked upon in complete acquies-
cence to a readymade social system of distribution itself.

While this passivity seems undead enough, zombie-like
in its total submission to the corporate or bureaucratic world,
Beshty has thought of these developments differently. "Blankness,
alienation, boredom, and disembodiment: white people love this
shit." We have returned to Beshty's text on the paintings of
Kelley Walker, "The Whiteness of the Whale," but the tone is
about to change. He continues: "This is not yet the end of the
story. We still have the press, we have the book, the magazine,
the painting, and the poster as hard currency; the scanner
itself hums with the factories that delivered it. All those hands:

the trucks, the labor, the oil derricks that give us the plastics, the store clerks who shelve and reshelve the units in
the networks of chain stores." An immense social field is being
imagined, an immersion in social context that at one point
Beshty calls a "complete reversal of the bourgeois readymade,"
the idea that he cites from an unnamed contemporary artist who
made the otherwise unbelievable claim "that the most important
artistic precedent in recent times [is] American Apparel," the
artist "asserting that it is effective as art because it sustains
itself outside of art." In an important moment in his essay
"Lesson: Notes for an Introductory Lecture," Beshty then
extends such social embeddedness, such social expansion, to his
own writing, and ultimately to all the texts collected here:

> This text, like all texts, conceals its collective nature.
> While it may be written in a singular voice, it is an
> amalgam of many entities. The voices of editors, design-
> ers, printers, binders, shippers, shop assistants who
> sold it to you or the web page you ordered it from are
> all at work in the text, covered over by inks and var-
> nishes, cellophane and UPC codes. All of these together
> constitute the meaning of this text. Yet we are taught
> not to think of all the mediations through which it has
> passed, changing along the way; we think instead of a
> single individual addressing us. When we consider that
> we are actually dealing with an object, an object with
> a history specific to itself that is comprised by a mul-
> titude, we are allowed a possible opening into expansive
> worlds within worlds.

We have come far on the trajectory begun by Beshty in <u>The
Phenomenology of Shopping</u>, thrusting his head almost erotically
into a field of readymade commodities, entering fully and completely into the undead life of the capitalist product, the
zombie-mode of the author as a pure, unthinking materiality.

    We have, in fact, come full circle. For the stake, we
might say, of the "revolutionary undead" ultimately could

be said to be life; it is reanimation; the "table-turning" of
the commodity fetishism long ago described by Marx followed
through its full panoply of inversions. And so we hear Beshty
describing the "minor photography" of Annette Kelm as a kind
of "parasite within the dormant body of its host," one that
"outlives its confines, drawing new life from dead flesh." We
hear Beshty's repeated call for what he calls a criticism that
would be "affirmative," distanced from the "language games"
of "negative critique": "Rather than insisting on looking into
pictures and asking what they might be 'of,' we should ask what
they do—or, more precisely, what we make them do and what we
do around them," Beshty insists, in a recent essay not collected
here. "In other words, one should ask how aesthetics organize
our relations to one another in concrete terms, which is to
discuss these issues affirmatively. This would be a discussion
of life rather than death—the life that we lend to depictions
of all sorts, the life that is plainly in view if we decide to
see it."[10]

The call for an affirmative criticism that Beshty issues
here emerges, actually, in its most radical form in the most
surprising subset of essays in this collection. I am thinking of
what can only be called Beshty's "feminist" criticism, the con-
certed attention to women artists and producers—from Annette
Kelm to Luisa Lambri, from Sharon Lockhart to Laura Owens,
Andrea Fraser, Jay DeFeo. This attention is striking enough,
sustained and intensifying over time, but more important would
be the manner in which Beshty's most crucial insights seem consistently to emerge in these specific texts: the essay on Fraser
inspiring a whole series of "introductory essays" in dialog with
her work, but also raising the confrontation with "one of the
most profound political questions facing the artist [...] whether
it is possible for art to propose a better world, a more ethical
world, despite it being so deeply implicated in inequity";
the essay on Lockhart returning us to the connections and social
extensions that Beshty has long been chasing, provoking the insight that "all practices contain other practices embedded within them, each telling provisional histories of art," provisional

histories that "are legible and exist in multitudes extending in every direction, if we choose to see them."

This vision of connections, of transitions and transformations, of social extensions, provisionality, contingency—all of this builds upon what might be identified as critical values and tropes espoused in Beshty's other essays. But they are values most often traced back to the feminist critique of art: the larger insistence on phenomenological concreteness, on a deep investment in corporeality, on empathic connection (all of this already in Beshty's critique of the postmodernist critique of documentary in his essay on Boris Mikhailov). To my mind, it finds its most radical statement in Beshty's reading of the work of painter Laura Owens, in the essay "The Story of O," where we hear the artist reflecting on Owens' rethinking of painterly gesture. This is an idea that she has articulated through an experience not linked to the clichés of male virility but instead a female erotics, to the female orgasm and sexual pleasure, with painterly gesture and gendered experience unthought together. This play with the terms of gesture and gender brings Beshty to invoke unexpectedly the figure of the seer Tiresias, turned from a man into a woman, from Ovid's tale of transformation that is the Metamorphoses.

And we remember Tiresias, stand-in for the artist, for the poet, for the writer, undead figure from the mythological past surveying the blasted heath of our modernity. We remember Tiresias, as he suddenly appears in T.S. Eliot's epic poem "The Waste Land":

> I Tiresias, though blind, throbbing between two lives,
> Old man with wrinkled female breasts, can see
> At the violet hour, the evening hour that strives
> Homeward, and brings the sailor home from sea,
> The typist home at teatime...

We remember Tiresias, hermaphroditic, hybrid figure of insight and foresight both:

> I Tiresias, old man with wrinkled dugs
> Perceived the scene, and foretold the rest—
> I too awaited the expected guest.

We remember Tiresias, filled by empathy, emptied like the undead, simultaneously:

> (And I Tiresias have foresuffered all
> Enacted on this same divan or bed;
> I who have sat by Thebes below the wall
> And walked among the lowest of the dead.)

Beshty invokes Tiresias as a description of Owens' painterly strategy. But the passage cannot help but sound self-reflexive, pointed at the other and the self simultaneously. For indeed the artist is describing, not himself so much, as the figure of the critic. We hear a profound description of the critical act as Beshty has here imagined it. We hear about Tiresias:

> ... who as punishment was turned into a woman by the god Hera. After spending eight years as a female, he would be called upon for the expertise he acquired to settle a bet between Hera and Zeus as to which sex derived more pleasure from copulation. To this, he responded that while male pleasure was as narrow as it was explosive, like a swiftly running stream, female pleasure was as wide and deep as the sea. His answer displeased Hera, making Zeus the winner of their bet, and as punishment Hera struck him blind, as though he, in confessing this, had betrayed a secret held in confidence. Blinding was unmistakably a sexual punishment, a second phallic smiting, a reminder of both the frailty and limitations of the masculine. To ameliorate this act, Zeus gave him divine insight, his vision no longer one that pierced and separated, but one that connected things together, that experienced the world as a sequence of trajectories rather than an accumulation

of finite things and impermeable surfaces; it was a
transformation from the divisive to the cursive. His was
now a vision attuned to fluidities.

NOTES

1. Sekula developed this take on the <u>New Topographics</u> by 1976, but in print the
statement post-dates Beshty's essays, see "Translations and Completions," in the
exhibition brochure <u>California Stories</u> (Christopher Grimes Gallery, Santa Monica
2011), n.p.

2. In a recent essay, I found myself describing certain forms of the current practice of art criticism as "zombie" modes, undead voices living off of a kind of apocalyptic self-annihilation of the possibilities that criticism once supported. See
"Late Criticism," in Daniel Birnbaum and Isabelle Graw, eds., <u>Canvases and Careers
Today: Criticism and Its Markets</u> (Sternberg Press, New York and Berlin 2008).

3. In "Notes on the Subject Without Qualities" Beshty's reflexive account of this
critical void becomes explicit at several points. For example: "Most Marxist social
critics operate within this paradox of positioning--while defining capitalism as an
expansive, all encompassing social system able to subsume any revolutionary opposition to its workings, the very act of writing in opposition seems an exception to
the rule. It seems these inquiries are launched from a kind of non-place, a voided
location from which critical distance and meta-operations can still function while
their very ability to do so is suspect. The limitless and displaced quality that
is ascribed to capitalism as a concept seems to mirror the very subjectivity from
which their critique is mounted, the dismantling of the authorial subject mirroring
the supposed dissolution of the nation-state under globalization. As we look outside, we see only the reflection of ourselves."

22

4. Allan Sekula, "Found Paintings, Disassembled Movies, World Images: Allan Sekula Speaks with Carles Guerra," Grey Room 55 (Spring 2014), p. 136.

5. See, for example, the collaboration with Eric Schwab, "Willkommen in Irak!" in Walead Beshty, Selected Correspondences 2001-2010 (Damiani, Bologna 2010), p. 113-121; and the texts such as "On the Conditions of Production of Pictures Made by My Hand with the Assistance of Light," or "On the Conditions of Production of the Multi-Sided Pictures Works," collected in "Procedural Texts," Walead Beshty: Natural Histories, 2nd ed., (JRP|Ringier, Zurich 2014), p. 190.

6. Kelley published an important consideration of the artist-critic position as his own introduction to the second volume of fellow artist John Miller's collected writings, see "Artist/Critic?" in Mike Kelley, Foul Perfection: Essays and Criticism ed. John C. Welchman (MIT Press, Cambridge 2003), especially p. 224: "I believe it is important to maintain that art still has a critical function in our society, no matter how much this notion is tested. The problem for the artist/critic now is to escape the present limitations of critical discourse. For the form of criticism itself is an aesthetic consideration."

7. See "Open Source: Walead Beshty in Conversation with Bob Nickas," Walead Beshty: Natural Histories, p. 108. A version of Press Release is reproduced on p. 111. "White Cow in a Snowstorm" has been included in the current anthology, published now as "Absolu Avec Vache (and the Spectre of the Gun)" in its latest—but perhaps not final—form.

8. Beshty prescribes a comically murderous fate for populist critics in the essay "Lesson: Notes for an Introductory Lecture." His essay on Michael Asher vehemently rejects the readings of Asher's work by his primary recent critics such as Buchloh and Kwon.

9. Someday I should perhaps write in detail about my specific disagreements with Beshty's reading of my essay; suffice it to say, contrary to the artist's depiction of the text, "Photography's Expanded Field" does not amount, as I see it, to a defense of the ontological category of photography but rather embraces its dismantling; it elaborates a model that would distance itself from medium-specificity; it celebrates rather than mourns the dispersal of practices that Beshty describes as the melancholic failure of the essay's model at its own end. It borrows an "old" postmodernist tactic for its re-use and transformation in the present, like Beshty has himself often done. My initial response to Beshty's "Abstracting Photography" was entitled "Photography and Abstraction," in Alex Klein, ed., Words Without Pictures (Aperture, New York 2010).

10. Walead Beshty, "The Looking-Glass Worlds of an Invention Without a Future: Some Notes on the Possibilities of Photographic Anachronism," published in Camera of Wonders, exh. cat. (Kadist Art Foundation, San Francisco 2015).

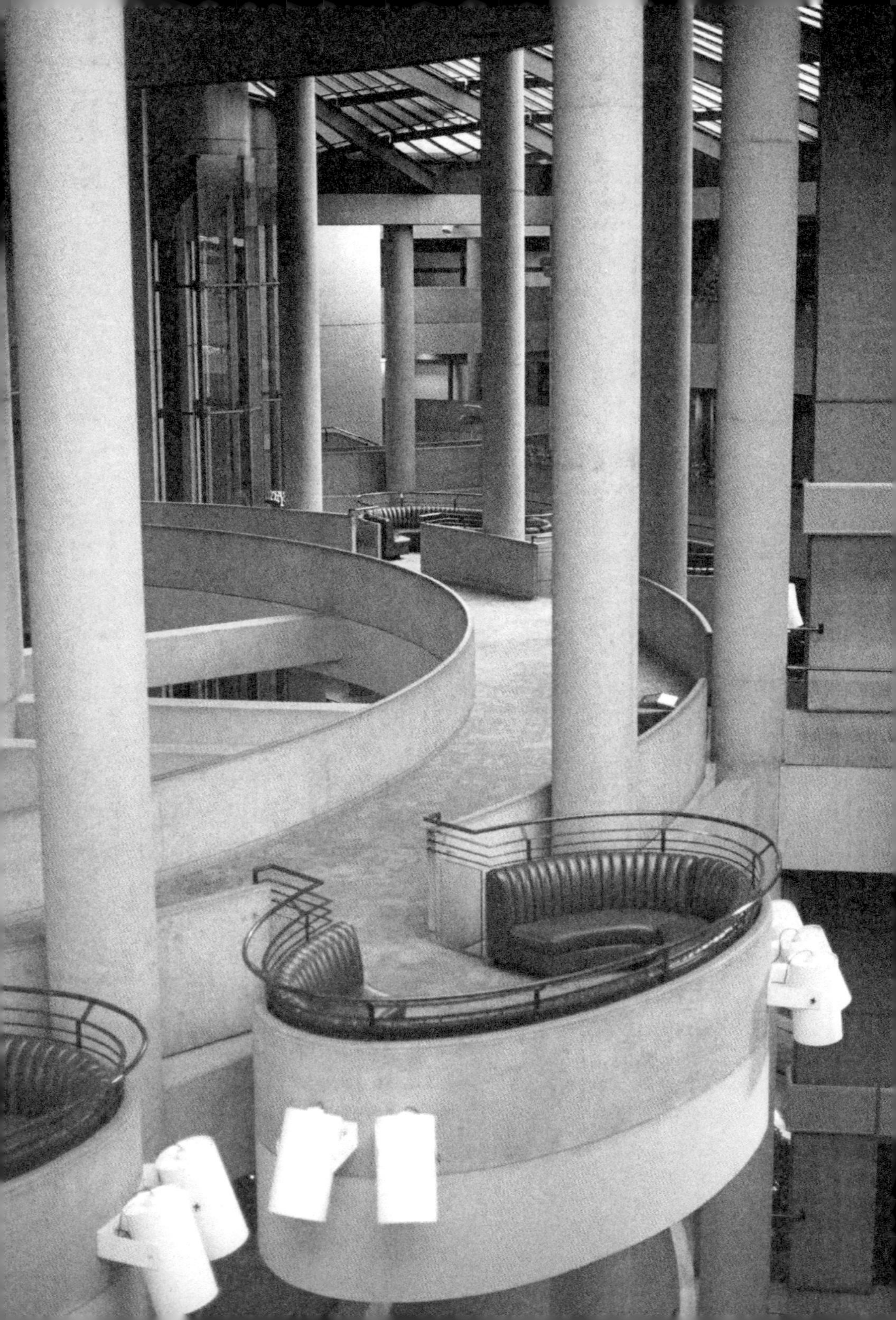

The City Without Qualities: Allegorical Landscapes and the Revolutionary Undead

First published as "The City Without Qualities: Photography, Cinema, and the Postapocaltyptic Ruin," <u>Influence Magazine</u>, issue 1 (October 2003), p. 50-61; reprinted in English and Swedish in <u>Site Journal</u> (Spring 2004), p. 2-4; reprinted in French in <u>Trouble</u> journal (Spring 2005), expanded for a lecture delivered at the Blanton Museum of Art, University of Texas, Austin, 2010.

LOCATION SCOUTING

I could not help thinking of the scene in which poor Gregor Samsa, his little legs trembling, climbs onto the armchair and looks out of his room, no longer remembering (so Kafka's narrative goes) the sense of liberation that gazing out of the window had formerly given him. And just as Gregor's dimmed eyes failed to recognize the quiet street where he and his family had lived for years, taking Charlottenstrasse for a grey wasteland, so I too found the familiar city, extending from the hospital courtyards to the far horizon, an utterly alien place. I could not believe that anything might still be alive in that maze of buildings down there; rather, it was as if I were looking down from a cliff upon a sea of stone or a field of rubble, from which the tenebrous masses of multistory car parks rose up like immense boulders.
—W. G. Sebald, <u>The Rings of Saturn</u>

Through the whole inner city run these streets … lined with houses that do not seem to be made for living in, but appear as a stone stage set for people to walk between.
—Walter Benjamin, <u>Briefe I</u>

> It is … fitting that in the center of a monstrous house,
> there be a monstrous inhabitant.
> —Jorge Luis Borges, The Book of Imaginary Beings

In the fall of 1966, Ed Ruscha hired a pilot and a photographer
to make images of what is arguably Los Angeles' most ubiquitous, yet also most banal urban location. From a mile up, Ruscha
recorded a vision of the car-infested metropolis through the
bombardier's scope, compressing the beige expanse of low flung
buildings into graphic black and white patterns. The resulting
book, Thirtyfour Parking Lots (1967), confronts us with something between the formal repetition of serial geometry and the
aerial reconnaissance of urban sprawl, as if enormous Sol LeWitt
wall drawings had somehow found their way into these cluttered
landscapes, only to be spotted by oil stains and garnished in
shrubbery. In a 1976 interview, Ruscha related his interest in
this bird's-eye view to a childhood desire to build a scale model
of all of the houses on his early-morning paper route, a model
he could "study like an architect standing over a table planning
a city."[1] It was the emptiness of his neighborhood streets at
dawn that inspired the young Ruscha's fantasy, a fascination
that later manifested itself in the one restriction he placed
on these pictures: that only completely empty lots be photographed. His aerial views of these mundane necessities of
contemporary car culture propose an expansive landscape of
desolately sprawling interstitial spaces: an endless maze of
deserted parking lots, vacant thoroughfares, and evacuated
strip malls. In Thirtyfour Parking Lots Ruscha posits a world
where the vernacular is devoid of life, the images appearing
as though they were taken just after some cataclysmic event
that had vaporized the population of Los Angeles, while leaving
the architecture untouched.

    Despite their contrivances, this collection of photo-
graphs resonates with a peculiarly uncanny aspect of Los Angeles
life in the late 1960s and early 1970s. Los Angeles County's
size and seeming prosperity notwithstanding, downtown Los
Angeles was virtually evacuated on weekends, when the population

26

of its office towers returned to their suburban homes, and its
streets lay empty save the homeless, a shadow population that
became all the more apparent when their workaday counterparts
were absent. This very phenomenon made downtown Los Angeles
the perfect shooting location for the first post-apocalyptic
science fiction film of the 1970s, The Omega Man (1971). Lacking
the funds to build expansive stage sets to simulate an abandoned city, or those required to cordon off acres of city blocks
during the workweek, the director and producer took a drive
through downtown LA on a Sunday to discuss their, at that
point doomed, film project. What they realized on that drive was
that downtown LA was already emptied, already postapocalyptic—a fact that made them able to follow through with the project despite their budgetary restrictions. The Omega Man's via-
bility as a production signaled a real crisis of the American
city that Ruscha recorded, one that mirrored the dystopic imaginings at the heart of the film. The desolation of downtown Los
Angeles was not unique; one could imagine many suitable locations for the film, if only in the all-too-common dead downtowns
of mid-sized postindustrial American cities. Detroit, Worcester,
Newark, Trenton, or Albany would all provide a suitable location for the escapades of Heston's violently estranged flaneur.
But Los Angeles was different; it was not a dying city, even
though its downtown looked, to quote Heston, like "the neutron
bomb went off." What the makers of The Omega Man understood
was that the city and the dystopic fantasy they were out to
create were in fact one and the same.

The late 1960s and early 1970s were marked by a radical
change in the character of the American city. Caught in a state
of violent flux between the swift decline of its old localized
industrial base and the rise of multinational corporate formations whose productive abilities no longer dictated their proximity to ports or railroads, its inhabitants were increasingly
polarized by class, race, and politics. Not surprisingly, this
conflict spilled out into our collective imaginings. The
American city came to embody the uncertainty of the time, as
both the literal and symbolic site for the clash of disparate

social groups, and an exemplar of the massive rift that was developing in the country as a whole. The road movie, whose run through the 1970s was kicked off by the surprise hit <u>Easy Rider</u> (1969), and followed by films like <u>Zabriskie Point</u> (1970), <u>Vanishing Point</u> (1971), <u>Two-Lane Blacktop</u> (1971), and <u>The Sugarland Express</u> (1974), directly addressed the desire for escape from the struggles of modern urban life. The troubled inner cities and the humdrum safety of suburbia inspired a yearning for the freedom of the open road and the simplicity of small-town living. This retreat, however, did not ensure the happiness it promised. The characters populating these films often found themselves alienated and detached, finding only temporary solace in the territories between urban hubs. More often than not what they end up finding, and are subsequently destroyed by, is more terrifying than what they sought to escape. The message being that away from the norms, mores, and control of modern society, life becomes just as Thomas Hobbes surmised, "nasty, brutish, and short."

With no where to escape to, it seems natural that fantasizing about complete collapse would be attractive to movie going audiences, prompting a parallel resurgence of the disaster film. These films provided the opportunity to escape through the cataclysmic collapse of the familiar, allowing us to relive historical catastrophes as in the 1975 film <u>The Hindenburg</u>, or imagine future ones, such as in <u>Earthquake</u> (1974) or <u>The Towering Inferno</u> (1974). Although the disasters varied in their form (either natural or manmade, either future or past) the message remained the same: mankind's hubris would be its own undoing—that is, if it was not already. As it progressively isolated itself in tract homes and suburban shopping malls, the American middle class fantasized about a cathartic end, all too aware that the war machine of the 1940s was directly responsible for the availability and low cost of new comforts, and the sense of security to which they had grown accustomed. Moreover, westward expansion itself had the air of horror about it, having been paved by the labor of the "invisible" and racially stratified migrant working classes who now found themselves isolated

in the dead downtowns of former metropolises. As the environmental historian Patricia Nelson Limerick duly notes, "the price
of progress [in the American West] had registered in the smell
of burnt flesh."[2] An undercurrent of apocalyptic anxiety thus
condensed around the mass-cultural fantasy of the television
set and the movie screen. The disaster film is a conservative
genre by nature, promising rebirth through cleansing fire,
a freedom from social ills through collective suffering, and the
possibility to reimagine society, typically in microcosmic form
through a cadre of heroic survivors who exemplify the most
noble qualities of the culture they left behind. In this context, the disaster film provides the perfect escape from historical memory: only from the ashes of total catastrophe can we
begin anew.

Jacques Derrida famously suggested that ours is the age
of the post-apocalyptic. By the time mass culture became cogni-
zant of Hiroshima and Nagasaki, the Holocaust, and Stalinist
purges, the apocalypse was no longer the object of morbid speculation, but a familiar historical fact, one that was hidden in
plain sight. The presence of these horrors unearthed the dark
side of modernity, the industrialization of death, which turned
technocratic utopian ideals on their head, and cut to the core
of any concept of humanist progress. It was an awareness that
could not be limited to psychopathic despots alone, too many
average people had to be complacent, and it implicated humanity
as a whole. The dictum that, if it happened to them it could
happen to us, transformed into the understanding that _if it
happened to them, it has happened to us_. In other words, the
worst we might imagine happening, the worst we might imagine
inflicting, has already come to pass. Peter Galison's argument
against the commonplace that the commercialist zeitgeist of post
World War II America was the sole cause for the radical transformation of the American urban landscape leading to postwar
suburbanization drives this point home. Galison emphasizes the
significance of federal tax incentive programs to major industries that effectively transformed what had been rural landscapes at the suggestion of the military industrial complex,

which were based upon the results of the strategic bombing surveys that were formed to assess the effects of Allied air power
on the landscapes of Germany and Japan. Unlike the oft-cited GI
Bill, which gave direct subsidies to young families purchasing
homes, these programs provided financial incentives to vital
industries that were deemed vulnerable military targets in the
event of nuclear war—encouraging them to spread out from traditional urban centers. The Strategic Bombing Survey was the
key document in this process of decentralization, and its conclusions often segued into morbid speculations about the effects
of similar bombing strategies within US borders. As Galison
states, "Looking at Hiroshima, Nagasaki, and Hamburg, Survey
personnel began to see their own cities," and as early as 1946
the Survey pushed for, "a reshaping and partial dispersal of
national centers of activities."[3] As a result of both their
direct and indirect influence on the shapers of public policy,
detailed guidelines were issued for identifying likely targets,
and their repositioning outside of densely populated urban
centers. This was closely followed by the initiation of billions
of dollars in tax incentives for the decentralization of the
American city, funding both the relocation of heavy industry,
and massive public building projects to provide the infrastructure they required, not least of which was the interstate high-
way system which enabled greater commuting distances and
increased interstate commerce, allowing for industries, and
those who worked in them, to move farther from the urban hubs
than had ever been possible. New sprawling industrial hubs
arose that were distinctly alien to the concrete jungles of their
19th century counterparts, flourishing in what had been the
fallow backwaters of the American landscape. Weapons of mass
destruction were designed for centralized targets, and the only
usable defensive tactic the shapers of public policy could discern was the fragmentation and decentralization of US industry,
in a network of rhizomatic and redundant centers of production.

    In his book _America_ Jean Baudrillard describes the
American West as a desert containing "cities which are not cities." "Irvine: a new Silicon Valley. Electronic factories with no

openings to the outside world, like integrated circuits … By a terrible twist of irony it just had to be here, in the hills of Irvine, that they shot <u>Planet of the Apes</u> … "[4] But it seems the philosopher of the simulacra missed the intimate connection between the landscape and the fantasy for which it was a backdrop. It was not irony that led the shooting scouts to choose Southern California's University of California, Irvine, campus as the stage set for the fourth installment of Franklin J. Schaffner's ape-infested vision of the future, so much as an understanding of the origins of the fantasy itself. The UC Irvine campus, built in the late 1960s, can be thought of as an architectural response to the fear of mass revolution of the underclass that the <u>Planet of the Apes</u> series tapped into. As students around the world were making headlines for taking over colleges and universities, and riots erupted in the urban centers of Chicago, Los Angeles, and Detroit, the planners of the newest addition to the UC system were designing a sprawling riot-proof citadel with no center for the over 10,000 students to congregate in, one of the many lessons the campus planners took from Berkeley. The makers of the <u>Planet of the Apes</u> could no more depict the exact dimensions of that cultural phenomenon than step outside themselves; they could only narrativize the desolation, represent it as metaphor, and realize it metonymically. Even in a hypertrophic world of simulations, behind the facade of fantasy lies the monstrous presence of the real.

The post-apocalyptic film is an odd hybrid of the morbid fantasy of the disaster film and the social alienation of the road movie. In <u>The Omega Man</u>, as the movie tag line indicates, "the last man alive is not alone." Charlton Heston stars as a relic of the once vibrant city, who is haunted by vampiric figures whose barely alive bodies cannot withstand daylight. Heston is caught in limbo, resolute in his devotion to bourgeois urban life in the shadow of its complete disappearance, intimately attached to a city whose last remaining inhabitants are openly at war with him. Despite their nightly attacks, Heston continues to live in his penthouse apartment in the heart of Los Angeles, a personal monument to technology and culture.

Engaged in a schizophrenic relation to his social world, he sips
fine wine and listens to Bach in the evening, and then roams
the streets with his machine gun hunting the other inhabitants
of the city. The communal order of "the Family" formed by these
post-apocalyptic night owls is a social group where class and
race distinctions are remnants of the past. In one scene, a member of the family comments on Heston's "Honky Palace," and the
leader is quick to correct him, saying, "Brother, those are the
old ways. They have no place here." Blatantly parodying the
promise of communist/socialist revolutionary movements of the
1960s, the solution offered in their communal life results in
total deindividualization, a fate that Heston's character comments is "worse than death." Heston's pursuers embody his dislocation from the urban milieu that defined and once surrounded
him. At the climax of the film, and the height of its absurdity,
Heston is crucified on a piece of modern sculpture, arms spread
out and head tilted down in a Christ-like pose, the blood that
pours from his wounds is revealed to be the only cure for the
zombie infestation; like Christ, redemption comes through his
suffering and his blood. The only remnant of the once-bustling
metropolis is erased with the memories of its last devoted
inhabitant. With him, the symbolic order of the old city is
eradicated. Yet, despite the impact that seeing Heston crucified
is meant to have, it is the opening sequence of the film depicting Heston cruising the streets of LA in complete isolation
that are the most haunting.

LIFE ON SET

> In the process of decay, and in it alone, the events of
> history shrivel up and become absorbed in the setting.
> —Walter Benjamin, *The Origin of German Tragic Drama*

In the summer of 1972, in the middle of the Vietnam War and on
the cusp of one of the deepest recessions in US history, Stephen
Shore ventured beyond the few square miles of New York City
by car for the first time. His project, to photograph his way

across the country, led him through the wide-open spaces that Shore later described as a "flat nowhere place of the earth."[5] Instead of photographing the bustling streets of his native New York as so many photographers had before him, the emptied avenues and vacant intersections he found on his trip became his chief photographic concern. One typical image of an intersection, <u>6th and Throckmorton St., Fort Worth, Texas, June 13, 1976</u>, is loaded with characteristically haunting absence. Traffic lights and street signs issue messages to drivers and pedestrians who are not there. A bus stop, what appears to be city hall, and a corporate high-rise surround the places where people are expected to be, but are not. In the background we can see the evidence of new construction, a crane atop a concrete and steel skeleton, but the desolate streets tempt us to ask who will fill the empty form. The trappings of modern life become unwitting proxies for isolation and anxiety, traffic signals continue to regulate nonexistent flows, buildings reach skyward with blank windows, and a bus shelter waits defiantly in the sun, all haunting the scene with their readiness to be activated. One might speculate what it would have required to produce such an image in Shore's native Manhattan. Contemporary Hollywood notably attempted this feat without the aid of special effects when, for one unprecedented day of shooting for Cameron Crowe's psychodrama <u>Vanilla Sky</u> (2001), Times Square was emptied of everyone but Tom Cruise. The director thought the impact of a completely abandoned urban center was an almost priceless spectacle. The Hollywood motto of "bigger is better" came full circle, as it was not the multitudes of choreographed extras that constituted the blockbuster money shot, but the equally choreographed evacuation of Times Square's 200,000 daily tourists, who waited along police barricades just outside of the camera's view. It was the most expensive location shoot in film history.

Shore did not have the advantage of a Hollywood budget: neither the support of city government to enlist uniformed officers to keep crowds at bay, nor the tortured wailings of Tom Cruise to register the desolation. The impact of a city devoid

of its inhabitants is compounded by the fact that at the moment
when Shore stood on the corner making his photograph, truly
no one was there. Cruise's dream sequence had already become a
reality on that sunny day in Fort Worth. It seems that in the
early 1970s the inhabitants of Shore's vision, like Heston's
assailants, had also developed an allergy to daylight.

The frenetic pleasure of urban life and the interactions
of its pedestrian actors are common in portrayals of New York
City. The opportunity for flânerie has also made its streets the
subject of many photographers, including of one of Shore's most
prominent contemporaries, Garry Winogrand. Winogrand's attraction to the movement of the anonymous masses is what probably
led many critics refer to his street photographs as testaments
to the character of urban life, "a casting inventory of the
essential city of modern experience."[6] Winogrand's images contain an almost typological collection of characters who operate
as stand-ins for the urban population as a whole. As photographer Tod Papageorge has posited, in Winogrand's images we
can identify "the Madison Avenue executive, the cripple, the
little old lady, the beggar, the celebrity, the artist … and
the crowd,"[7] continuing, "[Winogrand's photographs] describe …
a sort of urban minstrel show, full of interlocutors, end men,
shimmering women pulled in from the wings, bald one-liners,
missed cues, and a steadily growing gallery of the blind, the
halt, and the fallen."[8] Unlike Shore's quietly spare images,
Winogrand's richly populated frames seem to represent the
pathos of American urban life in the 1960s through the direct
representation of its subjects, and their immediate transformation into archetypes, stand-ins cast in a dramatic allegory
that evokes Jean-Paul Sartre's oft quoted phrase from No Exit—
"Hell is other people"—each player appearing trapped in a chain
of unrequited dependences and unsolicited animosities. For
Winogrand, and Robert Frank before him, the photograph was a
theatrical space—a proscenium arch that contained a world of
characters, struggles, and emotion. Take the overwhelming disaffection of Winogrand's image of American Legionnaires. A man,
presumably a veteran, crawls toward the camera with stomach-

churning desperation, as his fellow citizens gaze obliviously
over his head, engaged in their own personal dramas. Underlying
this image, like the majority of Winogrand's street tableaux,
is the seeming disconnectedness of the people involved, each
photograph presenting a gray wasteland of social relations.

In Shore's work, anxiety is marked by the complete
absence of interaction, and it reflects not only on the state
of anxiety and unrest surrounding the city, but also the difficulty of representing this circumstance through pictures in the
first place. The result is that Shore's photographs are occupied
by the haunting absence of Winogrand's rich assortment of
personalities. In contrast to the high-pitched drama and visual
irony Winogrand offers, Shore's images evoke the sense of a
stage set that will remain empty indefinitely. For example, in
his photograph of a seemingly innocuous scene of a car parked
in front of a rural storefront, US Route 10, Post Falls, Idaho,
August 25, 1974, the two open doors appear to be caught in
mid-action, as if the occupants of the car had suddenly evaporated in the afternoon sun, evoking the campy 1984 film Night
of the Comet, where Halley's Comet turns the population of Los
Angeles to dust. Or Shore's photograph of a campsite, Jackson
Wyoming, September 2, 1979, which feels like a modern version of
the infamously deserted early American colony at Roanoke, whose
inhabitants left only the elliptical phrase "Gone to Croatan"
on a nearby tree. In a recent conversation, Shore noted that his
book Uncommon Places (1982), composed of images from 1973 to
1979, ended up being edited in such a way that many of the city
views including people were left out.[9] The book's effect is a
serialization of this absence. As you turn each page, a new
image compounds the emptiness of the one before. When one comes
upon the few portraits in the book, it is surprising to find
that they demand the same type of attention as the architectural
views, as though the people in front of the camera were an
intersection, a building's facade, or a blank strip of asphalt.
They, too, seem to be waiting, poised on the edge of an occurrence
like the city that surrounds them, a similar sense of piercing
desolation haunting even Shore's images of family and friends.

        Bernd and Hilla Becher once likened Shore's work to
that of Eugène Atget, the canonical French photographer of pre-
Haussmann Paris, whose images Walter Benjamin famously noted
made its streets appear as though they were the recently evacuated scene of a crime.[10] As the Bechers go on to say, Shore's
project, like that of Atget, was initiated on the historical cusp
of radical social change, anticipating the disappearance of a
certain type of urban vernacular.[11] In Atget's case, this disappearance was the result of Napoleon III's desire to modernize
and control the population of Paris through the demolition of
labyrinthine medieval streets and the construction of grand
avenues. Shore's project marks a similar shift of economic and
social life: in this case, from the centralized urban downtown
to the decentered planned communities of suburban sprawl. Just
as Haussmann's reconstruction of Paris privileged surveillance
and police accessibility to ensure social order, the suburbs
offered safety in the form of easily policed neighborhoods of
largely homogenous and economically stratified populations
insulated from each other by an artificially imposed city plan.
The nascent urban anxieties were thus given form by real estate
developers, and enabled by governmental subsidies.

        Noticeably absent from Shore's archive are expansive
views of the surrounding landscape, where those who were able
to would eventually relocate. It is here that Robert Adams
defined the core of his project. In the photograph <u>City Center
of Denver from Ten Miles</u> (1968-1971), thousands of white roofs
fill the landscape as far as the eye can see, the tall buildings
of downtown Denver appear as a mere blip on the horizon. One
could imagine Shore's image of Fort Worth looking similar, if
only he had followed Adams's lead and stepped back ten miles.
Punctuating the landscape that inspired the long views of 19th-
century photographers such as Timothy H. O'Sullivan, Carleton
Watkins, and William Henry Jackson are houses laid out at equal
intervals, like rows of jewelry boxes in a department store display case. Their presence is an alien one, almost as if they had
been expelled from the landscape they now obscure. Although
the evidence of life is there—as much as a sequence of virtually

identical boxes can indicate life—the inhabitants are conspicu-
ously absent. Most importantly, the serial repetition of these
houses is the result of the same technological infrastructure
that allowed for the mass production of picture magazines and
advertising, each repeating identical box the product of the
same modernist industrial dream that gave photography, and its
nearly infinite reproducibility, a decisive role in the dissemination of ideology in the 20th century. The circulation of
images of attractive people living attractive lives in their
attractive tract homes seduced young families who sought the
security of home ownership and an escape from the increasingly
troubled urban centers. In this way the circulation of the
photograph is directly implicated within Adams's work. His
vision of an ordered wasteland of mass-produced homes is inextricably tied to the complimentary role photography played in
the formation of mass subjectivity, and the settlement of the
American West.

Often Adams's most direct images are his most haunting.
In the photograph <u>Tract House, Denver, Colorado</u> (1973), the mute
exterior of the building and its darkened windows betray nothing of its interior. Our desire to gain access to the house
through its many windows is met with the harsh contrast of the
noonday sun. A peek around the side of the house reveals more
of the same—staggered facades present themselves as equally
blank, and equally frustrating for the voyeur. When Adams does
photograph inside these buildings, as in his image of the claus-
trophobic wood-paneled corner of a tract home, there is no cor-
relation to an external world, no opening from which to escape
the enclosure (even the well-placed mirror, a potential break
in the gloomy walls, only reflects more paneling, and the photographer, like a vampire, goes unregistered in the mirror). This
image, like others in Adams's oeuvre, calls to mind a comment
made by Ed Ruscha regarding his interest in Los Angeles. As
Ruscha explained, "Los Angeles to me is like a series of storefront planes that are all vertical from the street, and it's
almost like nothing is behind the facades. It's all facades here—
that's what intrigues me about the whole city … the facade-ness

of the whole thing … "[12] The facade can be thought of as an
architectural analogue for the photograph, a scrim or screen
that alludes to an absent interior, which might explain why
photography was the medium Ruscha chose to describe the urban
vernacular of LA. It is easy to imagine that, like the empty
streets, the rows upon rows of houses in Adams's images are
empty as well. We find ourselves in a world of sprawling identical homes, inert and resolute in their repetition, a backdrop
for absent life.

Adams shot over 5,000 pictures of the sprawling Denver suburbs,
choosing to live in a tract home identical to those he photographed for the many years that were required to complete his
project. Fully immersed in this environment, he remained hostile
to it, commenting "I object strenuously to such houses as places
in which human beings are meant to live."[13] Yet he continued
to live and work in the conditions he found so reprehensible.
Reflecting on an early experience of a depopulated coal town,
Adams said, "the hills around were cut by abandoned coal mining
roads … it was brilliant, silent, full of <u>ghosts</u> … it had something Hitchcock about it." Adams transposes this sense of
hauntedness to the suburbs of Denver. But unlike the coal-
mining town enshrouded in reminders of its now-distant past,
the tract homes have little or no nostalgic potential, and do
not speak of life now absent, but of a life that seemingly
never was. Spaced evenly through the landscape, they lack the
American ghost town's aura of history, yet still they are
haunted. Whatever the reasons were to move to the suburbs,
they no longer matter. In Adams's work, the fantasy of suburban
utopia seems to have been severed from its roots. Like a lingering ghost, desire and memory have become separated from the
body that once supported them. What Adams recognized was that
the suburbs themselves were an apparition, an image and index
of a cultural mythology. Despite the endless flow of suburban
traffic (as he once lamented, "the cars never stop coming"),
Adams continued to produce views devoid of people, as though
the place itself precluded their existence. Even after all this

time in one of the most rapidly expanding suburbs of the 1970s,
Adams still saw only ghosts.

THE EXTRAS

> They're blue collar monsters, and they've always
> represented change.
> —George Romero

A similarly morbid fascination with suburban sprawl seems to
have inspired George Romero's second installment of his "Living
Dead" trilogy, <u>Dawn of the Dead</u> (1978). Romero chose the
newly opened Monroeville Mall in the suburbs of postindustrial
Pittsburgh as the film backdrop for his macabre fantasy.[14] When
Romero's characters arrive at the mall, it has been overrun by
zombies. But these monsters are not the standard fare of horror
films. Romero's zombies are the perfect citizens for the American
vernacular; liberated from history and social constraints, they
merely congregate and consume. Like Adams's tract homes, they
seem to develop spontaneously from the landscape, appearing
without explanation at the onset of the trilogy, and populating
successive scenes in progressively greater numbers. As Elias
Canetti reminds us in his magnum opus <u>Crowds and Power</u> (1960),
the masses of the dead always outnumber those still living.[15]
Similarly, the select few who grace the covers of magazines,
billboards, television, and movie screens are outnumbered by the
unseen who consume these products. In Romero's case, the undead
masses resonate as the invisible working class of the American
Rust Belt, the return of a public absented from popular depictions, as homogenous masses that haunt the shopping malls and
master plan communities to which they were delivered.[16] It is a
basic instinct that draws the Zombies there: as one of Romero's
characters surmises when the question "Why do they come here?"
is asked, gazing wistfully at the aimless zombies milling about
travertine tile and plastic flora like suburban teenagers killing time, waiting for the cavalcade of minivans and expectant
parents to pick them up, offering "This was an important place

in their lives." A similar question might arise about what drew
the inhabitants of the homes in Adams's photographs to Colorado;
as if to the mythical visions of unspoiled mountains, quaint
towns, and prairies found in common postcards that no longer
exist: a memory of an image of a place.

There is a deep awareness in Romero's film of the function of traditional genres like horror. As he states, "I find
there is an interest in horror because people think it's a safe
way to be made afraid—as opposed to relating directly to what
has happened."[17] For Romero, it seems, the most complicated relationship is that between media and its function as cultural
memory. The irony, of course, is that the movie theater is itself
a fixture of the postmodern mall, just another product it
offers. The shopping mall as a backdrop not only questions the
effect of a late-capitalist vernacular architecture that exists
exclusively as the location of consumption (the quasi-public
space that Rem Koolhaas has referred to as junkspace), but also
the equally key role that cinema plays in the landscape of commodity culture. A common interpretation of Romero's zombies
is that they represent the subjects of late capitalism, numbly
walking about in a consumerist torpor. But the zombies do not
shop; rather it is the people in Romero's films who do so, continuing to aggressively accumulate objects even after both
their use and their symbolic value is gone (the human survivors
in <u>Dawn of the Dead</u> acquire TVs, tennis rackets, evening wear,
and even money after the utility and the lifestyle they represent is gone). The immediate impulse of these survivors is to
continue to accumulate, to stock up. The zombies on the other
hand only take what they need, and they never victimize one
another to get it; instead, they are communal. It seems the survivors refuse to acknowledge that the accouterments of their
former lives now only have meaning as memento mori. Like the
scene W. G. Sebald sees from his hospital bed in the epigraph
that opened this text, from within the context of such a rift
everything has radically changed, even if the material supports
seem to present no mark of its passing. This territory is the
postapocalyptic, where past and future appear as a paradoxically

endless present. Here suburban sprawl can be the place where
you live, and yet seem like a sequence of empty shells, or the
heart of a city can exist for one blinking traffic light.

POSTSCRIPT: NOTES ON BLUE COLLAR MONSTERS[18]

> The only pleasure the melancholic permits himself,
> and it is a powerful one, is allegory.
> —Walter Benjamin, The Origin of German Tragic Drama

The voodoo beliefs that gave us the figure of the zombie were
equal parts the Roman Catholicism of the colonial occupiers of
Haiti, and African Animism. From their inception zombies were
an expression of colonial violence reflecting the transformation
of the Haitian people into disposable slave labor employed in
the sugar cane fields by privateers and colonizers. In short,
the zombie was a direct expression of a clash between occupier,
and occupied, thematizing the horror of indentured servitude.
One does not fear zombies, but instead fears becoming a zombie—
rather than the threat of death, they threaten life without
end—a life denied meaningful death, one where living itself
is the curse. The zombie is a worker, a slave, nothing more than
body without soul. William Seabrook, the early 20th-century
travel writer who popularized the figure of the zombie in the
Western world with his the quasi-journalistic account of his
travels in Haiti, The Magic Island, writes that, "My first
impression of the three supposed zombies, who continued dumbly
at work, was that there was something about them unnatural
and strange. They were plodding like brutes, like automatons."
He goes on to note that their eyes were vacant, uncanny. But
one has to wonder if this European adventurer simply didn't
register them as human beings, seeing none of what he knew as a
fundamental dignity of human life. Instead he saw an image of
resignation, domination, and the dehumanization characteristic
of imperialist enslavement. Rather than threatening figures,
they were what Giorgio Agamben has called, "bare life," which
he defined as a "human life … included in the juridical order

solely in the form of its exclusion (that is, of its capacity to
be killed)," in other words, a figure whom anyone had the right
to kill, whose lives were valuable only as labor, life reduced
to the status of body alone, like animate corpses.

Yet, as decolonization progressed through the 20th century, the zombie began to take on new meaning, not for the
inhabitants of Haiti, but for their white European occupiers
who clung to this fantasy first as an exotic example of primitive and mysterious culture, then later as a danger from
within, a specter of the brewing tensions between themselves
and the masses of the underclass. It seems no coincidence that
the transformation of the zombie in popular mythology from a
dumb, listless, beast into a violent aggressor occurred at the
very same time as revolutionary uprisings increasingly threatened
the hold European colonial governments had over the territories
they occupied. The revolt of the zombie became the revolt of the
slave, the revolutionary disruption of colonial rule, and the
ruling classes' fear of the power of the marginalized, for it was
not just the fear of losing the colonized lands, but a revolution from within that the immigrant populations and the working class came to symbolize.

The first period of runaway popularity for the zombie
film occurred during the depression, where the fear of the
indentured poor, who were doomed to lives of endless work,
exploitation, and suffering was brewing. Here the origins of
the American labor movement were sewn. The situation seems no
different in the late 1960s and 1970s, where in the era of stag-
flation the increasingly decrepit downtowns became a hotbed of
radical leftist activity, which, at its most extreme, threatened
a violent opting out of the working class that has been the
perennial fear of capitalism. From its inception, not only did
the figure of the zombie represent the worker, the poor, the
marginal, or outsider, but the entire filmic genre was that of
the poor man's horror film, for unlike other horror staples,
say that of Dracula, or Frankenstein, the zombie film exists in
the public domain. No expensive licensing fees were required,
because the first mention of the zombie was in Seabrook's sensa-

tionalist travel journals that, however farcical, paraded as journalism. This is only to say that as a subgenre, the zombie film both represents and enacts the category of the debased and the lowly. Thus the zombie presents one of the few progressive horror narratives, one that narrates popular revolution and exemplifies the idea of common ownership, and democratic populism itself.

These tendencies were evident in the modern urtext of the zombie film, Richard Matheson's 1954 novel, <u>I Am Legend</u>, set in the San Fernando Valley, which was then, as now, a sprawl of cookie cutter homes that were a precursor to those that Robert Adams would photograph in the 1960s. Matheson's novel tells the story of the last "man" on earth, a perfect tragic hero: a scientist with a love for culture, and reverence for the past, who is also mourning his family. He roams about the city killing the inhabitants, inhabitants who he sees as "murderous wretches," and every night is plagued by their taunts. Matheson calls these figures vampires, but in his description, and in the multiple film adaptations made (four strict adaptations and counting, along with numerous films that borrow heavily from the book), they are more like the contemporary figure of the zombie, with equal doses of the racial and classist undertones. As the protagonist's internal monologue goes:

Friends, I come before you to discuss the vampire: a minority element if there ever was one, and there was one. But to concision: I will sketch out the basis for my thesis: vampires are prejudiced against. The keynote of minority prejudice is this: they are loathed because they are feared … At one time … the vampire's power was great, the fear of him tremendous. He was an anathema and still remains an anathema. Society hates him without ration. But are his needs any more shocking than the needs of other animals and men? Are his deeds more outrageous than the deeds of the parent who drained the spirit from his child? … Really, now, search your soul; lovie-is the vampire so bad? All he does is drink blood. Why, then, this unkind prejudice, this

thoughtless bias? Why cannot the vampire live where he
chooses? Why must he seek out hiding places where none can
find him out? Why do you wish him destroyed? Ah, see, you
have turned the poor guileless innocent into a haunted
animal. He has no means of support, no measures for proper
education, He has not the voting franchise. No wonder he
is compelled to seek out a predatory nocturnal existence.
Robert Neville grunted a surly grunt. Sure, sure, he
thought, <u>but would you let your sister marry one?</u>

Matheson's novel is notable for a number of reasons: divine punishment is coupled with cold war anxieties and the dime store
horror genre where, for the first time, the mythology of vam-
pirism/zombiedom is lent a scientific explanation, positing it
as a communicable disease. It is impossible not to read his novel
in the context of the Red Scare, where social revolution is
repeatedly caricatured as a communicable disease, an epidemic of
moral erosion. But Neville discovers there are monsters who are
sentient, that he was killing individuals who have the ability
to speak, who view him as the true monster. It is only then that
he realizes that his understanding of the world was backward,
that he was the aggressor, and through this realization he
comes to grips with a society where infection is the new norm,
and he, Neville, is a murderous deviant. As he turns away and
accepts his death sentence, Neville grasps that just as vampires
were legend in pre-infection times now he, an obsolete exemplar
of old humanity, is legend in the eyes of the new race born
of the infection. Just as Dracula parodied the aristocrat who
fed off the bodies of his subjects surviving well past the age
to which he was native. It was Neville who was truly undead,
who continued to live after his natural death. The sheer ridicu-
lousness of it all causes Neville to chuckle as he dies: his
last thoughts being "[I am] a new superstition entering the unassailable fortress of forever. I am legend." Matheson lays
out an allegory for the generational clash of the 1950s, the
moral majority versus the leftist, de-individualized socialist/
communist youth, who ally themselves with the proletarian.

The distinction between them was lost on him. In the end, it is
a case of tragic comic misrecognition, Neville cannot see who he
is, cannot see the change that is happening, and continues on,
like a specter haunting the old city, all the while blind to the
new one that has taken its place.

The book inspired a film adaptation less than a decade
later, Ubaldo Ragona's <u>The Last Man On Earth</u> (1964), with
Vincent Price in the lead role. The film was shot in the EUR
(the Esposizione Universale Roma), a city on the outskirts of
Rome built by the architect Marcello Piacentini, and commissioned by Benito Mussolini as a monumental site for the 1941
World Fair, which to this day stands as the largest expression
of fascist architecture and urban planning in Italy, a city
invented from scratch. The site also provided a backdrop for
Michelangelo Antonioni's 1962 allegory of modern disaffection,
<u>The Eclipse</u>. To this day the EUR contains a museum of Italian
heritage, complete with scale models of the Roman Empire under
Constantine. Its opening was delayed until 1942, for the 20th
anniversary of the fascist regime, yet never fulfilled its original purpose due to the escalation of World War II. It is a relic
of a future that never came to pass. For the majority of the
film, Price as Dr. Robert Morgan accumulates a massive body
count of the groaning, almost mindless zombies who linger by
his home at night droning his name with impunity like persis-
tent street beggars—for him, they are a source of discomfort
more than threat. But the new, highly organized sect of young
zombies Morgan confronts at the end of the film are far more
dangerous. They are infected with the same disease, but with the
help of a serum have retained the ability to organize, operate
vehicles, and wield conventional weapons. More militia-like than
undead mob, their uniformly black dress is a thinly veiled reference to the fascist paramilitary Black Shirts, an association
emphasized by the use of the highly recognizable EUR that
serves as the action's backdrop. Morgan, skewered by one of his
assailant's spears after a military style raid on his home,
grumbles out his last words in a stupefied tone on the alter of
a nearby church, "I am a man … The Last Man … they were afraid

of me … " Again here the site of the film is key to its reading,
the echoes of fascism, the ruin of a hubristic past, and the new
society that is born from its ashes.

The next film to take inspiration from Matheson's novel
was Romero's <u>Night of the Living Dead</u>, which was groundbreak-
ing in a number senses, particularly for its oft remarked upon
final scene. Here the narrative of the loan survivor, who keeps
the history of the culture alive, who is outmoded, nobly tragic,
is upturned, because as the character Ben is finally freed
from his night of horror, he meets his end not at the hands of
a newly emergent mob of the undead, but of his own people, an
expression of the horror of the society he was native to. The
horror of the zombies is rivaled by the horror represented by
the living. Even in this last moment, the hero, the noble protagonist, is illegible to the mob of vigilantes hunting zombies.
He is misrecognized, his race making him indistinguishable from
the zombies, i.e. indistinguishable from the inhuman, from the
status of slave, nothing more than bare life, and he is killed
with little ceremony.

Each of the film adaptations of Matheson's <u>I Am Legend</u>
turns on a fundamental moment of misrecognition, a moment
where the main character confronts the truth, that he, as the
last vestige of the past, is the true monster in the eyes of
society at large. At the moment of death this fundamental confusion is confronted—manifest in the tragic inability to recognize the other, which is equally an inability to recognize oneself or who one is in the eyes of the world. As Benjamin wrote:
"Every image of the past that is not recognized by the present
as one of its own concerns threatens to disappear irretrievably,"
to which I would add that most often this disappearance is
complemented by history's return in a new and horrific form.

NOTES

1. Marshall Berges, "Interview with Ed Ruscha," <u>Los Angeles Times</u>, March 28, 1976.

2. Cited in Delores Hayden's essay "Urban Landscape History: The Sense of Place and the Politics of Space," in Todd W. Bressi and Paul Roth (eds.), <u>Understanding Ordinary Landscapes</u>, Yale University Press, New Haven 1997.

3. Peter Galison, "War Against the Center," <u>Grey Room</u>, no. 14 (Summer 2001), p. 13.

4. Jean Baudrillard, <u>America</u>, trans. Chris Turner, Verso, New York 1989, p. 123.

5. Heinz Liesbrock (ed.), <u>Stephen Shore</u>, Schirmer/Mosel, Munich 1995, p. 35.

6. Jonathan Green, <u>American Photography: A Critical History 1945 to the Present</u>, Harry N. Abrams, New York 1984, p. 98.

7. Ibid.

8. Tod Papageorge's introduction to <u>Public Relations</u>, exh. cat., The Museum of Modern Art, New York 1977; distributed by New York Graphic Society, p. 13.

9. <u>American Surfaces</u>, published in 1999, consisted of pictures that arose from his first cross-country trip in 1972.

10. Walter Benjamin, "Little History of Photography" (1931), <u>Walter Benjamin/ Selected Writings Vol. 2 1927-1934</u>, eds. Michael W. Jennings, Howard Eiland, and Gary Smith, Harvard University, Cambridge 1999.

11. Bernd and Hilla Becher in conversation with Heinz Leisbrock, op. cit.

12. Edward Ruscha, <u>Leave Any Information at the Signal: Writing, Interviews, Bits, Pages</u>, ed. Alexandra Schwartz, MIT Press, Cambridge 2002.

13. Carol Di Grappa (ed.), "Excerpts from a conversation with Robert Adams," in <u>Landscape: Theory</u>, Lustrum Press, New York 1980.

14. Notably, his first film, <u>Night of the Living Dead</u> (1968), used a deserted farmhouse as the stage for the return of the dead. Both films were shot just outside of Pittsburgh, and one could imagine that, in the time between films, the aging farmhouse was one of many replaced by cookie-cutter tract homes and regional malls.

15. Elias Canetti, <u>Crowds and Power</u>, Noonday Press, New York 1962, p. 63.

16. It is fitting that just as the regional mall was displacing the traditional urban centers at the time of filming <u>Dawn of the Dead</u>, currently the regional mall is in the process of disappearance. Across the country, an increasing number of malls like the one in Romero's film are either empty or near death.

17. Canetti, <u>Crowds and Power</u>.

18. This section was added in 2010 on the occasion of a lecture delivered at the Blanton Museum of Art, University of Texas, Austin.

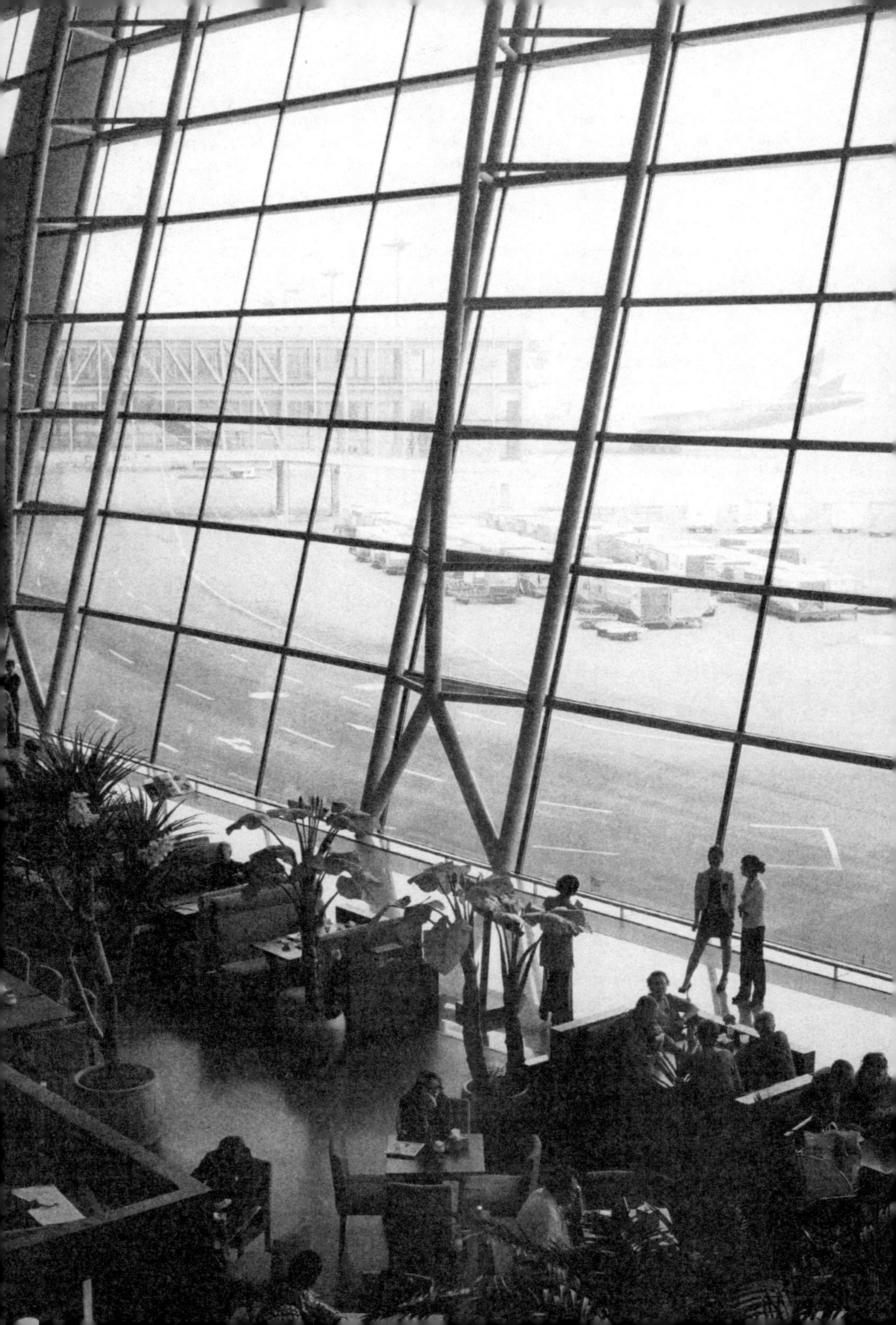

Notes on the Subject without Qualities: From the Cowboy Flâneur to Mr. Smith

First published in <u>Afterall</u>, issue 8 (November 2003), p. 125-134.

Every individual is on one hand the subject of cognition, that is to say, the complementary cognition of the possibility of the whole objective world, and on the other a single manifestation of that same Will, which objectifies itself in each thing. But this duplicity of our being is not founded in a unity existing for itself: otherwise we should be able to have consciousness of ourselves through ourselves and independently of the objects of cognition and willing: but of this we are utterly incapable; as soon as we attempt to do so, and, by turning our cognition inward, strive for once to attain complete self-reflection, we lose ourselves in a bottomless void, find ourselves resembling the hollow glass ball out of whose emptiness a voice speaks that has no cause within the ball, and, in trying to grasp ourselves, we clutch, shuddering, at nothing but an insubstantial ghost.
—Schopenhauer, <u>The World as Will and Idea</u>

[The Subject without properties is] the philosophical figure for what becomes, with increasing literalness throughout the 19th century, the global ubiquity of the white European. His domination is virtually self-legitimating since the capacity to be everywhere present becomes a historical manifestation of the white man's gradual

approximation to the universality he everywhere represents.
—David Lloyd, <u>Race Under Representation</u>

I am everyone, and no one. I am everywhere, yet nowhere.
—<u>Darkman</u> (1990)

Patrick Bateman, the protagonist of Brett Easton Ellis' novel
<u>American Psycho</u> (1991), may stand as the most polemical repres-
entation of American materialism during the Reagan years. In
Ellis' allegorical examination of the socio-pathology of commodity culture, the mechanisms of self are singularly constituted
in the right to consume. With increasing ferocity, Bateman
accumulates the names of others—Calvin Klein, Donna Karan,
Vidal Sassoon—to alleviate the nagging sense that his own name
has lost meaning. The distinction between people and objects is
thoroughly blurred, to him human beings are no different than
the products he acquires, uses up, and discards; a substitution
already manifest in the advertising that surrounds him. As
his transformation into a total sociopath becomes complete,
even the power over life and death cannot reaffirm his identity. At the close of the book, still no one can remember his
name.

Ellis' novel touches on the perennial anxiety of late
capitalism, as our own surroundings are tailored to our desires,
our sense of self is externalized to the point of complete
erasure. We fear becoming as inhuman as the objects that are
meant to reflect our deepest aspirations and desires. As we move
through the novel, we too must become numb like Bateman, as
indifferent to the random graphic acts of violence as we are to
the contents of his medicine cabinet. The most readily granted
expression of subjective agency in commodity culture is constituted as the right of consumption, and with this right comes the
promise of reattaining sovereignty over our domain. In short,
we are all promised that with enough money, we each could be
king. Ellis speculates about the endpoint of this becoming, the
moment of the actual assumption of the role of sovereign power

hinted at in advertising copy. In the end Ellis realizes this
consumptive fantasy in the ability to give and take life, or, as
more explicitly posited by Michel Foucault, a power constituted
in "the moment when the sovereign can kill" as the true realization of "his right over life."[1] In Bateman's case, this is his
attempt to control his own life. In Ellis' vision every act of
consumption is an allusion to death, and this forms our attraction to it. And its power—a power originating as the unique
right of sovereignty constituted as an exception to the rule of
law—provides a model for the individual as a form of absence,
in direct opposition to a contemplative reflexive model of the
self. As we each approach this sovereignty via consumption,
we must accept the inevitable side effect—that, in the words of
Giorgio Agamben "sovereign power is the very impossibility of
distinguishing inside from outside … "[2]

In this model of social anomie we lose ourselves in the
ebb and flow of a realized utopia of our desires. Our perpetual
movement between the limbos of non-places, such as airport
terminals, thruways, malls, housing developments, and pre-fab
homes—all realizations of some form of consumptive desire—create a sense of place wholly dissociated from previous ideas
of specificity, be they regional, historical, or temporal. Our
downtowns are made to appear and feel like the malls that had
once displaced them, our front yards are decorated with the
same wood chip and shrub islands we witness at corporate office
parks, our airports declare their own attractiveness as destinations in themselves, a status once limited to the cities they
are located in. Thus we fear we are defined by such places,
emerging as subjects who demand and are comforted by such
control, even empowered by it, and yet are simultaneously sub-
ordinated, and de-individualized through the aggregation of
our wants and needs. As we spread our culture everywhere, our
own identity becomes catastrophically generalized, diluted,
and at the moment globalization completes its mythical project,
completely dissolved. The sense of control and order we feel
when we can be sure that in any major city in the world we can
order a hamburger "just the way we like it" is coupled with

the afterthought that once everyone sees that burger as
their own, our tenuous connections to our own identity will
evaporate.

This is one brief formulation of a crisis of subjectivity, a poststructuralist apocalypse where all texts and sites
refer back to the ideological premise of a masterful subject who
stands in a perpetual state of its own erasure. An almost self-
deconstructing concept, the "universalized subject" arrives fully
formed in a state of disrepair; its dismantling follows the
circular chain of its development: the more we attempt to order
and control our own world, the more we are defined by it and
enact, symbolically and practically, our own absence. But with
every compulsive deconstruction of the "universalized subject"
we force ourselves back into this void. Repeated claims of the
depleted agency of the subject appear as the inescapable endpoint of contemporary culture. New technologies are said to
offer the complete domination of a society of control, as Jonathan
Crary puts it, in "new levels of mimetic 'fidelity' (holography,
high-resolution TV) there is an inverse move of the image toward
pure surface, so whatever drifts across the screen of either
television or home computer is part of the same homogeneity …
an infinity of routes and the equivalence of all destinations."[3]
This vision of an apocalypse of the subject is not limited to the
fixations of theoretical texts, but also a favored imagining of
the mass media. For this reason, the attraction we feel to this
idea and the anxiety that it engenders seems better addressed
as a kind of fantasy than a functional theoretical concept.

It might be why, as we desire the convenience of 24-hour
discount shopping and a Starbucks on every corner, we also
fantasise about seeing it all destroyed. Hollywood has offered
us ample opportunity to witness the apocalypse of the familiar,
and notably its favoured object of annihilation has been Los
Angeles itself. We have seen LA rocked by earthquakes epic in
scale, reimagined as an unlivable utopia, crushed by meteors,
ripped apart by dinosaurs, pierced by volcanoes, and even incin-
erated by UFOs. While this destruction is sometimes played out
in literal form, Los Angeles is often imagined as the site of

social apocalypse, a wasteland of immorality and alienation.
Los Angeles has been the backdrop for a multiplicity of destructions, easily molded to the worst we can imagine. As Ed Ruscha
once remarked about the city, "it's all facades here, that's
what's interesting about LA."[4] His emptied black-and-white
images of banal architecture—apartment complexes, fuel stations,
parking lots—are executed with an arbitrariness rivaled only
by the objects he points to, an aesthetic correlative of the
Angeleno fantasy of destruction. For Ruscha, people are "incidental," a "distraction," as though the Los Angeles he saw precluded the existence of its inhabitants.[5] With ominous vague-
ness, Ruscha posits this reading of his work: "It may be that
there's some sort of emptiness or stage play at the roots of
my work. Or at least it may be some kind of _final solution_."[6]
For all the playfulness of Ruscha's practice, the fearsome ring
of the phrase "_final solution_" should not be lost, nor should
its association with theatrical spectacle.

In the early 1970s the disaster film enjoyed a renaissance of sorts, beginning with breakthrough hits such as
Airport (1970), _The Poseidon Adventure_ (1972), _Towering Inferno_
(1974), and _Earthquake_ (1974), reemerging in the 1990s in
computer-enhanced form. These depictions of the complete destruction of the familiar, and of our collective punishment for
technocratic hubris, provided ample escapist fantasy. But the
disaster film never allowed the annihilation to be complete; the
cataclysmic always permitted redemption in which confrontations
with death culminated in a new beginning. We could then discard
the very history that lurked as the most troubling undercurrent of rationalist expansion in the service of modernity, free
to begin anew. Our debt to the past was now paid as a final
penance on the way to social utopia. From the ashes of disaster,
liberal-capitalist democracy could reinvent itself as the utopia
it promised but never delivered. The very real social inequa-
lities and economic challenges to American capitalism, the deep
recession of the early 1990s and urban unrest that struck
American cities echoing the situation of the late 1960s and
early 1970s. We could forget the Los Angeles riots because the

city was a now a smoking crater, with the survivors banded together around the American flag that now operated as a collective symbol of redemption and forgetting.

While these films sublimate and reconfigure the anxieties of western democratic capitalism, they are prefigured, both in the 1970s and the 1990s, by films that concern themselves directly with the construction of subjectivity within an apocalyptically amoral society. The social catastrophes our protagonists confront offer to reconstitute and reaffirm the macho retro-subject in jeopardy. The signature vehicles for such stars as John Wayne and Bruce Willis insistently assert this reemergence of the modern anti-hero. Moments of crisis are used to reveal our need for such "real men," whose alienation from society is marked by their reflection of the harsh realities that lie beneath the safety of social order. But Hollywood fantasy is not the only location for realizing this return. Shortly after September 11, the mythical "real" that were our working-class heroes were heralded as the new model for the masculine, the trend celebrated even in the sober pages of the <u>New York Times</u>. The traditional masculinity of men who spoke with actions and not words assured us that our rugged individualism could again double for our national identity. This mythology provided comfort, and gave us permission to ride the globe like cowboys searching for the ultimate villains of our consumerist polity.

The focus of this essay is not the repeated play of the collapse of the familiar: but, more explicitly, the fantasy of experiencing this collapse vicariously as the protagonist who survives as the echo of society itself. This, it seems, is the central fantasy and the source of our attraction to such films—such that we can fantasize at our becoming the embodiment of the dissolution of the social field in a dialectic metonymy. In his exemplary investigation, <u>White: Essays on Race and Culture</u> (1997), Richard Dyer convincingly argues the key role of the martyr fantasy as a tautological reassertion of the centrality of white subjectivity. The suffering of the white male subject, Dyer posits, "typically conveys a sense of dignity and transcendence in such pain … the white man has—as the bearer of

agony, as universal subject—to have dark drives against which
to struggle."[7] These "dark drives" often reflect the crimes of
society as a whole that are mirrored in the becoming of the universalized subject; thus the sins of man are possessed by this
subject and are his to embody and triumph over. This suffering
is often codified in an alienation from a world populated by
those who cannot fathom or complete their penance due to the
limits of their own perception. In bearing this weight of understanding, the white subject formulates this suffering in a
worldview marked by "disinterest—abstraction, distance, separation," mirroring a "public sphere that is the mark of civiliza-
tion, itself the aim of history."[8]

Film and television narratives enact the most overt play
of such fantasies, but despite their fictional and escapist
qualities, they are not a diversion from reality, but more accurately, they accentuate the aesthetics of these desires. In this
sense, they are more deeply implicated within positivist, empiricist representations of the "real world" than they are often
credited with. My contention is that the very basis of any realist endeavor is deeply intertwined with such mass-cultural
narratives, and moreover directly employs fantasy to define the
parameters of an objective reality. While film often asks to
be interpreted in terms of its immediate social context, only
recently have the implications of these fictions been directly
related to our construction of a worldview. Pictorial media
still have not undergone such analysis; the political and social
examinations of painting and photography usually rely on the
relationship to the real (its iconographic content) instead of
the construction of the fantastic. The important distinction to
make is that pictorial narrative is deeply tied to specific historical contexts, and its examination is not a tacit assertion
of a kind of urtext of experience, but of a relation of specific
social conditions from which such fantasies originate.

The most troubling dimension of the investigations of
subjectivity, and the postmodern and poststructuralist examinations of its collapse, is that they extricate their own fixation
from the milieu in which they develop. Such investigations stem

from a position defined in radical opposition to the dominant
ideology, while often claiming that the possibility of radical
practice has already been rendered wholly impossible. Most
Marxist social critics operate within this paradox of position-
ing—while defining capitalism as an expansive, all encompassing
social system able to subsume any revolutionary opposition
to its workings, the very act of writing in opposition seems an
exception to the rule. It seems these inquiries are launched
from a kind of non-place, a voided location from which critical
distance and meta-operations can still function while their very
ability to do so is suspect. The limitless and displaced quality
that is ascribed to capitalism as a concept seems to mirror
the very subjectivity from which their critique is mounted, the
dismantling of the authorial subject mirroring the supposed
dissolution of the nation-state under globalization. As we look
outside, we see only the reflection of ourselves.

It was such a death that Barthes saw as the foregone
conclusion of every photograph. Only after his lamentation of
his own mother's death could photography deliver him melancholic redemption in the form of the "punctum" or, in Lacanian
terms, the "ever-returning real." It was no mistake that Barthes
defined the punctum as a wound, an indexical trace of a collision. The effect of his unanticipated encounter with a photograph
of his mother reawakened visceral experience as a traumatic
void, an emptiness constituted by her fleeting, inexplicable
presence within the image. Death, for Barthes, lurks in every
image as this type of personal loss. In Siegfried Kracauer's
description of a familial photographic confrontation, he saw
something more absolute than death: total erasure. To his horror, his grandmother, just a young showgirl in the image, was
buried alive in a litany of banal detail. She became an "archeo-
logical mannequin" into which memories of the grandmother had
"dissolved." But it wasn't actually her absence he confronted,
but Kracauer's own memory, his own history. For Kracauer the
impenetrable surface of things was the wasteland of the photographic image. For both men, the lens pillaged this sense of
the personal, the real, reducing it to a catalog of things,

textures, and shapes. Memories and histories were successfully obliterated under the weight of its descriptive power.

The play of anxiety that plagues both Barthes's and Kracauer's interpretations of the photograph is located at the intersection of positivist empirical investigations of truth, and for lack of a better term, the poetic and mnemonic experience of the real. This dual model might be best described as the objective view, and the emotive or experiential (the first finds its correlative in the figure of the cowboy/explorer, the second in the flaneur). In both of these approaches, the concept of the real as an accessible and expressible constant is asserted. These modes of approach, as they are theoretically defined, make such a claim through their assumption of, first, a truth that can be ascertained by the photographic imaging of a subject and second, through the distillation of an affect or essential emotive quality that persist despite their repeated deconstruction.

In one of John Szarkowski's foundational attempts to define the nature of photographic representation in the catalog for the 1978 Museum of Modern Art exhibition <u>Mirrors and Windows</u> he writes that the core of its meaning lies between a "central and indispensable presence in the picture of its maker, whose sensibility is the photograph's ultimate subject," and a realist approach that "is used … to stand for a more generous and inclusive acceptance of fact, objective structure, and the logic of process and system."[9] Objectivity here is tacitly defined as an ability of the photograph to reveal a kind of latent truth through a positivist faith in perception as aided by machine. The historical conditions of this notorious deployment of photography are far too numerous to delve into here, but in this genre the geological surveys of the American West, the physiognomic studies of criminals, the motion studies of Étienne-Jules Marey, and Charles Marville's documentation of old Paris all come to mind. Each of these projects proposed that the documentation of facts was possible through pictorial organization, and were all equally consistent in the relegation of the conditions of their production (and most often the agendas that guided them) to a quiet subtext. They served these

unacknowledged ideological ends better by claiming "factual"
and universal ideals, claiming these pictorial models to be the
raw materials for social, economic, or scientific understanding.

Objectivity then is better understood as a claim made
from a position of power than as something implicit within the
images themselves. The lie in this assertion of objectivity
is that no singular subjectivity (or ideological belief) can be
found at its origin, but a universal concept operating as the
interminable defacto criteria for all relations, i.e. as absolute
and non-ideological. Moreover, these formulations of the external world and their conditions of production maintain a deep
relevance to our contemporary culture.

The American Survey image captured the expansionist
desires of a fledgling republic after the Civil War. The surveys
were meant to provide both valuable geological and topographi-
cal information about the West to the Congress, and were also
a means of indirect subsidy for the private sector—to encourage
land speculation and to attract the development of unsettled
territories. Through their pictorial organization these photographs demarcated land as possession, placing it under the singular view of a privileged eye. In demonstrating that the land
could be encompassed in the monocular gaze of the camera lens,
these images provided a subliminal reinforcement that man could
control it. Writing on the American West, Jane Thompson describes the power of these representations to locate an imperialist desire within the passive experience of the spectator, trans-
ferring an agenda in the service of a state apparatus to the
psyche of the individual citizen. As she writes: "[The blankness
of the plain] implies—without ever stating that this is a field
where a certain mastery is possible … the openness of the space
means that domination can take place virtually through the act
of opening ones eyes, through the act, even, of watching a representation on a screen."[10] As this experience of possession is
"shared" with the individual subject, the sense of triumph is
claimed as a democratic realization of personal freedom enabled
by the state and economic opportunism. This defined a distinctly American mythology of the West as an arena to be

mastered and colonized, and whose subordination could be experienced as a triumph manifest in the act of viewing itself.

This understanding of the effectiveness of the photographic image to disseminate universal ideals led in part to the
development of photographic models that chose the appearance of
participatory or experientially authentic reportage. Such images
announce their first-person observation through dynamic, asymmetrical, or seemingly arbitrary formal structures. As the opposing dialectical pole of positivist claims for objective reality,
the experiential model privileges immersion and intimacy over
detachment (most often realized as the "snapshot" style). As John
Szarkowski wrote in the introduction to The Photographer's Eye:
"[The photographer] learned that the world itself is an artist
of incomparable inventiveness, and that to recognize its best
works and moments, to anticipate them, to clarify them, and make
them permanent, requires intelligence both acute and supple."[11]
This "real" of experience is the mark of authenticity in the photograph, an echoing of the photographer's inner world, as it is
manifest in "his" chosen object. In this formulation, the work of
Garry Winogrand or Robert Frank operates as much as a comment
on life, as a dislocated self-portrait, and so the experience
of the specific auteur is presented as the cipher for universal
understanding. In essence, the photographer must become as
dynamic as the city itself, and in the end, be as capable of
experiencing and responding to its multiplicitous character,
internalizing it and excreting it as a picture.

As the quintessential Baudelairian flaneur, the photographer becomes "the passionate spectator," whose home is "at
the heart of the multitude, amid the ebb and flow of movement,
amid the fugitive and infinite,"[12] "a mirror as vast as the crowd
itself."[13] The flaneur is defined by Baudelaire in terms of
vision, the view of the scene encompasses his capacity to inter-
nalize the system around "him," from which he vacillates between
a mastery over the crowd and "his" own dissolution into its
flow. Walter Benjamin takes special note of this condition.
As he writes in his 1938 essay, "Paris in the Second Empire in
Baudelaire," "Baudelaire divorced himself from the crowd as

Hero … he set out to conquer the streets—in images."[14] This view
of the crowd is intertwined with a primal revulsion, as Baudelaire
goes on to say: "The idolatrous mob demanded an ideal worthy of
itself and appropriate to its nature—that is perfectly understood,"[15] and for Benjamin the primacy of vision in Baudelaire
amounted to a way of regaining control, to avoid "disappearing
forever."[16] As Klaus Theweleit observes, "command not only tames
the mass in its entirety; more importantly, it reconstitutes
the bodily mass … giving it direction, reassembling—or even
recreating—a body in dissolution."[17] These positions are again
drawn into direct conflict in the late 1960s and early 1970s
when, in the United States, a violent reconfiguration of the
urban was taking place, while simultaneously threatening bourgeois identity in terms of its authority within and identification with the city.

It was in the widespread urban unrest of the 1960s that
the street photograph had its heyday. The white male subject
found himself in a disturbing paradox, as Richard Dyer astutely
describes: " … white man has attained a position of being without properties, unmarked, universal, just human." For Dyer
this quality constitutes the quintessential anxiety of the white
male subject, as he continues, "to be without properties also
suggests not being at all. This may be thought of as pure
spirit, but it also hints at non-existence, or death."[18] Benjamin
Buchloh has argued that this might be the cause of a return to
the traditional pictorial genres within photography, identifying this precarious situation within Thomas Struth's portraits
of the "globalized" upper-middle class. Struth's portraits
appear problematically regressive, as "the condition of subjecthood appears … restricted to those that are fortunate enough to
have privileged access to …. the apparatus of subject formation
as much as to the proper conventions of representing subjectivity, i.e. to the Western European genre of portraiture."[19] But
Buchloh speculates that Struth may in fact be representing "the
dissolution which constitutes the subjective experience at this
very moment," an indication of the demise of the centrality of
the subjectivity that his archive first appears to be reifying.[20]

Marc Augé saw this as the paradox of the contemporary subject of "supermodernity." Writing of the world traveler in the modern age, Augé posits that "he is confronted with … an image of himself, but in truth it is a very strange image. The only face to be seen, the only voice to be heard, in the silent dialogue he holds with the landscape-text addressed to him along with others, are his own: the face and voice of solitude made all the more baffling by the fact that it echoes millions of others."[21] This might be why Robert Adams turned to the cluttered expanse of Denver's suburbs to redeploy the American landscape tradition (as it was originally constituted in the photographic surveys of Clarence King, with whom Timothy H. O'Sullivan, Carleton Watkins, and William Henry Jackson made some of their most renowned work). Lewis Baltz once commented that the formal composition of his images merely "mirror" the implicit logic of the landscapes he saw. The open space of the American West was "an apparently unbroken expanse of land [that] is, in fact, overlaid with a network of invisible lines demarcating ownership and indicating a pattern of future development … the arbitrary result of financial speculation."[22] Baltz's images depict the mythology of the American West as realized in the concept of "landscape as real estate," where the classical binary opposition of man and nature is displaced by the great equalizer, capital.

Even at the time of the American surveys, a capitalist restructuring of the open plain was occurring. One subset of the geological survey images was the documentation of mining projects in the American West, which designated territories of possession and use. While the photographs of the largely uncharted West not only was coincident with the naming of various features of the land, it was, as Alan Trachtenberg has observed, in fact one and the same act. He writes: "the name lays claim to the view … A named view is one that has been seen, known, and thereby already possessed."[23] With each act of naming and viewing, a reterritorialization of the boundaries of the self occurred, a self defined by the territories into which its expansion was a foregone conclusion. But this process of naming

was already being deployed by the mining industry to more
explicit ends, as Trachtenberg went on, "[names] were more
nakedly aggressive … outward signs of the act of appropriation
of the 'mining industry' if not the 'survey' itself."[24] Names
such as "Confidence," "Challenge," "Empire," and "Imperial" make
explicit the mythology they were establishing, and the sense
of empowerment and moral justification in its exploitation.[25]
Such names mirrored the subject position the views of the
West were meant to illicit, a model of subjectivity whose core
system was the "self-justifying ideology of competition and
expansion."[26]

The territorialization of open space through naming,
as it occurs first in the seemingly innocuous approach that
Clarence King engaged in and the more ominous capitalist/indus-
trial naming of the mining companies, is further complicated
in Baltz's series, The new Industrial Parks near Irvine,
California. In Baltz's images, territories are marked only by
opaquely bland monikers such as "PlastX" or "Semicoa," denoting
neither place nor conquest, but rather a moniker of "faceless,"
placeless capital. Essentially indicating these are nowhere
zones. Ideological implications are wrapped in isolated spheres
of self-referential, hermetic meaning, divorced from an outside
object, equally disengaged from the flow of production in
any material sense, just as their names are devoid of semantic
meaning.

The pictorial innovations of O'Sullivan and his contemporaries are located within Baltz's work as the first step
toward the numbingly bleak vision of contemporary life presented within New Topographics.[27] Baltz's highly regimented,
meticulously titled, gridded studies of the anonymous architecture of late capitalism, resonate as apocalyptic environments in
which the inhabitants for which they were built are completely
erased. Just as the survey images' "objective" ordering of
the landscape was underscored by economic interest, Baltz here
acknowledges that capitalism may offer the truest objective
order for the landscape, after all, the ether of capitalist
exchange value has no face. Just as the street photograph and

survey image formed the respective mass subjectivities of the time, the ideal bourgeois subject now may be the corporation, as described by Baltz's images of mute exteriors bearing no indication of life within.

This might have been the impetus for Miles Coolidge's series Safetyville (1994-1995), views of a three-quarter-scale city built in Southern California to teach children traffic rules. The city assumes oddly ominous qualities; empty facades, blank windows, and vacant intersections make one think more of postapocalyptic science fiction than a teaching tool. Unlike the New Topographics work, which played on absence in densely settled areas, Safteyville is an autonomous city never intended for living in. The only markers of the functional city that remain untouched in this mini version are the bright colors of corporate sponsorship, demarcating this land where there are no inhabitants, only potential consumers. Child-sized gas stations suggest a consumption that will occur years later, a Denny's restaurant brackets the main intersection hoping that the image of its logo will inform the mini passersby in their future decisions of where to take their as yet non-existent families. The city as a social network is relegated to symbols of consumption, freed from even the scale of the city it mimics; corporate logos are its monuments.

These representations of the city abandoned still leave room for the survivor, the photographer as the last witness to the destruction. While the narrative of the survivor has been explored in film, often he is a figure acted upon, trying to put up one last gesture of defiant resistance to chaotic collapse. Here we are given the postapocalyptic subject who is aware of the complete social breakdown that surrounds him, moving, flaneur-like, through the city as a reflection of its state of crisis. "D-Fens," played by Michael Douglas in Joel Schumacher's 1991 film Falling Down, is just such a vehicle: mild-mannered, heroically average, and permeable. Moving through the marginal spaces of a disintegrating Los Angeles, he encounters every social and racial stereotype imaginable, from the greedy Korean shopkeeper to Chicano gangsters and neo-Nazis. Each time he

declares his own separation, dispensing violent "justice" to
those he meets, and finally, after making his way across the
city, he takes his own life. His dislocation from the city that
surrounds him is calibrated by the name he assumes, cribbed
from his car's vanity plate—once a pathetic celebration of his
profession, and now a sign of white male subjectivity in a state
of retreat. The violence done to him, and that he has done to
others, is prefigured by the corporation that defined his life
and then set him adrift.

A similarly dystopic imagining of Los Angeles gave birth
to Liam Neeson's character Darkman in Sam Raimi's 1990 film of
the same name. Neeson, a noble scientist and inventor of a synthetic skin turned misanthropic crime fighter, is hunted by a
malevolent real-estate developer and his band of ruthless thugs.
They incinerate him and his laboratory and he is left disfig-
ured on the banks of the Los Angeles River. He is then found
and miraculously given super strength, which, along with his
own invention, gives him the ability to seek revenge. He inhabits, albeit briefly, the very identities of his tormentors, in
order to infiltrate their ranks and hunt them down. Taking to
the sewers, abandoned warehouses and other marginal spaces of
Los Angeles, he becomes a metaphor for the city itself, a seamless facade that obscures the scars that lie beneath. In the
final scene in the film, after sending the real-estate developer
and his henchmen to their deaths, Neeson flees the fiancée
he has just liberated. She screams his name, "Peyton," and he
replies, "Peyton is gone." With that he runs into the street and
merges imperceptibly with the crowd. She tries in vain to find
him, but soon realizes the futility of her search. He has disappeared into the rush of commuters, and as the camera pans over
the crowds, settling on one anonymous face, Neeson's voice-over
begins and we learn that he has become "everyone, and no one."
Neeson's character reemerges as a heroic survivor of the city
mired in corruption and crime, a transformation that occurs in
this complete loss of his previous individuality. Unlike the
schizoid model of superhero and alter ego, he is the totalized
combination, a third term that doubles as a void.

Within these two films, the transcendence and martyrdom
of the main characters is marked by their floating names. They
are set apart from the city, their bodies acting as a material
manifestation of alienation. More recently, some action films
propose a similarly restrictive image of society, but assure that
the transcendence offered by the heroic martyrdom of the white
male can reinstate his subjective autonomy. In <u>The Matrix</u> characters are renamed when they ascend from the simulated world
that acts as their prison, proposing the renaming as their rec-
onnection with their true selves. <u>The Matrix</u> follows Keanu
Reeves' ascension from a lowly computer programmer who moon-
lights as a hacker, to the Kung-Fu-fighting Jesus-surrogate,
Neo. In a world that is a computer-generated fantasy, the other
inhabitants are semi-disposable zombies who are not cognisant
of their own imprisonment and the life-and-death struggle that
is occurring all around them. Like the main character from John
Carpenter's film <u>They Live</u> (1988), Neo is gifted with an awareness of the delusion subduing the masses. While in <u>They Live</u>,
Nada (whose name provides ample evidence of the stark contrast
between these films) sacrifices himself to bring a world controlled by interplanetary bourgeois capitalists, whom he discovers accidentally, to a point of collapse, Neo is the redemption
of a unified subject who has been almost divinely "chosen" to
be a saviour. Nada begins the film as nothing, and ends up in
much the same state, while Neo is the embodiment of redemption
itself. In Neo, the white male subject has gained life after
death with the conclusion of his worldly character; he ascends
to a higher plan of existence.

The Matrix Reloaded (2003), follows a distinctly more
complicated form of transcendence. This time the most radical
metamorphoses occur not to our savior in Prada, but to the computer program in human form, Mr. Smith. In the first film Smith
is a predictably evil agent—with a deep disgust for everything
human, he is little more than a de-individualized villain.
Clothed in a variation of managerial professional attire (boxy
black suit with white tie), Smith's dress is understated compared to the black vinyl, shiny euro-trash aesthetic of the

gang of protagonists. But through the course of the film we
learn that Smith has in fact undergone a radical and unforeseen
mutation. Through his contact with Neo his programming has
changed, gaining new powers and an autonomy from the computer
system that created him. With equal ferocity, he combats both
the agents of the synthetic world and the human rebels lead by
Neo. Smith's mutation is a function of his ability to replicate
himself in others—in essence to take over other bodies, not
assuming their appearance, but instead making them identical
to him. Each individual is not a vehicle to be controlled by the
original Smith, but an identical sentient copy, a completely
decentralized subject. Smith is the serialized model of white
subjectivity, here presented in ubiquity. Like the endless
reproducibility of the commodity, Smith is a succession of
selves, each arriving fully formed. This mob is an inversion of
the Baudelairian metonymy of the flaneur, a crowd as singularity. One might imagine armies of Mr. Smith returning from
work to the sprawling identical houses photographed by Adams
or Baltz, or the serial displays of vernacular architecture
of Ruscha's frames. The perfect subjects for the mass-produced
home. What is key here is that the process of naming, as was
the case with the survey image, creates a new body for the dominant subject. The crisis of Patrick Bateman is realized in figures who violently enact their positions as voided characters,
and evolved into those whose process of naming is their final
redemption as a transcendental subject: a subject that passes
through the void, and reemerges as divine.

NOTES

1. Michel Foucault, <u>Society Must Be Defended: Lectures at the College de France, 1975-76</u>, ed. Mauro Bertani and Alessandro Fontana, trans. David Mace, Picador, New York 2003, p. 240.

2. Giorgio Agamben, <u>Homo Sacer: Sovereign Power and Bare Life</u>, trans. Daniel Heller-Roazen, Stanford University Press, Princeton 1998, p. 37.

3. Jonathan Crary, "The Eclipse of the Spectacle," in <u>Art after Modernism: Rethinking Representation (Art Criticism and Theory)</u>, ed. Brian Wallis and Marcia Tucker, David R. Godine, New York 1994, p. 143.

4. Edward Ruscha, "LA Suggested by the Art of Ed Ruscha," in <u>Leave Any Information at the Signal: Writing, Interviews, Bits, Pages</u>, ed. Alexandra Schwartz, MIT Press, Cambridge 2002, p. 223-224.

5. Howard Pindell, "Words with Ed Ruscha," in <u>Leave Any Information at the Signal: Writing, Interviews, Bits, Pages</u>, p. 61.

6. Ralph Rugoff, "The Last Word," in <u>Leave Any Information at the Signal: Writing, Interviews, Bits, Pages</u>, p. 299 [emphasis added].

7. Richard Dyer, <u>White: Essays on Race and Culture</u>, Routledge, New York 2002, p. 37.

8. Ibid., p. 39.

9. John Szarkowski, from the introduction to <u>Mirrors and Windows: American Photography Since 1960</u>, exh. cat., The Museum of Modern Art, New York 1978, p. 19.

10. Dyer, <u>White: Essays on Race and Culture</u>, p. 34.

11. John Szarkowski, from the introduction to <u>The Photographers Eye</u>, exh. cat., The Museum of Modern Art, New York 1966, p. 4.

12. Charles Baudelaire, <u>The Painter of Modern Life</u>, trans. Jonathan Mayne, Phaidon, London 1995, p. 9.

13. Ibid., p. 10.

14. Walter Benjamin, "Paris in the Second Empire in Baudelaire," in <u>Walter Benjamin: Selected Writings, Vol. IV, 1938-1940</u>, trans. Harry Zohn, ed. Michael W. Jennings and Howard Eiland, Belknap Press of Harvard University, Cambridge 2003, p. 39.

15. Charles Baudelaire, "The Salon of 1859," in <u>The Mirror of Art: Critical Studies by Charles Baudelaire</u>, trans. Jonathan Mayne, Phaidon, London 1955, p. 60.

16. Walter Benjamin, <u>Walter Benjamin: Selected Writings</u>.

17. Klaus Theweleit, <u>Male Fantasies, Volume II: Male Bodies—Psychoanalyzing the White Terror (Theory and History of Literature, Volume 23)</u>, trans. Erica Carter and Chris Turner, University of Minnesota Press, Minneapolis 1989, p. 42.

18. Dyer, <u>White: Essays on Race and Culture</u>, p. 39.

19. Benjamin H. D. Buchloh, "Portriats/Genre: Thomas Struth," in <u>Thomas Struth: Portraits</u>, Schirmer Art Books, Munich 1998, p. 160-161.

20. Ibid., p. 162.

21. Marc Augö, <u>Non-Places: Introduction to an Anthropology of Supermodernity</u>, Verso, New York 1995, p. 103.

22. Lewis Baltz, "Lewis Baltz," in <u>Landscape: Theory</u>, ed. Carol Di Grappa, Lustrum Press, New York 1980, p. 29.

23. Alan Trachtenberg, <u>Reading American Photographs: Images as History, Matthew Bradey to Walker Evans</u>, Noonday Press, New York 1989, p. 125.

24. Ibid., p. 153.

25. Ibid., p. 152-153.

26 Ibid.

27. The name "New Topographics" comes from the 1975 George Eastman House exhibition that brought together a number of photographers who were imaging contemporary built environments, as curator William Jenkins wrote: "The detailed and accurate description of a particular place, city, town, district, state, parish, or tract of land." The name stuck for all but the Bechers, the only artists in the show who were not Americans. Among the other participants were Robert Adams, Lewis Baltz, Joe Deal, Frank Gohlke, Nicholas Nixon, and Stephen Shore.

Neo-Avantgarde and Service Industry: Notes on the Brave New World of Relational Aesthetics

First published in German as "Neo-Avantgarde und Service Industrie. Die schöne neue Welt der relationalen Ästhetik," Texte zur Kunst, no. 59 (September 2005), p. 150–157.

The conglomeration of strategies and artists that fit under the heading relational aesthetics indicate, if only for recent history's lack of "movements," a pronounced shift in the topography of contemporary art, and the urgent need for the realignment of the theoretical models addressing the politics of aesthetics. Despite its amorphous set of conditions and tenets, as they were expressed by Nicolas Bourriaud in his 1997 collection of essays Esthétique relationnelle (translated into English as Relational Aesthetics in 2002), relational aesthetics is manifestly distinct from interventionist precedents (i.e. institutional critique, identity politics, performance, and installation) if only for its intersection with the broad topography of contemporary vernacular, and its aversion to declarative political assertions.

Bourriaud's collection of essays loosely maps an ideological shift as it took place in the early 1990s, a transformation he ascribes to the general sense that methodologies associated with political and socially engaged art of the previous generation were no longer viable as strategies for contestation. From a theoretical perspective, classical models of critical opposition (those associated with the prevalent 1970s and 1980s politics of representation and the discourse around institutional critique) provide an untenable set of compromises between the institution and practitioner, between the opening up or revealing of dominant structures, and the naturalization or reification of those

powers. In other words, "political" art of the 1970s and 1980s
all too often took on the voice of the authority it was seeking
to destabilize, even if only as parody, reinforcing and naturalizing the relations between the dominant and the subordinate
despite its supposedly revelatory content. Such work reinscribed
conventional power relations even as they sought to destabilize
them, a paradox evidenced by the relative ease that institutions
had in accepting and adopting such work. Furthermore, through
the repeated "revelation" of the monumental or unassailable
power that lay behind the facade of cultural production, such
work further mythologized dominant forces to the point of
becoming sublime while offering little support for the agency
of the individual or modes of resistance other than the blunt
articulation of this state of affairs. Michel de Certeau pin-
pointed this problem when he wrote that the discourse around
repression and ideology is a self-inflicted chastening that has
the cumulative effect of "family stories," of "devils and boogey
men." As he wrote, "ideological criticism does not change its
(repressive force) function in any way, the criticism merely creates the appearance of a distance for scientists who are members
of the institution."[1] This is, for all intents and purposes,
the crux of the argument levied against the traditions of insti-
tutional/ideological critique and the Pictures Generation,
and even more explicitly, the theoretical models that developed
in tandem and were received in concert, rehearsed by Bourriaud.

But to claim that the largely American movements of
identity politics and institutional critique were the only impetus for the formation of relational aesthetics would be misleading. Taken on its own, relational aesthetics is born from a
distinctly European circumstance. Formed in the increased importance of the European regional institution in contemporary art
in the midst of the erosion of the commercial art market of the
1990s, relational aesthetics tends to treat all art venues as
neutral arenas which are both autonomous from the mechanisms
of the commercial art world, and are predicated on the democratic promise to facilitate the open interaction of individuals
and ideas.

That is to say, the institutions in which relational
aesthetics developed are not the centralized expression of national culture evidenced in traditional museums, or the quasi
corporate complexes prevalent in the US, but were instead the
European network of kunsthalles and kunstvereins, which have
a regional municipal modesty about them. To those who come from
a US context, which lacks that form of civic infrastructure for
art, relational aesthetics' assertion of the democratic potential
of art institutions seems rather naïve, if not saccharine. But
seen from a European vantage point, the US traditions which
grappled directly with institutional contexts are simplistically
moralizing, if not morosely melodramatic. Bourriaud's claim that
relational aesthetics is about, "learning to inhabit the world
in a better way,"[2] evades the implication that the artist is a
morally superior messianic figure who takes on the sacrifice of
revealing inequities, and issuing edicts on the repressive power
of institutions. Rather, according to Bourriaud, relational
aesthetics presumes to create "open ended" contexts for self-
determination that are seemingly freed from the restrictions
of the state and capitalist structures. They do not treat the
institution as a privileged location, but as yet another locale
in the postmodern geography, just one of many points where
social relations are activated. In short, the institution is simply a social node rather than an assertion of state power, or
class ownership over culture. And so, the question is less that
of what form opposition might take, as it was usually construed
in the US context, but how to operate within restrictions,
reimaging the site of exhibition as a viable location for public
discourse and aesthetic production.

Despite the relative successes of a number of artists
within Bourriaud's groupings in the US (most notably, Pierre
Huyghe, Maurizio Cattelan, and Rirkrit Tiravanija), the American
response to the movement itself has been minimal, and when it
has been taken notice, it has been tepid at best. In the Summer
2005 issue of Artforum, Joe Scanlan opined, "Why is relational
aesthetics so boring?" going on to say, "time and again I have
found myself in a room full of people … yet the group always

ends up exchanging pleasantries, and planning dinner … "[3]
The only extended critical response published in an American
journal came from Claire Bishop (who hails from the UK) in the
pages of October. Bishop's article matched Scanlan's derisive
tone, albeit in markedly different terms, faulting Bourriaud's
mantras of community and exchange as "rest(ing) too comfortably
with an ideal of subjectivity as a whole, and community as
immanent togetherness." Both writers insinuate larger problems
contingent upon questions of verifiable "quality," as Bishop
pinpoints, " … how are we to measure or compare these relationships? The quality of the relationships in 'relational aesthetics' are never examined or called into question … all relations
that permit 'dialogue' are automatically assumed to be democratic or good."[4] But if the criterion by which the efficacy
of relational programs are to be judged is absent from the discourse surrounding it, a more problematic set of implications
are alluded to by Scanlan, who, chidingly, writes, "Indeed,
firsthand experience has convinced me that relational aesthetics
has more to do with peer pressure than collective egalitarian-
ism, which would suggest that one of the best ways to control
human behavior is to practice relational aesthetics." He continues, "Peer pressure is effective because it uses one of our most
basic fears—public humiliation—as a built-in mechanism for
controlling behavior."[5] In short, actions and the mechanisms
of sociality are put on display and thus become self-conscious,
subject to an internalized policing, which transforms Bourriaud's
notion of "conviviality" and the development of an "art based
on interactivity and the creation of relationships with the
other," into divisive systems of control, producing a reification of the dominant model, rather than an alternative to it.

   Before launching too deeply into the theoretical issues
surrounding Bourriaud's collection of texts, one needs to note
some important mitigating factors. Firstly, the quality of the
translation of the first English edition of Esthétique relationnelle leaves much to be desired. Often relatively vague English
terms take the place of more precise French philosophical terminology (such as dispositif being translated as "mechanism"

rather than the more accurate "apparatus," which evokes the Foucauldian and Althusserian Marxist lineage, central to Bourriaud's thought), and the book is filled with typographic errors and language constructions that are not only grammatically suspect but often almost incomprehensible. Furthermore, Bourriaud's book was never intended as a single treatise, rather it is a series of essays written throughout the 1990s that directly responded to their moment. These circumstances create a great deal of difficulty for anyone looking to locate a concrete or fully formed methodological structure or consistent theoretical argument within the book, as the position Bourriaud adopts shifts over time as does his mode of writing (from the more theoretical to essayist). Thus, without such qualification in mind, to an English-speaking audience, Bourriaud seems to frequently oversimplify the work of the artists he discusses offering a largely schematic lineage to accompany it, often excluding characteristics that do not fit comfortably within the relational program. While these omissions are problematic, they are part and parcel of the spirit in which the original texts were written, and distributed. For example, he makes Tiravanija's work sound like an experimental kindergarten, describing it as a place "where people once again learn what conviviality and sharing mean," overlooking the moments of awkwardness, and even out right alienation that take place in his work. Similarly, Bourriaud's critics rely on similarly reductive readings of these artists. Claire Bishop claims Tiravanija is simply creating new networking points for "art dealers and like minded art-lovers … because it evokes the atmosphere of a late night bar," citing a 1996 account by art critic Jerry Saltz that details his social escapades with art world insiders and random flirtations in Tiravanija's first New York solo show <u>Untitled (Free)</u> from 1995 (where Saltz chatted with David Zwirner, Paula Cooper, and Lisa Spellman, and met some young artists), as evidence. While this criticism is partially true—Tiravanija's exhibitions do reinforce preexisting social networks, and have at times taken on a saccharine surface of togetherness—this dismissal obscures a more comprehensive understanding of the

complex of subject formulations operating in Tiravanija's work.
Some of these more complicated aspects are at least hinted at by
Saltz himself, in the paragraph immediately preceding the one
that Bishop quotes. In that passage, Saltz wrote that,

> A sense of uneasiness was always close by. Once when I
> went to the gallery I ate alone, and I felt that old fear
> of doing something wrong. I remember pausing outside the
> door and thinking, "Maybe I shouldn't do this—they'll
> think I'm a moocher." I felt sheepish, guilty, like I was a
> freeloader. I don't usually feel this way when I go back
> to a show more than once.[6]

Certainly this does not satisfy the question of accessibility, or
the passive relationship Tiravanija has with the mode of social
interaction he creates, but it does attest to an important societal contradiction, and a specifically capitalist anxiety typi-
fied in the free market mantra: "there's no such thing as a free
lunch." But the investigation of the nascent anxiety presented
by Tiravanija, and the potential implications that follow are,
for Bourriaud and his critics alike, patently off limits. After
summarizing critiques deriding relational programs for their
art world insularity, Bourriaud asserts:

> … do we deny Pop art because it reproduces codes of visual
> alienation? … What these critics overlook is that the con-
> tent of these artistic proposals has to be judged in a for-
> mal way … bearing in mind the political value of forms …
> They are aimed at the formal space-time constructs that do
> not represent alienation, which do not extend the division
> of labor into forms … the purpose is not conviviality,
> but the product of conviviality … [7]

Bourriaud, in evading what he sees as a threat to the political
project of the work, also abandons the most complex, and provocative dimensions of those practices. By dismissing these questions, and displacing the emphasis on some later, unexaminable

"result," the scope of Tiravanija's work deadends in a simplistic notion of community. But in fact, it seems that Tiravanija
invites that very query into the specific contradictions
implicit in an art that is concerned with large sociopolitical
issues, and yet is largely entwined with a system of privilege.
"Alienation," and "the division of labor" are exactly what
Tiravanija is proposing we question, both the ubiquity of low
paid service labor in the art world and its invisibility, alongside the anemic and simplistic conception of the public at work
in a field predicated on private ownership, and he does so sub-
tly without resorting to spectacularized circuses of victimiza-
tion. Firsthand accounts often allude to "the product of conviviality" as constructed by Tiravanija as being less than utopic.
As one reviewer wrote, "[w]e are now the wallflowers at the
party, and our old-fashioned spectatorship is just sad," articulating the friction between the seeming freedom of the work,
and the sense of anxiety it is capable of producing. Saltz
describes this effect as a "subversive, unsettling hospitality."
The specific character of this form of "unsettling" needs to be
examined, because the core of relational aesthetics' critical
program seems to lie here. The anxiety described by Saltz in his
repeated interactions with Tiravanija's work both in his 1996
and 1999 shows at Gavin Brown's Enterprise provide a useful
jumping off point.

In his accounts, Saltz describes an almost adolescent
angst, as he writes, " … being there can be difficult. I experienced unwanted waves of shyness, affection, and irritation
there,"[8] and the social restrictions (i.e. peer pressure) of the
environments appear continuous with a society of surveillance
and their self-policing rigid codes of conduct which occupy all
transactions without being firmly locatable. This nascent anxiety derives much of its energy from the very real privatization
taking place in the Post-Fordist era, a conflation of leisure
and work time, and the increasing exposure and display of the
private lives of individuals in the public sphere through social
media; the personal and social realized through Twitter feeds
and Myspace pages is presented for public scrutiny and is, in

this constellation of forces, inextricable from the corporate
and governmental occupation of public space. This has affected
the institutions of art as well, which have seen a sharp
decrease in state funding and a geometric expansion of private
support, a phenomenon that began in the US, but is swiftly
transforming the public sphere in Europe. Yet the most disturbing dimensions of relational programs is that they not only
amplify late capitalist anxiety, but facilitate the corporatiza-
tion of public space as they draw attention to it. On this point
Bourriaud is quite correct in his construction of a reactionary
evolution of relational aesthetics. What in the previous generation's practices often appeared as a rather repressive set
of moral assertions, is replaced in relational aesthetics by an
almost radical complicity, which chooses neither to comment
nor intervene in the functioning of power, and instead seems
to magnify the permeation of private interests in the public
sphere. In short, relational aesthetics mirrors the erosion of
both the commons, and the private through the increasing occupation of leisure time by capitalist exchange.

This is in evidence in the events following the recent
Guggenheim Museum acquisition of Tiravanija's <u>Untitled 2002
(he promised)</u> in 2004, which was supported by American Express.
For the project Tiravanija turned over the event programming to
the museum, who then worked in tandem with American Express'
PR department, and created a sequence of events which were more
advertisement than microtopia. As the press release read:

> To celebrate the new IN:NYC Card, Amex will present a free
> interactive art exhibition at the Guggenheim Museum cre-
> ated by internationally acclaimed artist Rirkrit Tiravanija,
> which will engage visitors with a variety of programming
> elements that respond to the culture of the city in which
> it is displayed. In addition, award-winning music artist
> Wyclef Jean will perform live for invited guests.

Or, as it was later described by the fashion wire service:

Fashion Wire Daily October 8, 2004—NEW YORK—In the New York universe, installation art by 2004 Hugo Boss prize-nominated artist Rirkrit Tiravanija is in the same room as celebrity guest DJs Nicky Hilton and Nicole Richie; Wyclef Jean performs and sings about his political leanings to a well-heeled crowd of girls in Chanel jackets drinking lychee martinis from Latin fusion restaurant Calle Ocho. Canadian Press—Fri Oct 8, 11:16 AM ET LONDON (AP).

Similarly, at his recent exhibition at the Serpentine Gallery in London, the communing of art world insiders morphed into an event that sounded more like a Hollywood Oscar party (with a few art stars mixed in) than a site of participatory exchange. Stuart Comer's Artforum.com diary entry describes processions of celebrities—Kid Rock, Rod Stewart, Farrah Fawcett, Mariah Carey, David Gilmour and Roger Waters (Pink Floyd), Alex James (from Blur)—which crescendoed in "[a] flurry of pale yellow chiffon, [as] Paris Hilton made her entrance into the kitchen."[9] Here the insiders privileged in Saltz's account, and chidingly observed by Bishop, are themselves shut out for the Hollywood celebrity. Instead of creating a new zone of interactivity, social divisions are reenacted in heightened spectacle, a further distancing of the public from the creators of the mass culture which they are subjected to.

Tiravanija, and others who invoke these "free" zones of conviviality, not only run the risk of transforming the communal into the estranged but, more importantly, by claiming these sites as open and free they naturalize the hierarchies that become manifest there, locating them as the urtext of experience. Much as the institution became an accepted and inescapable platform for aesthetic production, the power relations of the art world and the cadres of insiders and outsiders are received in the work with acceptance. Rather than positing "living a better way," it seems to say that the current way of living is inescapable.

Perhaps conscious of the ambivalence of these works, Bourriaud defends the liberatory dimension of these practices

by repeatedly conflating the freeing of the artist from traditional divisions of labor with the liberation of the viewer.
Such assertions are specious as best, for these are two positions
within the production of art could not be more different. He
conflates Michel de Certeau's depiction of an individual's means
of resistance in daily life (mini revolts that gum up the works
of monolithic powers through willful inertia or ambivalence),
with the artist's adoption of ruses, operating as curator,
interior designer, caterer, public relations manager, and event
organizer (quite different from the parodic adoption of these
roles in institutional critique, with Marcel Broodthaers as
museum director, Andrea Fraser as Docent, or Michael Asher as
exhibition designer). While relational aesthetics programs adopt
these roles, they do not reflexively dismantle them. Bourriaud
defends this adoption, and refers to it as democratic, but democratic for whom? While these approaches open up new territories
for artists, it is deeply problematic to assume these mean more
ethical or valuable contexts for viewers to interact in, or that
viewers are given more agency simply because the artists have
more authority, unless that authority is transformed in some
way, an outcome Bourriaud fails to mention if he does indeed
see that taking place. The viewer is not presented any further
occasion for agency other than that which is already present in
the commercial sphere. In fact it is the institution, with the
artist facilitating, that engages in the broadest range of ruses
and disguises, manipulating categorical divisions and masquerading as one of many other cultural venues within the commercial
environment (bar, restaurant, dance club, etc.). Tiravanija's
practice demonstrates this in particular, as the instrumentalization of his work by whatever power is close at hand is often
adopted without friction by the work (which is diffused by
its inherent complacency, i.e. anti-didacticism). While viewers
operate simply as occupants of a circumstance, fixed in their
subjection to the circumstance, the artist is allowed to remain
a moving target, acting in a continuum of professions, while
never being fully accountable to any particular criteria for
efficacy.

In this sequence of deceptions, reappropriations, and play, the viewer continues to be merely the object acted upon, enticed to engage in a series of banal activities such as eating, talking, listening to music (in seeming acknowledgment Tiravanija lists "lots of people" as one of his materials. This incidentally parallels the business model adopted by social media corporations, who broker user-provided content to large financial gain). This is why Bourriaud concerns himself more with describing how the artists act, their intentions, and the distinctions between their approach and previous practices, and avoids, almost completely, as Bishop discerns, the "quality" of those interactions the work produces. He simply assumes these new relationships are positive because they have been enacted, not what contexts for behavior they are activated within, or their relationship to external mechanisms. Often the occupation of various roles, like Jorge Pardo's foray into store design at the Dia Art Foundation, indicates a seamless, almost cynical, conflation of disciplines, and the metamorphosis of the institution into a commercial space. Pardo's Dia merges the design of the expanded bookstore into the first floor gallery, making no aesthetic indication of a difference between the two. This may in fact be an articulation of the truth that lies beneath the surface, but it also acts to reify their fusion together, naturalizing it by pointing to this transformation, but never questioning or creating a friction with it. Most importantly, in the conflation of public and consumer space it leaves the role of the artist as an agent unexamined.

The current trend in mall design is to accent traditional shopping spaces with "communal meeting points," "settings for festive interaction," "space to roam, to sit down, and to talk," and, with increasing regularity, mall managers are creating public events, employing large open "park-like" spaces, and free attractions to entice consumers, fully displacing its less seductive relative, public space. Museums have realized that their "public" space can bolster revenue streams from their shops. If at one time museums were autonomous and naturalized power centers, in the US the climate of curtailed governmental support radically changes the situation, as " ... both the museum and the entertainment complex are, today, sustained by the transactions of shopping."[10]

Far from utopic, relational aesthetics often leaves us in a decontextualized social world, where repressions are naturalized by their being wrested free from their origins. In the rejection of strategies of institutional critique, which always reasserted the material conditions of space, the relational aesthetics conception of social interaction mirrors the recent shift in urban planning's understanding of the city. As Sze Tsung Leong has noted, the spatial term "map" has been jettisoned in favor of terms like "scenario analysis systems," a "science of spatial modeling," a "decision support system," or a tool for "forecasting space time dynamics," terminology that emphasizes social relations over geographic space. Such terms are echoed in relational aesthetics' appropriation of terminology like "laboratory," "station," "matrices," and "sets of information strata," (among others), intermittently signaling data structures, industrial forms, and economic categorizations. Similarly, the relationships that occur in relational aesthetics are invisible to the material understanding of the institution, or physical locus of power, by their very imbeddedness. This revision of the city map foregrounds the relations between pockets of the city, privileging usage over topography, networks over space, all in service of "the primary engine of urbanization: the market." Bourriaud's "interstices" in "the social corpus" are just such invisible points of communion where divisive separations between classes occur through social pressure rather than physical partitions, and the complete irrelevance of private vs. public space is realized. The proposed liberatory conflation of domestic space and gallery space, and the real world progression of the art institution into entertainment complex, creates both a disturbing endpoint where domestic space becomes indistinguishable from commercial space (for Bourriaud only considers the transition going one way, not the other), and masks the understanding that this is already happening. The new digital behaviorist topography of the city completely dissolves the

symbolic divisions between personal and public. The city itself
becomes an expression of interrelations, consciousness of material conditions evaporates, creating systems of control invisible to those who are placed inside them. More importantly, those
for whom material concerns are a grave matter (i.e. for the poor
and disenfranchised who must constantly negotiate to acquire
the bare necessities for sustaining life) are rendered invisible
for they offer little if any untapped revenue. And for those
for whom this system is intended, with the onset of the satellite monitoring and real time statistical mapping, the panopti-
con has become as ubiquitous as the sky itself.

Nan Ellin argues that this dematerialization is the
foundation of a distinctly postmodern anxiety of the city,
"[w]here modernist fear and the positivistic climate in which it
occurred led to efforts to detect causes and effects … postmodern fear amid the refining anti-technocratic climate has incited
a series of closely related and overlapping responses including
retribalization, nostalgia, escapism, and spiritual return."[11]
Or in Bourriaud's words, "we are hoping for the return of the
traditional aura … "[12] The understanding, or reflection, of these
evolutions of subjectivity and space are important to consider
in reexamining the subjectivity of the viewer, and how control
can be disrupted, but the methodological tools of relational
aesthetics and its surrounding discourse seem to go only so far
as to acknowledge and/or replicate these systems, literalizing
their movements without providing any moments of resistance.
By dissolving the boundaries between cafes, bookstores, or
nightclubs, and the space of exhibition within the museum, the
possibility that the museum could be reimagined as a bulwark
against the expansion of spaces of commerce is further eroded.
Instead such practices take part in staging the impossibility
to imagine a site outside of financial exchange, deploying the
transformation of public space into spaces of commerce as a
foregone conclusion by reinscribing existing structures of control and renaming them "a realm of possibilities," of a "possible
future," evidenced in the construction of "microtopias." This is
exactly the system of domination that Gilles Deleuze and Félix

Guattari describe in <u>A Thousand Plateaus</u>, when they wrote that
"[a]ttention has recently been focused on the fact that modern
power is not reducible to the classical alternative 'repression
or ideology,' but implies a process of normalization, modulation,
modeling, and information that bear on language, perception,
desire, movement etc. and which proceed by way of microassem-
blages."[13] And despite the long overdue acknowledgment of the
radical transformation of public space that relational programs
bring to the fore, they have, up to this point, been marked by
a corrosively passive attitude to them. The problem is not their
naivety, for this awareness is far too well executed to be
unknowing; rather it is its complicity, verging on cynicism,
which proves its most troubling quality.

NOTES

1. Michel de Certeau, <u>The Practice of Everyday Life,</u> trans. Steven Rendall, University of California Press, Berkeley, p. 41.

2. Nicolas Bourriaud, <u>Relational Aesthetics</u>, Les presses du réel, Dijon 2002, p. 82-83.

3. Joe Scanlan, "Traffic Control: Joe Scanlan on Social Space and Relational Aesthetics," <u>Artforum</u>, vol. 43, no. 10, 2005.

4. Claire Bishop, "Antagonism and Relational Aesthetics," <u>October</u>, Fall 2004, no. 110, p. 65.

5. Joe Scanlan, op. cit.

6. Jerry Saltz, "Resident Alien," <u>The Village Voice</u>, July 6, 1999.

7. Nicolas Bourriaud, <u>Relational Aesthetics</u>, p. 82-83.

8. Jerry Saltz, op. cit.

9. Stuart Comer "Diary: Park Life," Artforum.com, July 6, 2005, <u>http://artforum. com/diary/id=9216</u> (last accessed September 2015).

10. Sze Tsung Leong, in <u>Harvard Design School Guide to Shopping</u>, Chuihua Judy Chung, Jeffrey Inaba, Sze Tsung Leong (eds.), Harvard Design School, Taschen, Cologne 2002.

11. Nan Ellin, "Shelter from the Storm," <u>Architecture of Fear,</u> Princeton Architectural Press, Princeton 1997, p. 26.

12. Nicolas Bourriaud, <u>Relational Aethetics</u>, p. 60.

13. Gilles Deleuze and Félix Guattari, <u>A Thousand Plateaus</u>, University of Minnesota Press, Minneapolis 1987, p. 458.

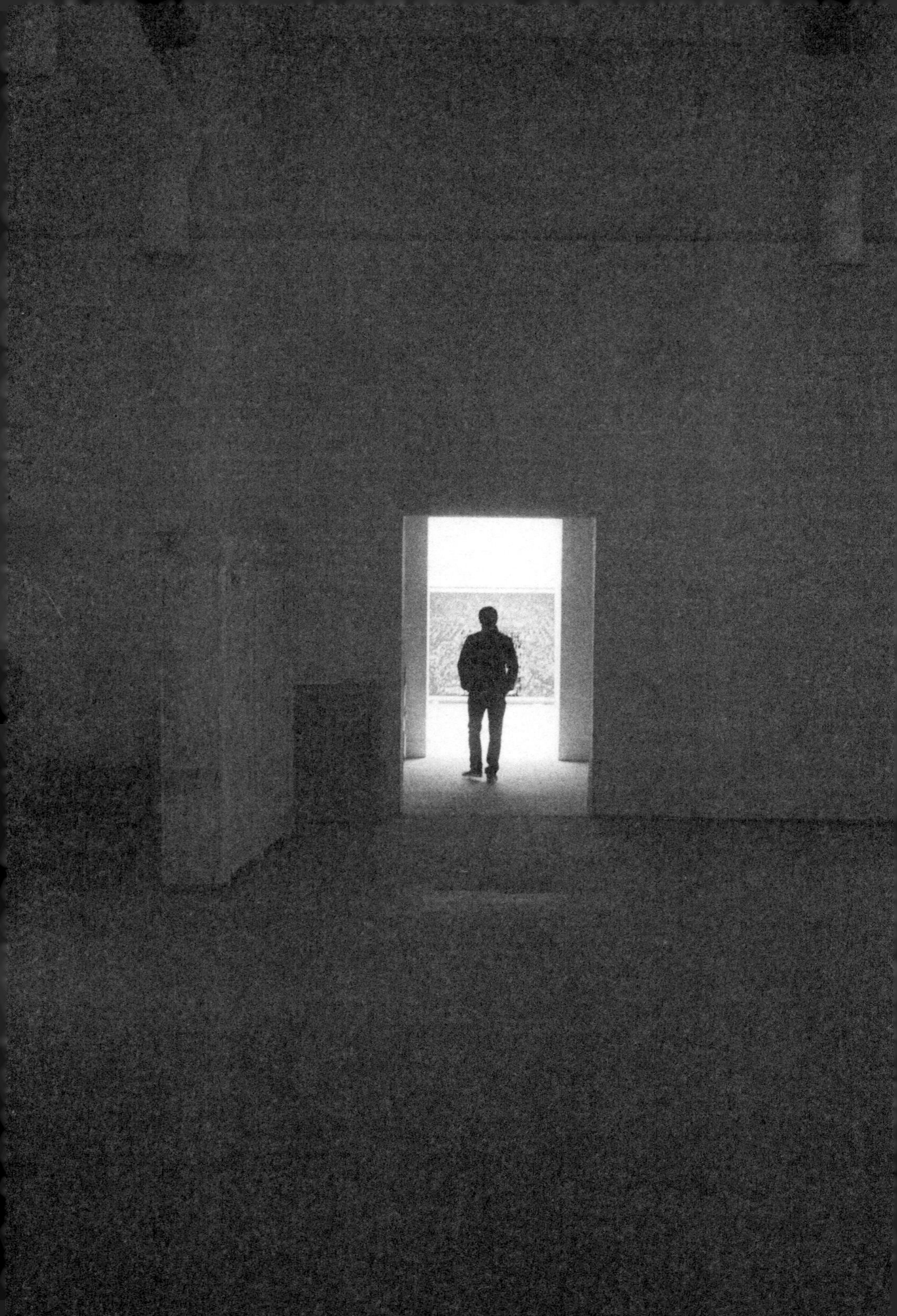

ABSOLU AVEC VACHE[1]
(and the Spectre of the Gun)

First published as "A White Cow in a Snowstorm," Bunch Alliance and Dissolve, exh. cat., Public Holiday Projects, Contemporary Arts Center, Cincinnati, Ohio 2006, p. 209-220; revised and republished as "Air Made Solid," Dot Dot Dot, vol. 15, 2007, p. 57-64; revised and republished as "Fenestration," The Grey Cloth, Das Institut im Glaspavillon/Galerie Meerrettich, Berlin, Germany; revised, expanded, and republished for Material Presence, Project Space 176, September 2008, p. 21-39.

The redemption of an epoch assumes the structure of an awakening, thoroughly governed by artifice. Only with artifice, and not without it, do we free ourselves from the realm of dreams.
—Walter Benjamin[2]

THE PROBLEM OF THE READYMADE

The proposition of materialist aesthetics carries with it a seductive promise, not only that the world of appearances can be punctured, shedding light into its darkened recesses, but also that there is something to be found lurking behind the curtain, a repressed "truth" at work within all things. Such a revelatory proposition is nowhere more embraced and confounded than in Marcel Duchamp's innovation of the readymade—an object which, in its moment of display, skirts between concrete literalism and imagistic spectacle. Fountain (1917), perhaps the most notorious example of the readymade, is often reduced, by proponents and detractors alike, to a testament of the artist's ability to arbitrarily confer value onto any object, and an irreverent disruption of the division between high and low. Yet this legacy cloaks a far more corrosive and unforgiving revelation. While at a first glance the readymade represented the power of the work of art to reflect and problematize its context, positing what would prove to be one of its most disarming critical abilities—i.e. its capacity to reflexively examine its own social function as it is tied to the conditions of exhibition—it preemptively refuted the direct political efficacy of anything that called itself art. For if a gesture as simple as the recontextualization of a common object could obliterate its use value, thus transforming it into an effigy of its past function, it also made clear that this quality of uselessness was alone the thing that made art art. This intervention into instrumental meaning was not simply a negation, but a distillation of the art object to its base social condition—a quality Rosalind Krauss called "exhibitionality."[3]

Far from democratizing and demystifying, as many of Duchamp's more stridently ideological contemporaries claimed as their aspiration, the readymade proposed art as an institutional gesture—the expression of a silent agreement. What constituted the readymade was not the object on display, but the frame that surrounded it. To follow the logic of the readymade, each art object, equally dependent upon the frame of exhibition, was also equally mute when it came to the address of an external state of affairs, the art object's enunciatory power being, if not simply a manifestation of its conditions of display, then at least wholly dependent on them to be recognized as art. In this gesture, the radical proposal of the avant-gardes, for both a materialist transparency and the utopian merging of artistic production with the quotidian, was simultaneously parodied and rendered moot. The disjunction that the readymade exploited—between the utopian aspirations of art, and art's relation to the everyday—was more than simply the byproduct of exhibition. It was the very foundation of it.

In, "Paris, Capital of the 19th Century," a text that would become the foundation for his epic and unfinished treatise on modernity (the _Passagen-Werk_ or _Arcades Project_), Walter Benjamin echoed Duchamp's insight into the exhibition with similar irony. Benjamin surmised that the impetus to collect and display objects derived from the desire to evoke "a world that is not just distant, and long gone, but also better—a world in which, to be sure, human beings are no better provided with what they need than in the real world, but in which things are freed from the drudgery of being useful."[4] In both Duchamp's and Benjamin's constructions, the making and displaying of cultural artifacts and their associated abilities to imagine an alternative to the status quo are inextricably tied to their incompatibility with the world of instrumental use. We thus have a paralyzing double bind: the proposal of a transformative utopian vision of functionalist and materialist aesthetics required the absence of instrumental use to even be spoken, a seemingly unacceptable trespass upon the very ideal that defined the productions of the avant-gardes (and political art in general). Conscribed to a limited field of possibilities, a producer who acknowledged the implications of the readymade was forced to position themself within an array of equally bleak options: either being resigned to a general attitude of bour-geois complacency, a naive zealotry, or an engagement with a prolonged negative characterization of their own crisis of effi-cacy by rephrasing it in a multitude of equally deadened forms.

If there is any lesson to be learned from Duchamp's innovation of the readymade, it is that no object within an exhibition can be taken literally. In concrete terms, making an exhibition is to work by analogy, to work via a model. Extricated from the world of use, exhibitions operate allegori-cally—no matter how one defines the parameters. To confuse this is to fall into the looking glass—to live life within a phantasmagoria. Exhibitions act as hypotheses, and perhaps this is why they have become affixed to the mute tabula rasa of Cartesian grids, far removed from sites of common exchange, cloaked in museum white.

The Great Exhibition of 1851, held in London's Hyde Park, defined the conditions of exhibition in the modern sense. From the early 1500s onward the term "exhibition" had only specialized legal meaning, referring to a giving of evidence: literally to "hold out." But with the Great Exhibition, and in World's Fairs that followed, the antiquarian meaning and impli-cations of the term blossomed. Born of the nascent consumer

culture of Victorian England, the World's Fairs were a key
distillation of modernity, uniting technological innovation,
immersive spectacle, nationalist ideology, and a forewarning
of the borderless world of global capital. In short, they
were an instrumental expression of modern life by symbolic
metonymy.

The late 19th century also gave rise to the modern corporation. The corporation, which would achieve the most radical
redefinition of personhood in a legal sense by the end of the
century—reimagining the very qualifications of the term "individual" as constituted by the state—was in its earliest stages
at the time of the World's Fairs. The subjectivity that arose in
this period is typically characterized as fractured and anomic,
an optically-centric incorporeality initiated by a constellation
of discursive forces that are far too expansive to discuss here.
However, the invention of the modern corporation as an individual under the law is perhaps the clearest and most complete
expression of this transformation, although with the terms
transposed. Instead of seeing what we thought was a unity fractured into disparate parts, the corporation as citizen-subject
arises out of discursive fragments. What for the humanist was
the indelible and ineffable fact of the individual, was rendered
porous and contingent, stripped completely from the notion
of the body (a term corporations semantically contain, i.e. corpus). Corporations are instead a multitude of voices congealed
into a singular entity—a transcription of an ephemeral set of
compromises and competing agendas given a singular voice. It
seems perverse for the groundwork of humanist democratic ideals
to be deployed in this manner, an uncanny proposition, because
if the same rule of law endows an immaterial entity the status
of autonomous individuality as guarantees our own, then our
own selfhood becomes troublingly precarious. This is why
McDonald's can now speak in the first person, but it also provides for the possibility of a series of ruses, provocations,
and liquidities.[5] As Gilles Deleuze noted, the corporation is "a
spirit, a gas," and we must wonder what it means for this ghost
to speak—for daily life is filled with such voices.[6]

Joseph Paxton's Crystal Palace, which housed the Great Exhibition of 1851, was a singularly remarkable material manifestation of this paradox posed architecturally. The Crystal Palace was the prototype of the modern steel and open-frame, glass curtain-walled architecture, providing the template for what would become the modern museum, the corporate complex, and the department store. The structure took the industrial dream of endless production and limitless expansion as defining principles; innovating a design that eschewed the monolithic stone construction and the revivalist pastiche popular in its time, opting instead for a modular structure of four-foot-square cells comprised of wrought iron. Despite its immense scale—it was over 1,800 feet in length and covered 19 acres—and industrial construction, it had an overall feeling of "lightness," the glass panes alternating between reflections of blue sky and surrounding greenery. Its sheer ephemerality so perplexed contemporary critics that it was denied even its existence as architecture.

The Crystal Palace was not of the world of buildings and monuments. It was a machine, a container for vistas, a scrim upon which spectacle could occur; a proposal that was alien to the public affirmation of cultural stability that architecture had come to represent. It was perpetually new; a structure whose modular construction allowed endless substitution. Or, more exactly, it was an embodiment of newness. At every turn, its interchangeable serial components shone with a "fairy-like brilliance," as if dropped from the heavens.[7] Architecture and vision became a singularity rendered in iron, as though Leon Battista Alberti's diagram of Renaissance perspective had been made concrete. When it was gone it would leave no auratic ruin for tourists, burning up in an explosive fire that was all too fitting for a building seemingly made of gas. But the structure persisted, built and rebuilt with little concern for the authenticity of an original. As Dostoyevsky wrote, "You believe in a crystal edifice that can never be destroyed, an edifice at which one would not be able to stick one's tongue out, or to thumb one's nose, even on the sly. And I am afraid of this edifice

because it is of crystal and can never be destroyed, and because
one could not stick out one's tongue at it on the sly."[8] The
only true damage that could be done to it could not come from
the material world of fires and explosions, but from the symbolic order from which it gained its authority. The fickle
wavering of consumerist tastes marked its demise.

General consensus denied the Crystal Palace a place in
the esoteric battle over architecture's identity.[9] It was the
work of a technician, not of an architect (artist). Paxton was
not ideological enough to be labeled a heretic. There was no
manifesto for the Crystal Palace; that project could be left
to the high practitioners. He was simply making do—problem
solving—there was no program, no doctrine. Its effect was
an "intoxicating" and disorienting experience. As one critic
explained, "It is, in my opinion, extraordinarily difficult to
arrive at a clear perception of the effect of form and scale
in this incorporeal space." Or as another visitor wrote, "There
is no longer any true interior or exterior, the barrier erected
between us and the landscape is almost ethereal." He continued,
"If we can imagine that air can be poured like a liquid, then
it has, here, achieved solid form."[10]

The threat that the structure posed to architecture
proper was its challenge to humanism and the authorial mark.
It contained no singular architectural event—no recognizable
style. It was, instead, a frame, a guide by which discontinuous
objects could be laid out as though in a picture. The structure
embodied not only a technological sublime in its modular and
serialized industrial form, but exemplified the very concept of
exhibition, of display. While its chief attribute was invisibility—its grand halls described as a container for "a perspective
so extended" that it appeared to be "a section of atmosphere
cut from the sky"—as a site, it was a microcosmic image of the
reach of the Western world, an egalitarian fantasy that invited
visitors to engage in virtual transport, offering a compression
of time and space, a short walk bringing visitors from contemporary South Africa to the Holy Roman Empire.[11] It was a safari
of capitalism staged in an interior.

It was some 50 years later that architecture succeeded
in cleaving the visual from the corporeal. Long before Le
Corbusier's <u>Maison Dom-ino</u> (1914-1915) ushered in an era of func-
tionalism and the "international style," the ubiquitous contemporary form of the art exhibition space, architecture, and
time travel were one and the same, already having been born
as a Cartesian virtual reality. The speculative fantasy of
glass architecture is nowhere better articulated than in Paul
Scheerbart's manifesto <u>Glass Architecture</u> (1914), itself a celebration of materialist transparency adhering to all the conventions of manifesto writing even as it undermined them, veering
between an earnest yet hyperbolic utopianism, and parodic science fiction. Its excesses were something the self-valorizing
Corbusier could never manage, and only obliquely allude to. Yet
for both men, everything within the architectural field, from
the accumulation of objects to the world framed by its windows,
was an element in an expansive order, an abstract topography
that inhabitants are invited to float above and through like
ghosts in an indefinitely expanding world within a world.

Le Corbusier's 1952 United Nations Secretariat Tower was
the first glass curtain-walled architecture in Manhattan. The
jeers were not unfamiliar, nor were the myriad technical problems. In fact, Corbusier was so frustrated by the difficulties
that he abandoned the project. Glass architecture found its
ultimate form here: an international style for international
compromise. Here was a building, which simultaneously stood out
and blended in—reflecting what Michel de Certeau called "the
city as text" on the surface of its modular panes. This was a
peculiar brand of hiddenness, all too fitting for a practitioner
who opted to produce under a well-publicized alias, just as so
many of his contemporaries who gave form to modernist principles chose to do (notably, all businesses begin with the adoption of a "fictitious" name, even if that name happens to be
your own). Bertolt Brecht famously stated that the image of the
exterior of a factory could tell you nothing of the lives it
contained. The Secretariat was no different, despite its glass
facade. When the lighting conditions of the Secretariat building

were reversed by night, after working hours, the modular interior was displayed devoid of its labor force. Le Corbusier allowed this desire to see in, without revealing anything more telling than what the reflective modular exterior offered by day: a procession of blank boxes.

Theater operates in this way—feeling both near and far, transparent and opaque—a living likeness that is more akin to a reanimated corpse than the social field it duplicates. If the Crystal Palace was the first building that fully capitalized on the theatrical spectacle of exhibition, the readymade was the first art object to be solely constituted by theatrical distance. Here the ritual act of viewing became the artwork's material—the object itself a hollow shell—a decoy. Thierry de Duve put it succinctly when he wrote that, in the wake of the readymade, the only truth to which the art object could attest was the power of its own name, rendering palpable the "pact that would unite the spectators of the future around some object … that added nothing to the constructed environment and did not improve on it, but quite the contrary, pulled away from it, bearing no other function than that of pure signifier."[12] Art was, in this liminal state, simply a category—nothing more than a name.

It seems no coincidence that just as Duchamp brought the foundational theatricality of art objects to the fore, the "zero point" of painterly materialism would surface thousands of miles away as a theatrical backdrop. In 1913 Kazimir Malevich was asked to contribute costumes and set designs for the Cubo-Futurist play Victory over the Sun. Aside from the almost unwearable costumes, Malevich produced a series of concept drawings for the sets, which in stark black-and-white appear like preparatory sketches for the Suprematist canvases he would begin producing two years later. When asked about his tautologically titled Black Square (1915), and its placement at 45 degrees in the top corner of the room of the 1915 exhibition 0.10 (Zero-Ten, Petrograd), Malevich referred back to these early set designs as its origin. The monochrome was simply a placeholder, a gap, a black hole—identifiable only by its event horizon.

While <u>Black Square</u> is often credited with being the first monochrome, this is not actually the case (not that being first matters). Some 30 years earlier this totem of total materialist refusal was realized by the poet Paul Bilhaud, in an exhibition staged in the apartment of the writer Jules Lévy in October of 1882 in Paris. Such modernist notables as Édouard Manet, Pierre-Auguste Renoir, Camille Pissarro, and Richard Wagner were given a peek at what would be framed as their legacy.[13] For the exhibition, Bilhaud contributed a small black painting titled <u>Combat de négres dans une cave pendant la nuit</u> (<u>Negroes Fighting in a Cellar at Night</u>), a joke that was stolen not once but twice: first by Alphonse Allais who produced a book titled <u>Album Primo-Avrilesque</u> (1897), which expanded the series to a range of color swatches and contained no mention of Bilhaud despite their acquaintance; and later by Malevich, who in the same year as <u>Black Square</u> produced the painting <u>Red Square</u> which included a particularly Bilhaudian parenthetical addendum in its title (<u>Painterly Realism of a Peasant Woman in Two Dimensions</u>). The invisibility of the site of work was here matched by the invisibility of the marginalized, both relegated to infrastructural obscurity. Daily life's representability was again scathingly parodied; the quotidian again displayed in absentia. Such mistrust of images has become a staple of modern life, although photography—not painting—has been the primary recipient of this ritual derision for the past half-century. Stoic deconstructive critique and hedonistic celebrations of nihilism often result in identical outcomes; it is just the captions that change. One is prompted to wonder how many times we can restage this anxious war on images to satisfactory effect?

David Robbins warned us about playing these games of total opposition for too long. Characterizing the Cold War as, "the war between Fun and No-Fun," and going on to surmise, "Eventually the American-led forces of Fun won, of course … Had its contribution only been limited to the recognition that, at certain moments, people want nothing more than to Do The Monkey—moreover, that they have the right to Do The Monkey, and should have the right to do it—by itself it would have been

something … [but] can a culture keep a moment, even one derived
from authentic inspiration and need, going that long? To respond
in the affirmative is to suppose that a culture can keep Doing
The Monkey <u>indefinitely</u>, and that there's no point beyond which
the Monkey-Doing culture will suffer damage or hurt itself … "[14]
Robbins ends this essay, "The Compass is the Map" with a claim
for entertainment as the last possibility for artistic efficacy.

In the late 1980s and early 1990s, many artists were
going corporate, sweating out the entrenched polarization that
fueled the critical debates of the preceding decades. The para-
gon of 1960s artistic radicalism, the art worker, received a
promotion to bourgeois entrepreneur. Warholian dandy-nihilism
is now less provocation and parody—becoming earnest was the
trump card to an earlier generation's irony—and more so, a viable business plan. At its worst this is cynical realism; at its
best it is a reflexive understanding that the traffic of a work
of art, its role in the market, is a key element of its meaning.
Recently one contemporary artist said in a lecture that the
most important artistic precedent in recent times was American
Apparel—asserting that it is effective as art because it sustains itself outside of art—a complete reversal of the bourgeois
readymade. But this example forces the question of whether any
art can exist outside the frame of exhibition by simply stepping to the side—by resigning the title "art"; and even if it
operates outside the literal context of a book, museum, or gallery space can it exist without an implied "exhibitionality"?
Or in Duchamp's words, "Can [an artist] make works that are not
'works' of art?"[15] Still, with the erosion of the mythology of
a white cube, or the printed page as a pure site of experiential
exchange, the backstage machinations of the marketplace, and
its relation to the network of exhibition spaces, remains an
impolitic topic of discussion. This despite the fact that the
proposition of art as a vehicle of reflexive critique no longer
seems quite so radical.

While art has proven hesitant to veer into pure didacti-
cism, science fiction displays little reticence. In the 1968 episode of <u>Star Trek</u>, "Spectre of the Gun," Captain Kirk and crew

set out under strict orders to contact an advanced yet unknown
race called the Melkotians. Warned off by an automated buoy,
they proceed to the surface of the planet, since their mission
of peace came with the stipulation from their superiors that
this contact must be made "at any cost" (peace at any cost being
an American hallmark). On the planet the crew are transported
into a schematic version of the American Old West, specifically
the very moment of the shootout at the OK Corral—finding they
occupy the role of the losers of this fight. Although the scene
is notably fictitious, even to the crew, death is not. As Dr.
McCoy observes, "In the middle of what seems so unreal, a harsh
reality. This is not a dream."

No matter what claims they make to the inhabitants of
this virtual world, no one believes they are who they say they
are, instead referring to them by the names of the men that
the Earp brothers and Doc Holliday had vanquished on that day.
Instead of being seen as purveyors of peace, they are seen as
familiar enemies who refuse to leave despite the townspeople's
warnings. The world was wrested from Kirk's mind, released when
the aliens scanned his brain, and Kirk goes on to explain that
the history into which they had been thrust was a character-
defining moment in his ancestral line. That the Old West town is
partial (missing walls, facades, and other architectonic necessities) is explained within the narrative as being the result of
missing information in Kirk's knowledge of the site and his own
history. Yet the true reason for the town's appearance was the
show's budgetary restrictions, which forced the producers to
recycle parts of the Old West sets on Paramount's studio back
lot. The scene of the crew's confrontation with its own historical mythology (they were, after all, space cowboys, colonizing
"the final frontier") occurs in remnants of past Hollywood narratives, a bricolage of the ruins of past fantasies, past scenes,
and past viewpoints.

As the crew waits for the impending showdown, it is rea-
soned that the only way to transcend this prison is to reject
the fiction altogether. As Spock goes on to warn, "I know the
bullets are unreal, therefore they cannot kill me. The slightest

doubt, and the bullets will kill you … " continuing, "The bullets
are unreal, without body, they are illusions only, shadows without substance. They will not pass through your body for they do
not exist. Unreal, appearances only, they are shadows, illusions,
nothing but ghosts of reality. They are lies, falsehoods, specters,
without body. They are to be ignored." But realizing this is
not enough, for the human members of the crew cannot remove the
kernel of doubt about the reality of what they see, and this
doubt, or more exactly, this belief in the facticity of images,
is exactly what will kill them. Only after each Vulcan receives
mind meld from Spock is the crew immune to the weapons used
against them, the "false consciousness" of the world of images
transcended; only then are they allowed audience with the timid
yet advanced aliens, an audience we never see in the episode,
for we are still in the world of sets and allegories, just as was
the crew when they landed on the planet, capable perhaps of
understanding fictions, but not able to ignore them. An alien
world that is beyond images is also beyond representation—a
zero point that the crew of the Enterprise proved itself worthy
of, but that we have yet to earn as mere viewers.

But what of Malevich's zero point, and its proposed
transcendence? With the climate in postrevolutionary Russia
progressing into Stalinism, the proposition of materialist
abstraction had become a symbol of bourgeois elitism. Malevich
returned to his pre-Suprematist foundations, producing canvases
that aped those of his antecedents, first the Cubo-Futurists,
and, most extreme, the Impressionists. Stranger still, Malevich
backdated these works, so that his Suprematist works remained
the forgone conclusion of these styles—turning his own progression into an ellipse—doubling back on itself. Since he held
to the conviction that he had reached the endpoint of painting,
the height of purism in form, there was nowhere to go but backward. He was trapped in his own Wild West origin story of false
starts and primordial violence.

The endless circulation of purisms in a culture of copies
always seems to lead to the same place: back into the blank,
which leaves the sites of production camouflaged in plain view,

like Paul Bilhaud's preemptive joke on monochrome painting's
radicality. In the debris of such battles, one is prompted to
ask where the ground of the real that these struggles are supposedly in the service of actually lies. In the wake of these
double negations, individual producers are relegated to one
more modular element, the social field appearing as a static
constellation of interchangeable parts. The citizen subject realized as a relational component, a unit of measure, an abstraction. But what of the visceral residues of work? Where labor's
vulgar bodily exertions are required, it exists out of view, in
off-hours, backrooms, cellars, and distant factories, negotiated
in private communications and invisible transports, sanitized
by aggregation, illegible in seductive surfaces.

As viewers, our role is to dissolve into these frames,
into an aggregated mass: out of time, out of space, and into
an abstract gleaming world. Yet seeing ourselves as part of
the mass, our individuality in a perpetual vacillation between
disappearance and reappearance, does not have to be debilitat-
ing. Rather, it can be a source of strength. Autonomy has
historically emerged from marginal zones: pirates and radicals
hide like rats in the walls, housewives stage mini-revolutions
in their kitchens, office workers in their cubicles. An understanding of this can make it clear that production is a common
fact, a daily ritual of compromise enacted with various levels
of awareness, but present nonetheless as a lingering force.
We can be both inside and outside of the picture, one of its
parts, and one of its producers; there need not be a stratified
hierarchy in our relationship to aesthetics. The embedded
compromises and negotiations present in any production and
their subsequent lack of authorial solidity need not be seen as
dirty secrets. This would not be an absolutist proclamation
of the corruption of authorship, but rather an assertion that
this authorial position is a communal one of transparency
and subterfuge at once. In this realization, there is a middle
ground of negotiation. All production—even "authorship"—
is comprised of myriad transit points and competing forces,
which deceptively assume the appearance of solidity.

The world we see from transitional spaces—the world outside the window; the world from the perspective of escalators, people movers, monorails, and shopping centers—has become an intellectual bogeyman—a storage container for all our alienations. These infrastructural interstitial zones stand as compromised, indeterminate way stations between chimerical destinations. As an open field they occupy the space of bare fact, which we should approach with suspicion, but they are also undecoded, unprocessed, and this has potential. Perhaps it is our presumption that all things, in order to exist, must have a determinable authorship and a plausible origin story that renders these plays of compromise inscrutable.

Railing against architecture has become a noble leftist cause. Perhaps this is because architecture's seeming solidity offers the hope for a stable and dominant ideological power to fight, a metaphor for the patriarchal institution, social and otherwise, a wall to bloody one's knuckles against. As Georges Bataille wrote, "The storming of the Bastille is symbolic of this state of affairs: it is hard to explain this mass movement other than through the people's animosity … against the monuments that are its real masters."[16] From a distant vantage point all action is symbolic, but models such as the Crystal Palace are unstable; they float, they are collusions of mass culture. Seemingly monolithic expressions of power are a similar accumulation of compromise and negotiation containing gaps where any visitor may assert their own agenda. We too are collaborators, even if we choose to relinquish our place in the credits. These momentary openings, the pockets between, their ruins, their transitory spaces, their ignored seams, and forgotten vistas promise a site from which the either/or of utopian and apocalyptic thinking—or a political/formalist opposition—can be dismantled, and production can be both symbolic and literal at once.

NOTES

1. The title, "Absolu avec Vache" is derived from the following passage written by
Arthur Danto, in "Paint it Black" in <u>The Nation</u>, August 18, 2003: "Hegel likened
the Absolute in Schelling to a dark night in which all cows are black, so a clever
student in Jena might have had the bright idea of painting an all-black picture
titled <u>Absolute With Cows</u>—witty or profound depending upon one's metaphysics."

2. Walter Benjamin, "Erfahrung und Armut," in <u>Gesammelte Schriften</u>, Surkamp
Verlag, Frankfurt, 1972, p. 234, as translated in Detlef Mertins, "The Enticing
and Threatening Face of Prehistory: Walter Benjamin and the Utopia of Glass,"
<u>Assemblage</u>, no. 29 (April 1996), p. 18.

3. Rosalind Krauss, "Photography's Discursive Spaces," <u>The Originality of the
Avant-Garde and Other Modernist Myths</u>, MIT Press, Cambridge 1985, p. 131-150.

4. Walter Benjamin, "Paris, Capital of the Nineteenth Century: Expos. of 1939,"
<u>The Arcades Project</u>, ed. Roy Tiedemann, trans. Howard Eiland and Kevin McLaughlin,
Harvard University Press, Cambridge 1999, p. 9.

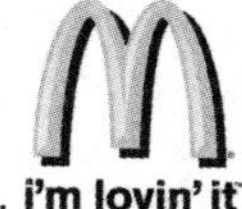

5.

6. Gilles Deleuze, "Postscript on Societies of Control," <u>October</u>, vol. 52
(Winter 1992), p. 4.

7. Patrick Beaver, <u>The Crystal Palace, 1851-1936: A Portrait of Victorian
Enterprise</u>, Hugh Evelyn, London 1970, p. 34.

8. Fyodor Dostoyevsky, <u>Notes from the Underground</u>, trans. Jesse Coulson,
Penguin Classics, New York 1972, p. 35.

9. " … the conviction has grown upon us, that it is not architecture; it is engi-
neering—of the highest merit and excellence—but not architecture." From, "The
Design of the Crystal Palace," <u>Ecclesiologist</u> 41 (1851), p. 269, as cited in Louise
Wyman, "Crystal Palace," in <u>Project on the City 2: Harvard Design School Guide to
Shopping</u>, Taschen, Cologne 2001, p. 236.

10. Cited in John McCean, <u>Crystal Palace: Joseph Paxton and Charles Fox</u>, Phaidon,
London 1994, p. 4.

11. Ibid., p. 32.

12. Thierry de Duve, <u>Pictorial Nominalism: On Marcel Duchamp's Passage from
Painting to the Readymade,</u> trans. Dana Polan and Thierry de Duve, University
of Minnesota Press, Minneapolis 1991, p. 115.

13. Phillip Dennis Cate, "The Spirit of Montmartre," in <u>The Spirit of Montmartre:</u> <u>Cabarets, Humor, and the Avant-Garde, 1875-1905,</u> ed. Phillip Dennis Cate and Mary Shaw, Rutgers University Press, New Brunswick 1996, p. 1-94.

14. David Robbins, "The Compass is the Map," in <u>The Velvet Grind: Selected Essays,</u> <u>Interviews, Satires (1983-2005),</u> ed. Lionel Bovier and Fabrice Stroun, JRP|Ringier, Zurich 2006, p. 270-272.

15. Thomas Hirschhorn offered an answer to this question in <u>Somebody Cares About</u> <u>My Work</u> (1992): placing a series of collages on the street outside his studio, Hirschhorn photographed garbage men hauling his works away. In relinquishing the frame the exhibition, the works he deposited met the same end as any other object freed from use: the dump.

16. Georges Bataille quoted in: Dennis Hollier, <u>Against Architecture: The Writings</u> <u>of Georges Bataille</u>, trans. Betsy Wing, MIT Press, Cambridge 1992, p. 15.

Toward an Empathic Resistance:
Boris Mikhailov's Embodied Documents

First published in <u>Afterall</u>, issue 12 (Fall 2005), p. 80-88.

A sort of umbilical cord links the body of the photographed thing to my gaze: light, though impalpable,
is here a carnal medium, a skin I share with anyone who
has been photographed.
—Roland Barthes[1]

The beauty of looking into these places without actually
being present there is that the excursionist is spared
the vulgar sounds and odious scents and repulsive exhibitions attendant upon such a personal examination.
—Jacob Riis[2]

The contradictory claims of the above quotations capture the
ethical conundrum that has plagued documentary photography
since its inception—between Barthes's assertion of empathic
visceral connectivity, and Riis's celebration of an almost clini-
cally discrete voyeuristic verisimilitude. It is difficult to
imagine that any practice could have received a more complete
dismantling and demotion by the 1970s art world discourse than
the tradition of documentary photography. Ceremoniously stripped of its currency, the social-documentary project found itself
under siege from both aesthetic formalist and structuralist/
poststructuralist positions, which vied for dominance over the
nature and history of photography. The former—whose clearest

voice was that of John Szarkowski, the highly influential curator of photography at The Museum of Modern Art—cited its woe-
ful insistence on narration, which was "generally achieved at
the expense of photographic discovery," and its claim of transparency, which distanced the photograph from the validity
of authorship and personal expression that would deliver the
medium a more auspicious painterly pedigree, as justification
for his disdain.[3] A perhaps even more damning critique emanated
from the latter camp, which took specific issue with documentary photography's positivist claims for objectivity, and ironically dismissed it on the very social, moral, and ethical
grounds upon which the tradition had been founded.

While some semblance of the tradition remained (the most
provocative examples of which were produced by the most vehe-
ment critics of its liberal humanist naiveté), the majority of
practitioners who clung to the possibility of a direct response
to social milieu within a museum context did so only under a
literalization of the program put forward by Szarkowski, most
notably in his seminal 1967 exhibition New Documents. This
exhibition heralded artists who had once worked in journalistic
formats and turned the document to distinctly "personal ends."
Opting for a more pronounced declaration of the presence of the
maker within the image, and a dismissal of the sociopolitical
dimension as something directly representable, later practitioners veered toward a mode of production best exemplified by
William Eggleston. In his centrally framed color images of evacuated interiors, isolated figures and objects displaced the radical upheaval going on in the American South (one that just so
happened to directly question his own position as a southern
white aristocrat) in favor of personal ciphers of alienation.
Another trajectory, best represented by the New Topographics
photographers, dealt with this ethical quandary by focusing on
the alienation of the figure from the contemporary landscape,
systematically depopulating traditional sites of social exchange
(for example, downtowns, factories, businesses, suburban developments, etc.).[4] Photographs that were still predicated upon
their ability to see into the hidden world of others, and thus

claim an empathic connectivity, increasingly turned to the isolated realm of the personal. Thus in the snapshot roughness of Nan Goldin, later exemplified in the practices of Wolfgang Tillmans and Richard Billingham, the problematic assertions of total transparency and social efficacy were diffused by the metamorphosis of documentary into diary. These artists avoided the contentious claim for the stable and relevant transcription of "reality" in favor of stylistic familiarity (for example, the family photo album), thereby reaffirming their own immediacy and proximity to the viewer through the simulation of the debased vernacular of the snapshot. In this sense photography relinquished its long-held position as the aesthetic preserver of history, as if taking Siegfried Kracauer's famously pessimistic appraisal that photography "sweeps away the dams of memory … threaten[ing] to destroy the potentially existing awareness of crucial traits" as a bare fact, not as a warning.[5]

The art world's photographic taste for these faux-naive diaries, the revivalist formalism of monolithic transcriptions of evacuated postmodern geographies, and the glazed stares of alienated figures indicates its almost unanimous hesitance to reopen sociopolitical questions of representation. It suggests we are trapped in a prolonged lamentation over the defeat of liberal humanism, and the subsequent erosion of its core terms— "liberty," "freedom," and "democracy"— in a jingoist hijacking by neoconservative elements. The photographic repertoire of strategies appears reduced to the symbolic insinuation of external conditions, and an abandonment of direct intervention and contestation. In contradistinction to other practices, photography seems to have embraced a role as the conservator of a rarified aesthetic tradition, one that will likely, in time, be spoken of with the same derision that the early avant-gardes reserved for salon painting.

Under what was, to some extent, a parallel condition of resignation—both by the direct repression of the Soviet Union and in the post-Soviet sanitization during the shift to capitalism—the work of Boris Mikhailov found its form. Evasive and multivalent, Mikhailov's practice moves between a range

of stylistic approaches. I first came upon his images at the
opening of the politely austere exhibition <u>Cruel and Tender</u>
at Tate Modern (2002). Amid the processions of contemplation,
punctuated by pleasant chitchat and lazy strolls of the opening's attendees, I noticed people emerging from one of the exhibition halls more briskly than others. There I found the almost
floor-to-ceiling prints from Mikhailov's <u>Case History</u> (1999):
rough-hewn photographs tacked directly to the wall, depicting
the <u>bomzhes</u> (which he defines as "homeless without any social
support") of his native Ukraine in various states of undress.[6]
The tension in the gallery was palpable. People seemed to stand
at attention around the photographs, resting uncomfortably in
the center of the space, careful to keep their distance from the
images, as if actually being confronted by half-naked homeless
men and women. The harsh grain of the 35mm film enveloped the
print, matching the battered and sometimes diseased bodies that
presented themselves so willingly to the camera—a condition of
bodily dissolution that had been neatly expunged from the saccharine visions of a post-Soviet democracy. Mikhailov paid each
of his subjects and asked them to disrobe; the vulgarity of this
transaction is made evident by the confrontational images. The
acknowledgment of the trade in bodies and the interplay of dominance and subordination in the act of viewing were inscribed
on their surfaces, a difficult pill to swallow on a leisurely
stroll through the museum. The social contract, in its moment
of harrowing disintegration, brought forth a vision of the body
that echoed that of a medical examination, and simultaneously
unearthed the history of physiognomic investigation sublimated
in contemporary portraiture. The images are as violent in their
unblinking transcription of suffering as in their insistence
on the necessity to take notice, even if only to upend the conditions that made them possible.

The particularly precarious contemporary problem faced
by those who seek to directly confront and undermine dominant
ideological structures is the danger of reinforcing the very
thing they oppose. This situation was succinctly described
by Judith Butler when she wrote, "dominance appears most

effectively as its 'Other,'" outlining that the dialectic of "dominance and opposition" is rendered illusory though the "instrumental use that the former makes of the latter."[7] Most problematic of all, we run the risk of affirming an authority synonymous with that dominant structure through the inhabitation of its prescriptive voice, a strategy that Allan Sekula surmised, "preclude(s) the possibility of anything but affirmation" regardless of the ends to which it is put, and subsequently naturalizing a mode of address whose primary function is that of subordination.[8] This is, for all intents and purposes, the crux of the argument levied at the tradition of documentary photography—through its instrumentalization at the hands of the dominant classes, it re-victimizes those it proposes to save, reifying their otherness, and affirming the juridical procedures that excluded them in the first place.[9] That is perhaps because photography is founded on the impenetrable scopic remove of spectacle, enacted in the techno-mediation between photographer and subject, and recreated at the safe distance of its audience; whether they are readers of a magazine or visitors to a museum, they are given tacit permission to revel in a fetish for character and form that is the true culprit here.

The figure of the aloof flaneur haunts photography, providing its cool distance and voyeuristic proclivities. But Mikhailov is no flaneur; rather, he rummages through the refuse he is presented with in search of something he can put to his own use. It is physicality that is his interface; he is something of a guerrilla <u>bricoleur</u>, a scavenger. Mikhailov collects his materials as his subjects do, searching in the forgotten and discarded, piecing together minor histories and totemic memorials.

Such scavenging was in large part a necessity within the former Soviet Union, where the territories available to the photographer without journalistic sanction were limited to the zones the state did not have access to, or chose not to trespass upon. Materials were often in short supply, dictating that artists employ both an economy of means and the rough assemblage evidenced in their production. Despite increased availability after the fall of communism, Mikhailov continues to work within

these limitations. He persistently employs objects that betray
their former uses, operating both as a memory trace and a dual
refusal of the homogenizing effect of Soviet prescriptions and
late capitalism's endless procession of the new. In <u>Unfinished
Dissertation</u> (1985) a series of photographs are fixed onto
a discarded and incomplete academic text found in the street,
turning it into something of an aesthetic treatise and a personal diary. <u>Look at me I look at water</u> (2002) also employs found
materials. Both reintegrate personal texts into the matrix of
photographic representation, but the results are fragmentary;
passing thoughts and second-hand accounts litter their pages.
Arranged in a piecemeal reconstruction of subjectivity, they are
developed from scraps and represented in a form traditionally
used in the black-market traffic of pornography (an appropriate
reconstitution for the personal proclivities repressed in the
Soviet era). There is an equivalence between the ragged yellow
pages adorned with annotated snapshots and passing memories
transcribed in ballpoint pen. Gracing the margins of the
stained pages are recollections of news stories and people
Mikhailov photographed, along with more elliptical poetic notations and laconic humor. Ever present is a practice of "making
do," evident in Mikhailov's appropriation of refuse as the staging ground for the personal, and in his attraction to the
interstitial sites he photographs, which offer both the privacy
needed to produce out of view of the State, and the occasion to
document the multiple negotiations and appropriations required
in adapting to the strictures of the former Soviet Union. In
short, they not only recount the conditions of repression,
they materially attest to it.

In the summer of 1986, Mikhailov began documenting a
summer ritual practiced by the proletarian population of the
city of Slaviansk. Working-class families crowd the unsightly
beaches amid industrial detritus and the passing of freight
trains. In his photographs, the plump bodies of the ailing and
the elderly gently float in the pools of salt water, a byproduct
of the soda ash factories that frame the horizon. In the shadow
of an industry that has ravaged the landscape, the communities

formulate their own strategies of coexistence and even counter-
mythologies to the industrial secularism (many share the belief
that the pools have medicinal and even spiritual effects).
The photographs themselves are dark, over-printed, and deeply
toned, as if stained by the landscapes they depict. Flecks of
dust, hairs, and nicks in the emulsion are framed by the dark
smudges of gelatin silver directly exposed to light, giving them
an echo of nostalgia while insistently foregrounding the material conditions of the photograph, even as we become immersed
in the scene.

Mikhailov applied this approach again in his first
post-Soviet series, By the Ground (1991). Far bleaker than its
earlier counterpart, By the Ground consists of similarly dark-
toned black-and-white photographs. Freed from the prohibition
of photography in public spaces, the streets of Kharkov and
Moscow became his subject. Still, moments of lightness touch the
images: young girls are caught playing in an alley, lovers tus-
sle in a public park, and passersby are caught in awkward personal displays on the street. But ever-present in these images
is the increasingly bleak city that surrounds them. Empty
streets and back alleys strewn with rubble form the backdrops
in which his subjects go about their routines. With increasing
regularity, isolated figures appear adrift along the concrete
boulevards, the dissolution of Communism's "great experiment"
creating its first wave of abject poverty. The signs of isolation that begin to surface in By the Ground dominate his next
series, At Dusk (1993). Shot exclusively in Kharkov, At Dusk
presents what would seem to be highly populated areas as abandoned macabre stage sets waiting to be activated by the onset
of liberal democracy. Individuals cling to the shadows, or are
found slumped on benches, or sprawled at bus stops; the inhabitants of the city appear to be perched precariously on topographies from which they might slide off into oblivion, the landscape seeming more postwar than newly democratic. It is here
that the corrupted documentary genre—at its moment of complete
disappearance from the economy of contemporary artistic production—is recovered and redeployed in a form that betrays the

simultaneous erosion of both its efficacy and the ideals it
strove for. The communal intimacy that marked Salt Lake (2002)
appears all but evacuated. It is in this series that we begin to
see the focus of Mikhailov's next body of work, the desperate
conditions of the bomzhes.

Case History was originally intended to be the third
part of a trilogy. In chromatic progression from By the Ground's
deep brown and At Dusk's modeled cyan, Case History was to be
Mikhailov's pink work. As he writes, the pink "corresponded to
a revival of new life, like during a sunrise, when the light is
evenly covering the whole surface."[10] But upon his return to the
city, he was confronted with something altogether different.
New prosperity had been born, but only with deepening levels of
desperation. The gray streets were adorned with foreign adver-
tisements, and brightly colored kiosks brandishing the names
"Agfa," "Konica," and "Fuji" offered the newly arrived color
photography as if providing ground-floor entry to the spectacular vistas held aloft on billboards. The shiny signifiers of
the arrival of the free market matched the ubiquity of their
neighbors' abject bodily existence as the newly expanded class
of the homeless grew. Mikhailov referred to the proliferation of
color photographs and their new availability as a "rash on an
ill body."[11] The abject bodily trauma of the images comprising
Case History resonate in the dissolution of the once-idealized
totality of the proletarian body politic of the Soviet regime,
fractured and stratified into those who were able to integrate
into the free market, and those who were abandoned in its margins, everywhere present, yet uncannily invisible in the images
of the now "liberated" society. Mikhailov's staged return of
the body in a state of disrepair contrasts starkly with his
playful earlier investigations of the mundane body of the average Soviet citizen. Both unmake the hermetically sealed body of
the totalitarian ideal, expert in its pure transformation and
control of carnal drives, while upsetting the sexualized fig-
ments of free-market imagination by their direct depiction of
poverty and disease, intertwined with a similar invitation of
the viewer's gaze. Here Barthes's famous comparison of the

fleeting power of the photograph to a wound seems most apt,
as though it were now festering, an infestation of the "common
skin" that he saw as the greatest promise of photography.[12]

Boris Groys has commented that the reason Mikhailov's
Case History is so disturbing is that the "frail, ruined, and
repulsive bodies of the homeless people in these photographs
are … presented as erotic bodies."[13] The relationship we have to
these photographs, as with the personal snapshot, is one of
immediacy, in this moment reversing the benevolent stewardship
of our personal memories and inscribing the chaos and trauma
our collective histories so expertly sublimated. In this sense,
Mikhailov recovers—as he does with his reuse of discarded material—the visceral phenomenological connectivity of the documentary photograph and the mnemonic potential it once presumed
to maintain, reopening the ethical and social questions that
persist despite their contemporary collective disavowal. As
Mikhailov wrote, "I was interested in the borders of a new
morality which would suit the new borders of survival."[14] Such
investigation is long overdue, and while his work is far from
solving many ethical contradictions, its repeated emphasis on
the necessity of an active engagement in these debates provides
a viable pathway out of the anomic retreat of contemporary art
at a moment when the stakes appear to be unusually high. If
nothing else, Mikhailov's work proves that photography is still
in possession of its capacity for visceral effect despite the
theoretical consensus that it is the harbinger of disaffection.
In his hands it once again offers an emphatic resistance that
the practitioners of this most "carnal medium" once wielded so
effectively.

NOTES

1. Roland Barthes, _Camera Lucida_, Hill and Wang, New York 1981, p. 81.

2. Jacob Riis, quoted in Maren Stange, _Symbols of Ideal Life: Social Documentary Photography in America, 1890-1950_, Cambridge University Press, Cambridge and New York 1989, p. 16.

3. John Szarkowski, _The Photographer's Eye_, The Museum of Modern Art, New York 1980, p. 6.

4. Numerous examples are called to mind, such as the emptied vistas of the New Topographics photographers, including Robert Adams, Bernd and Hilla Becher, Joe Deal, and Stephen Shore, as well as post-Pop conceptual investigations such as the work of Jan Dibbets, Dan Graham, Ed Ruscha, Michael Schmidt, and Robert Smithson.

5. Sigfried Kracauer, "Photography," in _The Mass Ornament: The Weimar Essays_, Harvard University Press, Cambridge 1995, p. 58.

6. Boris Mikhailov, _Case History_, Scalo, Zurich 1999, p. 5.

7. Judith Butler, "Restaging the Universal: Hegemony and the Limits of Formalism," in _Contingency, Hegemony, Universality: Contemporary Dialogues on the Left_, ed. Judith Butler, Ernesto Laclau, and Slavoj Zizek, Verso, London 2000, p. 28.

8. Allan Sekula, "On the Invention of Photographic Meaning," in _Photography Against the Grain: Essays and Photo Works, 1973-1983_, Nova Scotia College of Art and Design, Halifax 1984, p. 1.

9. Martha Rosler, "In, around and afterthoughts (on documentary photography)," in _The Context of Meaning: Critical Histories of Photography_, ed. Michael Bolton, MIT Press, Cambridge 1984, p. 305-308.

10. Mikhailov, _Case History_, p. 4.

11. Ibid., p. 10.

12. Barthes, _Camera Lucida_, p. 26-27.

13. Boris Groys, "The Eroticism of Imperfection," in _The Hasselblad Award 2002: Boris Mikhailov_, Hasselblad Centre, Gothenburg 2002, p. 77.

14. Mikhailov, _Case History_, p. 8.

Wolfgang Tillmans

First published in German as "_Die Dichte Des Unfertigen_" in _Texte zur Kunst_, no. 64 (December 2006), p. 218-221.

While art audiences had become increasingly accustomed to a plurality of approaches aimed at disrupting, or at least redefining, conventional forms and approaches to installation, most photographic practices favored a more conservative agenda, embracing the staid genre forms of the premodern Beaux-Arts, exemplified in an almost obsessive adherence to Renaissance pictorial formulae. The architectural tropes of contemporary photography—ubiquitous in both its presentational affect and its subject matter—performed a pictorial affirmation of the cold geometries of the white cube, as if reassuring spectators of the works belonging to the museum's hallowed halls. Still, the most prevalent art photography relies upon heightened artifice, depopulated expanses, and cinematic fantasy, distant from the snapshot's banal depictions, appearing all but ignorant of the implications of the similarly plasticine views that grace billboards and magazines. It was as if, in the wake of the troubling recognition of photography's malleability in the hands of instrumental use, and its critical reappraisal by artists and critics in the 1960s and 1970s, the contemporary production of photographs required turning back to a time before avant-gardist debates or postmodernist dismantling.

Within this milieu, Wolfgang Tillmans work is something of an anomaly. Tillmans' earliest photographs found their home in the pages of picture magazines, subsumed within the editorial

strictures that had come to represent the very incompleteness
that the neo-pictorialists were hard at work to correct. Within
his images we find neither the densely packed, allegorically
loaded struggles that characterize American street photography,
nor the quality of epic disaffection characteristic of the New
Topographic or Düsseldorf School. That is, Tillmans' photographs
are distinctly nontheatrical constructions: his formal predilec-
tion is not for spatially illusionistic microcosms of the world,
but instead for pictorial flatness, a matter-of-fact or seemingly offhanded compositional arrangement that sits tenuously
within the photograph's flat field. Tillmans' work thus has the
sensation of incompleteness, which is often mistaken for the
ill-considered or undeliberate naivety of the snapshot. In snapshots, this sensation is an indication of a missing subject, a
figure that serves as an elusive codex that gives the images
their meaning. Siegfried Kracauer identified this quality of
incompleteness with memory, as it is opposed to gestalt history,
and further placed the totalized "banality of detail" of photography at odds with memory's "flowing expanse." While many
have noted the mnemonic allusions of Tillmans' work, an observation clearly articulated by Gil Blank when he wrote that
Tillmans' photographs cohere "through an unending accretion
of multiple and imperfectly formed instances," the construction
of memory is not simply the diaristic notations with which
Tillmans is often associated, but a hybridized memory culled
from popular culture as much as personal experience. In his
exhibitions, the faces of the anonymous are as likely to be
found as images of the famous, a conflation of private memory
and the public sphere that renders the membrane between these
seemingly opposed mnemonic repositories more porous than our
sense of interminable individuality usually allows.

This signature strength of Tillmans' practice is perhaps
nowhere in better evidence than in his first museum survey in
North America, a traveling mid-career retrospective originating
at the Museum of Contemporary Art in Chicago, and currently
on view at the Hammer Museum in Los Angeles (co-organized by
Russell Ferguson and Dominic Molon). Even to say the show

traveled is something of a misnomer: a minority of the work
appears in identical form at both venues. Images from as early
as 1993 appear along side unfamiliar images, while still others
have been remade in radically different form. In Empire (Punk)
(2005), one of Tillmans' iconic earlier photographs appears
as a blown up fax transmission, and the photograph of pop icon
Morrissey, itself originally presented on the cover of Index
Magazine, was installed on the wall in Chicago; only to resur-
face on the expanse of unassuming tables in the Truth Study
Center in Los Angeles. These momentary echoes within Tillmans's
work, the calling back of previous moments of reception, situate
the photographs as objects in a recombinatory system that constantly performs a reexamination of its own procedures, retell-
ing its origins within the immediacy of its new moment of presentation. Each iteration of Tillmans' work becomes a specific
reconfiguration in a moment time, a stable form drawn from a
repository of images that, like celestial bodies, are organized
figurations drawn from a seemingly vast reservoir. Tillmans'
editorial experience might also explain the often misinter-
preted form of his earliest installations, which favored densely
clustered thematic groupings whose exhibition logic was somewhere between the taped up mementos of a teenager's bedroom
and the salon style configurations of a magazine page bereft of
text. Those earliest procedures evoke Sarah Charlesworth's April
21, 1978 and Hans-Peter Feldman's Sunday Pictures (1976) in
equal parts, both of which emphasized the sorting mechanisms
that construct photographic meaning in spatial terms, directing
the viewer to a recombinant (and in these cases readymade) logic
often obscured from view. Tillmans' choices are less prescribed,
alluding to a private field of references from which the groupings originate, sharing the greatest affinity with the hybridized cinematic practices of Hollis Frampton, Morgan Fisher,
Chris Marker, and Yvonne Rainer, each of whom wove together
found images, quasi-autobiographical narration, and materialist
abstraction into a materially based subjectivity—a sensitivity
to repressed connections to which Tillmans seems acutely aware.
Frampton likened this indirectly manifest mnemonic field to

"a ghostly freight of possible films," each film a singular
manifestation of "directly implied possible films" that form a
"cloud or cluster of films that exist virtually." Tillmans similarly describes a field of images that are in a constant state
of "becoming," proposing a similarly metalogical form whose
irregular agglomerations and tangential threads offer a metonymic allusion to the field from which it originated, and a
formal analog for their potential reframing within almost limitless formations.

It was this quality that Craig Owens associated with
photography's operation en abyme, specifically its ability to
not only exemplify its own reduplication, but depict it simultaneously. Owens saw this as the void from which the photograph
could not escape, an endlessly reduplicated failure of meaning,
leaving only "an overwhelming feeling of absence" in its wake.
But Tillmans' repetitions eschew this seemingly inescapable reiteration of nihilistic failure by expanding the epistemic features of photography and its display, both by rejecting the
totalizing implications of pictorial form (as he said in a recent
interview, "the camera always lies about what is in front of it")
and by emphasizing the territorial mapping that occurs in
between images (continuing, it "never lies about what is behind
it"). In this way Tillmans expands on the common understanding
of photography as a melancholic receptacle, a photography characterized as unable "to convey anything but a sense of loss, of
absence," and instead of relying on the pictorial interdependency of objects within the frame, extends this reduplication to
the site of exhibition. This process incessantly resists the proposal of a naturalized singular contextual reading of the work,
while never slipping into relativist nihilism or an amnesiac
reclamation of humanist individuality. What Tillmans deploys is
an exhibition that contains within itself a memory of its past,
not only present in the photographs as mnemonic deposits, but
also because the entirety of the exhibition behaves as a spa-
tialized allegory for recollection.

What returns, in Tillmans, is not simply the procession
of sameness, but, as Eduardo Cadava elucidated, a "movement

through which something other is inscribed within the same, which is now no longer the same, name(ing) what is always other than itself," in other words a "return of returning." In Tillmans' hands, exhibitionality becomes a distinctly photographic enterprise, a reformulation of past conditions, within the static immediacy of the exhibition itself, and a reflexive operation that neither falls victim to a melancholic celebration of social anomie, nor a reactionary affirmation of naturalized meaning or transparency. Instead, the exhibitions take on a diminutive and porous form, proposing a method of production that is both distanced from totalized spectacle and yet expansive, that neither engages in a negative masquerade of categorical objectivity nor mires itself in a hermetic personal sphere. The sheer variation in his photographic program—from portraits to performative scenes, landscapes, enlarged punctures in sheets of film, wily gestural abstractions, and serial monochromes—develops a practice that at once embraces the range of procedures that constitute a photographic episteme, and ties these together through an equally rich exhibition rhetoric. Much in the same way, the conditions that defined opposing camps in experimental film were redefined in the hands of Frampton, Rainer, Marker, and Fisher, recovering documentary, materialist abstraction and narration from self-anointed purists, and thus formulating a synthesis that emphasized the possibility for a politicized subject amid a field that was preoccupied with taxonomic separation. The very urgent need for a reconfigured affirmation of possible subject positions and political becomings that allow for some semblance of autonomy renders these the direst of questions. It is specifically the need for a movement away from alienated paralysis, which, at least in the US, is overdue. It is this sensibility that Tillmans' perfectly timed exhibition draws to the fore, without proclamation or prescription.

Parallax Views: Michael Asher at the Santa Monica Museum of Art

First published in English and German in <u>Texte zur Kunst</u>, no. 70 (May 2008), p. 168-171, 205-209.

Winding through the flickering latticework of Michael Asher's temporary exhibition at the Santa Monica Museum of Art, Albrecht Dürer's statement "Perspectiva ist ein lateinisch Wort, bedeutet ein Durchsehung"[1] came to mind, which resonated both with the experience of tentatively peering through the exposed stud walls filling the gallery, and the revelatory promise of institutional critique with which Asher is inextricably identified. Stepping carefully through the skeletal walls, one is subject to a sequence of disquieting perceptual transformations: the intersections of the stud walls optically reordered the gallery space along a multitude of planar confluences, reconfiguring the bedrock of exhibition design, the sight line, into a strobing view that rearranged itself with the slightest shift in physical position. The initial effect was visually disorienting yet corporeally grounded. I found myself slowly rocking from side to side, alternating eyes, sensitive to the disruption of my stereoscopic vision, a chance stumble or scrape against the exposed metal studs drawing me out of the optical detachment familiar to any exhibition goer.

It is no revelation that exhibitions have disembodying effects. It was, after all, Joseph Paxton's Crystal Palace—a transparent modular exhibition hall made of glass sheets and iron beams—that would define the most spectacular qualities of the exhibition, thrusting the term itself into the cultural

imagination.[2] Yet in trying to reconcile the spatial and optical
conditions of Asher's work, I experienced firsthand what I had
assumed was merely theoretical flourish: the alienating cleavage
of the corporeal from the visual, a potent reminder that, at
least since Leon Battista Alberti's treatise on perspective, architecture has had literal and metaphoric governance over vision.

Organizational systems always run the risk of obliterat-
ing what they try to preserve: Renaissance perspective and
exhibition mechanics are no exception. The attempt to define
rational space in the terms of infinite, reproducible, and
homogenous Cartesian parameters required the repression of certain aspects of how we actually see (for example, that we see
stereoptically, or that we see in curved rather than straight
perspectival lines), their existence amounting to a tangible
threat to the reality such models propose. Similarly, the standard exhibition design tends to favor static, portable works of
art and is less welcoming to those that deviate from these conditions. In the intersecting planes of Asher's work—derived
from the overlaid floor plans of the 44 exhibitions held at the
"museum"[3] since 1998—such attempts at organizational clarity
become contingent, providing a phenomenological immersion that
rests tentatively between the spectacular and the materialist,
all the while presenting a history of the space as an array of
intersecting fragments. As one moves through the exhibition,
one passes through an almost infinite sequence of interlocking
vantage points, their visual and physical containments rendered
unavoidably palpable and curiously incoherent.

Asher's excision of instrumental meaning, by recontextu-
alizing and overlaying the past configurations of temporary
wall supports, appears continuous with processes Benjamin H. D.
Buchloh outlined as the core operational logic of allegory,
characterized by "appropriation and depletion of meaning, fragmentation, and dialectical juxtaposition of fragments," which
has the effect of "ruins".[4] Furthermore, Asher's current exhibition is remarkably analogous to the procedures Buchloh observed
in Dadaist poetry, which "deplete[d] words, syllables, and sounds
of all traditional semantic functions and references until they

bec[a]me visual and concrete."[5] Yet in Buchloh's formulation, the political efficacy of allegory is suspect, leading irrevocably to resignation. In a polemic, two years earlier, Craig Owens succinctly argued that allegorical works of the postmodern period "enact a deconstruction of the museum … [that]—like Daniel Buren's — can take place only within the museum itself … We thus encounter once again the unavoidable necessity of participating in the very activity that is being denounced precisely in order to denounce it."[6] Here Owens argued that allegory leads to a "complicity" that is irreconcilable with the political project of critique (an insight that is never extended to the critics engaged in deconstructive modes despite their equal susceptibility to this problem).

On closer examination, Asher negotiates a way out of this critical dead end. While Asher's work is a cacophony of fragmented systems, piled, conflated and re-presented as an inscrutable whole, the work's re-combinatory logic resists allegory's melancholic reiteration of alienation, without presuming that authoritative structures can be simply ignored—enacting a bricolage logic, which is distinct from the allegorical due to its insistence on active rather than passive reception. In other words, one must actively navigate through the ghost walls, step over and through them, rather than stand back and observe them from afar. Such re-combinatory activities are evocative of what Claude Lévi-Strauss proposed as the asymmetrical oppositional model of the <u>science du concret</u>, a mode of resistance that eschews open opposition for subtle transformation and misuse. Asher reorders the mechanisms of the exhibition into a pastiche of spatial rhetorics that divert their performance of cohesion into a series of experiential contingencies. In this, Asher avoids the mute stasis of Walter Benjamin's formulation of "allegorical seeing" (notably Benjamin's arguments offer the theoretical basis for both Owen's and Buchloh's writing on allegory) by proposing a dynamic re-combinatory visual and spatial experiential model in an active site of participation. In Asher's work for the SMMA, the result is a fracturing of the seeming unity of the institution into a multiplicity of irreconcilable intonations,

opening up the possibility for alternate modes of vision and
production that operate despite the presence of a hegemonic
order. Thus, the naturalized authority of exhibition rhetoric
is transformed through a recombinant logic that is corrosive
to any authoritative prescription regardless of origin, here
realized as a contingent spatial harmonic that asserts the possibility for political practice beyond simple revelations of
dominance and subordination. In this proposition, Asher rejects
the melancholic generalities that usually pervade the argumentation around artistic critique, imbedding his production in
active social systems.

As early as 1976 Asher began making use of the exhibition
site in increasingly contingent and socially dynamic ways that
extended into a larger sociopolitical field. From the insertion
of a lounge area for viewers to "communicate on a social level"[7]
at the 1976 Venice Biennale to his work for a three person
show at the Los Angeles Institute of Contemporary Art in 1977
in which he employed paid participants to occupy the space,[8]
and through numerous exhibitions including those held at the
Nouveau Musée in Villeurbanne in 1991, and the 2004 project
Asher initiated with students from Fairfax High School in Los
Angeles to reinstall the modern and contemporary galleries
of the Los Angeles County Museum of Art, Asher's work has completely rejected the idea that the exhibition space could be
dealt with as a static model.[9] It is worth mentioning that these
tactics are all the more prescient in light of recent interven-
tions in the performative social field of the exhibition space
by artists like Rirkrit Tiravanija and Tino Sehgal.

In light of these developments, one is prone to agree
with the sentiment Miwon Kwon expresses in her catalog essay,
that Asher's work currently "seems all the more important and
necessary." Unfortunately, Kwon misses the opportunity to reex-
amine the implications of Asher's practice from the perspective
of 2008, offering familiar analyses of his past work, and then
repurposing well worn conclusions: Asher's practice, in Kwon's
summation, is "nothing short of the radicalization of the exhibition situation … an antidote to the forgetfulness or willful

blindness that refuses to see the gallery walls for what they really are and what they really do."[10] How Asher's stripped down walls, emphatically tied to the specific history of a small institution, support such a broadly didactic claim is left for the reader to assume. But the proposition is most disturbing for the qualities of the work it chooses to ignore, if not completely repress, confining Asher's practice to architectonics and the staid polemics of quarter-century-old arguments and their static models of power relations. A similarly sweeping appraisal was made by Buchloh in the conclusion to a talk given on the occasion of Asher's exhibition entitled "Voiding the Void." Asher's work was again reduced to a lamentation of artistic efficacy, a negative revelation of alienation in the "prison-like" halls of the museum.

Deploying Asher's work as a definitive treatment of the condition of "gallery walls" or a revelation "of the institution of the museum itself"[11] reduces it to a vague metaphor, one no less absurd than the confusion of the regional, idiosyncratic Santa Monica Museum for an organization with expansive institutional authority, a role that is both clearly beyond its means (it does not collect and is a museum in name alone) and an indication of the all too common abstraction of Asher's careful practice into impotent generalities. Tired metaphoric tropes—like the "void" of institutional power or the singular monolithic Museum (which is not unlike the transcendental and transhistorical presentness Asher's work is often called upon to counteract)—aggregate and spectacularize the work's sensitivity to the specific conditions of the exhibition site, regardless of its relative dominance or scale. It is this sort of generalization that lends power to a potent mythological facade of impermeability, while also lending intellectual laziness a heroic edge. The deepest irony is that it is this very formulation of power that Asher upends in his work, eschewing the antiquated generalization that all arts institutions are functionally identical as expressions of "institutionality," and revealing the propensity of critique to elevate and universalize its object of inquiry as chimera.

It is difficult, if not nearly impossible, to extricate Asher's work from the voices of his most outspoken supporters or vice versa, but it is urgent that we do so. For just as Asher contextualizes the authority granted to any object in a site of exhibition within a sequence of ever-changing concrete and quotidian mechanisms, the sharp contrast to the ideologically over-determined readings it inspires reveals the woefully anti-quated critical models that had initially developed in tandem, yet unlike Asher's work, refused to evolve. As Asher wrote of his close collaboration with his editor, friend, and supporter Buchloh in his 1983 collection of writings, "Our collaboration has been essential for the analysis of individual works as well as for an understanding of the general historical context. Yet I hope that the fusion of the two approaches has not resulted in a seamless text, but rather reveals the parallelism that exists within the two enterprises of art production and criticism that are generally considered separate, if not opposi-tional."[12] If this distinction remains unacknowledged, and if writers continue to confine themselves to admirably cogent, historically significant, yet wholly dated theoretical models, what is sacrificed is a viable record of productions that, like Asher's, operate in subtle, contingent, and nuanced con-crete rather than abstract terms. It is the assertion of any trans-historical proposition of "transparency," "exhibitional-ity," or "institution" (whether it is defined in the instrumen-tal use of architecture or certain modes of exegesis) that Asher's work summarily dismisses. His work's assertion of an affirmative rather than negative model for aesthetic produc-tion, despite the prescriptive confines of the institution, exemplifies the practice's most radical and incendiary proposi-tion, one that is distinctly manifest in his work at the Santa Monica Museum.

NOTES

1. "Perspectiva is a Latin word which means 'seeing through.'" Cited in Erwin Panofsky, <u>Perspective as Symbolic Form</u>, trans. Christopher S. Woods, Zone, New York 1991, p. 27.

2. One critic described it as an "incorporeal space," and another commented that "there is no longer any true interior or exterior," that the structure had a "perspective so extended" it appeared "like a section of atmosphere cut from the sky." As quoted in Louise Wyman, "Crystal Palace," <u>Project on the City 2: Harvard Design School Guide to Shopping</u>, Taschen, Cologne 2002, p. 240.

3. The Santa Monica Museum lacks a collection and the institutional scale usually associated with the term "museum."

4. Benjamin H. D. Buchloh, "Allegorical Procedures: Appropriation and Montage in Contemporary Art," <u>Artforum</u>, September 1982, p. 45.

5. Ibid., p. 46.

6. Craig Owens, "The Allegorical Impulse: Toward a Theory of Postmodernism (Part 2)," <u>October</u>, vol. 13, Summer 1980, p. 71.

7. Michael Asher, <u>Writings 1973-1983 on Works 1969-1979</u>, ed. Benjamin H. D. Buchloh, The Press of the Nova Scotia College of Art and Design and the Museum of Contemporary Art Los Angeles, Halifax and Los Angeles 1983, p. 138.

8. Ibid., p. 147f. Importantly, in Asher's words, "[t]he paid participants were free to pursue their day-to-day activities as usual in as much as the context of the situation would allow them to do so," leaving the viewer with "[…] the responsibility which, in traditional aesthetic practice and perception, was deferred to either author or object."

9. Ibid., p. 202.

10. Miwon Kwon, "Support and Decoration: Michael Asher's Critique of the Architecture of Display," in <u>Michael Asher</u>, ed. Elsa Longhauser, exh. cat. Santa Monica Museum of Art, Santa Monica 2008, p. 55.

11. Ibid.

12. Ibid., p. ix.

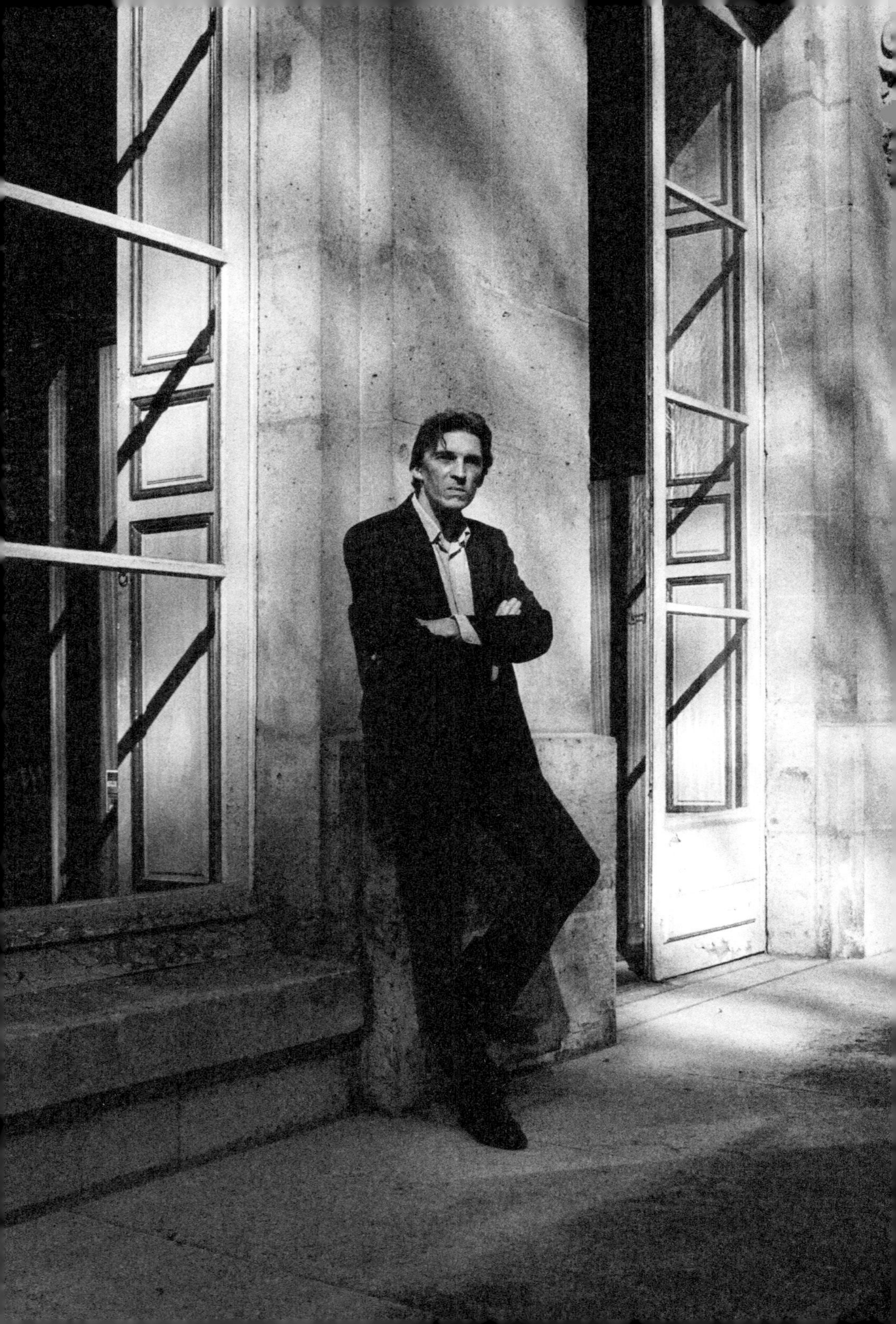

Interview with Nicolas Bourriaud

First published in <u>Altermodern: The Tate Triennial</u>, exh. cat.,
Tate Publishing, London 2009, p. 54; excerpted in <u>Chance</u>, Documents
of Contemporary Art, MIT Press/Whitechapel Gallery, Cambridge and London
2010, p. 223; excerpted in <u>Chinese Photography Magazine</u>, 2011, p. 44-49.

NICOLAS BOURRIAUD: Two questions. Firstly, how does traveling (and displacement) function in your work? Would you say that you are inscribing forms in space, rather than on paper or canvas? Secondly, in history, "Modern" moments have always been linked to uprooting, nomadism, exodus. Do you think postmodernism is therefore coming to an end?

WALEAD BESHTY: In the airport, the airplane, in customs and security queues, abstraction is forced to reconcile itself with materiality, where the relation between the abstract rule of Law and the movement of bodies is realized with banally vulgar immediacy. I am not speaking in the classic sense of abstraction or materialism within art (especially not in the sense that the term "abstract" is misused to mean "non-figurative," or that materialism has come to be synonymous with a claim for ontological purity), but in how abstractions are manifest in compromised form within the quotidian, how they govern our experience of the "real," or, more exactly, how they become concrete, and how this becoming produces moments of friction and error. In transit, concepts as amorphous as subjecthood (as constituted in the right to privacy, personal property, free speech etc.) are rendered specific and given edges simply by their being momentarily subject to revision. In these marginal connective tissues, tacit hierarchies become spatial, physical: one's

belongings are inspected, one's body relegated to queues,
numbers, compartments, "class." Normally, the fragility of the
state's guarantees manifest themselves only in moments of direct
conflict and massive collapse (such as the recent credit crisis,
or the revelations regarding the conditions at the American
military prisons at Guantanamo Bay or Abu Grahib), but in the
case of air travel, the fragile malleability of social order
is always close at hand, delineated by temporary post and rope
stanchions, bracketed by pavilions and kiosks in linoleum
topped chipboard, in color-coded wall-to-wall carpeting, and the
eye of the x-ray machine. It is a commonplace that the reason
one is more likely to cry while watching a movie on an airplane
is the implicit trauma of air travel, i.e. the fear of death,
of crashing, which leaves us emotionally vulnerable. But the
trauma of air travel is quite literally one's confrontation
with one's tenuous grasp on autonomy, its little humiliations
emphasizing the conditional nature of self-hood: an alchemical
transformation that allows inalienable rights to become suddenly alienable, subject to revocation. In this constellation
of forces, the x-ray has pride of place, delineating the edge
between the "real" world, and the site-less limbo of air travel.
Its accidental discovery in the late 1800s fits seamlessly into
modernity's fascination with transparency: the desire to capture the minutiae of movement (cinema), to turn objects into
surface (photography), to see inside (x-ray). For me, these machinations become palpable in moments of error, when there is a
friction between modes of vision (i.e. organizational systems),
as when enlightenment principles rub up against airport security, or x-rays damage vacation photos, or the distance an
object travels results in damage. Abstractions have reached the
level of facticity. Financial markets, national sovereignty, the
corporation as individual under the law, international airspace,
property rights: all are interwoven ephemeral constellations
that delineate the rights of the citizen subject and the conditions of the social sphere. The Bush Administration understood
this fully, bending this abstract foundation to its whim. As a
senior White House aide told a reporter for the New York Times:

"We're an empire now and when we act, we create our own reality. And while you're studying that reality—judiciously as you will—we'll act again, creating other new realities, which you can study too … " (One is left with an image of former President George W. Bush as a character akin to Neo from <u>The Matrix</u>, able to reform the solid world—to which the unenlightened are subject—to his messianic whim.)

Old notions of critique seem rather quaint in light of this formulation. The modernist transformation from the tangible to the intangible, from the object to the image, the haptic to the visual, is only half of the contemporary equation. With the passing of the last century and a half, these abstractions have been naturalized, entrenched, and built upon to such a degree that they have the quality of concreteness and stability. It makes no sense to claim them either as "real" or a "fiction." These have always been false oppositions; the actual circumstance is far less discrete. After all, the solidity of objects is as much an abstraction of the social systems that produced them, as the social systems are abstractions of these objects: a kind of capitalist realism. Classic critiques of power, some of which fall under the umbrella of the "postmodern," rely on a "reality principle," an idea that the real and fiction can be separated, that the revelation of power can threaten (not simply reify) dominance, that there is even something behind the curtain to be revealed, but these categorical delimiters are untenable. Monolithic expressions of power are simply an accumulation of compromise and negotiation, they all contain gaps; we, too are collaborators, even if we choose to relinquish this role. These momentary openings, the pockets between, their transitory spaces, ignored seams, and forgotten vistas, promise a site from which the either/or of utopian and apocalyptic thinking, or the political/formalist opposition can be dismantled, and production can be understood as embedded and at stake in all things, not at the level of grand abstraction, but as a bare fact evidenced in every moment of life. I think part of the problem is the search for "endings," the desire to cleave the past from the present, to hope for a liberatory rupture.

Abandoning this search might be the way to an affirmative
proposition of critique, rather than a negative one. This is the
choice between presence and absence, ascetic refusal and active
negotiation. Perhaps, as the documentary filmmaker Hito Steyerl
put it, "the closer to reality we get, the less intelligible it
becomes," but still this "reality" is what it seems it is most
important to confront, one that is camouflaged in plain view,
the unintelligible that is everywhere around us.

Untitled Response
"Is Photography Over?" Symposium
San Francisco Museum of Modern Art

First delivered as response to prompt on the occasion of "Is Photography Over?" symposium, San Francisco Museum of Modern Art, April 22-24, 2010.

"Since its invention, photography has almost always been in crisis. In the beginning, the terms of this crisis were cast as dichotomies: is photography science or art, nature or technology, representation or truth? This questioning has intensified and become more complicated over the intervening years. The crisis of photography has become intertwined with those of other areas of culture and society, whether visual, theoretical, museological, economic, technological, or geopolitical. At certain times the issues have become sufficiently urgent to require a profound rethinking of what photography is, does, and means. This is one of those times. Given the nature of contemporary art practice, the place of photography in current visual culture, the advent of new technologies, and the eclipse of others, this symposium will explore such questions as: what is at stake today in seeing something as a photograph? What is the value of continuing to speak of photography as a specific practice, medium, or discipline? Is photography over?"

Before one could address the questions above in good faith, one would need a serviceable definition of what "photography" (and here, its hypothetical exemplar, a "photograph") is. Without veering into convoluted ontology, this "photography," regardless of what might be argued to fall within its boundaries, seems best described as a type of "medium," or "an agency or means of doing something," and in its specific case, "the intervening substance through which impressions are conveyed to the senses or a force acts on objects at a distance." Defined in this way, a medium is constituted by a dialectic of applied use and technological development, and is further defined by the conventionalization of the relationship between the two, a process that occurs over time and is in a state of constant revision. It would follow that a medium is never freed from its use, nor is it freed from its position between some agents in a transaction, and it is always steeped in the inertia of its conventions, for this is how, by analogy, each new relation between shifting technologies and new applications is self-historicizing and legible. This is the unending "crisis" of all media, the struggle between adherence to convention, and new relations between technology and use. This would describe the transformation of a series of relations between technology and use, to the becoming of a "medium," in short, the institutionalization of these instances of negotiation, which is consummated by the use of its name in an abstract trans-historical sense, as in when its name is invoked in and of itself as a stable entity. The identification of a medium is an act of institutional reification par excellence, in fact it is _the_ institutional act, that which makes the institution concrete—like air made solid.

The means by which this conventionalization is distributed is either practical—such as vocational training or apprenticeships—or disciplinary, i.e. localized within—from the perspective of media—a meta-discourse such as the museum or art history (a hybrid form of these is reflected in most art school curricula). But the process of development and institutionalization mentioned above is internal to the "medium" itself, and it would be appropriate to add that only an outside agent (a disciplinary agent) would be concerned with the nature of one medium's distinction from other media, and in so doing, is attempting to situate that medium within a larger array specific to that institution. In short, a medium is always relational, and the attempts to isolate it and treat it as discrete is to institutionalize it; and to further attempt to place it

within a larger schema is to institutionalize it a second time,
rendering it further abstract. While a medium is always a play
between the spectral hold of its name, and the material minutiae
of its development, the disciplinary must cling to the spectral
alone and make it tangible. This is always tenuous. So it seems
safe to say that when we speak of a "crisis" in the way asserted
above, we speak of the trouble in institutionalizing photography within a broader field as a discrete entity, here specifically the field of art, and whether or not this category, in and
of itself, is still useful for these purposes.

So we have a question above that tacitly pertains to
ontology, that points to the status of "photography's" being—
here of being "over"—and thus, it is not only "photography's"
position within a larger constellation of aesthetic production
residing under the umbrella heading "art," but the entire
structure of differential media within the institution of art
that is called into question. When we ask "what is at stake
in seeing something as a photograph?" we ask that of all media
(it would be just as sticky to ask the same of painting or
sculpture). In other words, when we ask the value of the term
beyond its provisional utility, and moreover, when we ask these
questions from the perspective of the maintenance of the disciplinary institution of art (pertaining to taxonomic areas of
study, and theoretical objects or objects of discourse) alluding
to the need to reevaluate its parameters, we are implicating
the categorical systems applied to all art objects, questioning
the way medium specificity is applied on an institutional level.
"Photography" becomes, in this instance, a way to name this
institutional anxiety, and any perceived crisis is really that
of the disciplinary structures applied to it. In the case of
photography, this difficulty has inspired several admirable
attempts at reconciliation which are germane to the current
debate, from John Szarkowski's foundational The Photographer's
Eye, to Rosalind Krauss' "Photography's Discursive Spaces," to
Peter Galassi's Before Photography: Painting and the Invention
of Photography, to the more recent "Photography's Expanded
Field" by George Baker, all of which attempt to negotiate a

position for photography within the museum or art history
as a discrete and identifiable "medium," one with a coherent
identity. In so doing, they constitute a defense of the institutionalized categorical delimiters of art historians, curators,
and critics respectively.

The questions posed for this conference neither relate
to practices that we might call photographic, nor do they point
to the theorization of those practices, as these practices are
all specific sets of relations and do not operate at the level of
abstraction. Instead the condition of "crisis" is realized on
the level of abstract institutional categories invented to delineate one set of practices from another, a crisis pertaining
to whether or not the current structure of disciplines is able
to identify and dutifully manage the traditions they are called
upon to preserve and maintain; it is about creating a criteria
for what is excluded and what is included in the hypothetical
warehouse called "photography." It is less a crisis for the
medium, and more a crisis of the institutionalization of art
itself. Actually, it is even more mundane than that. When
medium specificity is staged from within academia or museums
it is really a question of paying the bills, of funding lines,
departmental autonomy, curriculum, intellectual fiefdoms,
library tabs, allotted real estate, and canons wrapped in the
guise of a broad philosophical conundrum. When these debates
are realized on the level of abstraction, such as "What is
photography?" or "Is photography over?" the details of this
bureaucratic topography are glossed over; we are reduced to the
intellectual equivalent of theorizing empty filing cabinets, of
treating the terminology and categories as fixed, and searching
for some hidden meaning within them. A more pointed question
might be: How is the current means of understanding the institutionalization of these conventions useful for the maintenance
of the organizational structure of cultural institutions? For
example, why do photography departments exist in institutions
alongside regional or historical specialties? Or why do we maintain photography departments within art schools, most absurdly
graduate art programs, when these professional distinctions

barely exist within contemporary art? We could also ask if
these departmental divisions continue to serve any purpose, or
if they are the institutional equivalent of the appendix, slowly
evolving away. Is that what we are worried is "over"? Or is it
possible to leave behind the empty essentialization of categorical delimiters without sacrificing an awareness of historical
development? These are not ontological questions, but questions
of logistics, of bureaucracies and their historical development,
of how the contemporary field is an accumulation of minute
negotiations. These are the questions pertaining to the quotidian, and the incremental formulation of history, the same incremental formation implicit within the course of any medium's,
or discourse's life. This would be a pathway from abstract argumentation to the real political stakes of the production and
reception of aesthetics, and more specifically, a means to confront the widespread confusion of a disciplinary reckoning
with a crisis in its object of study.

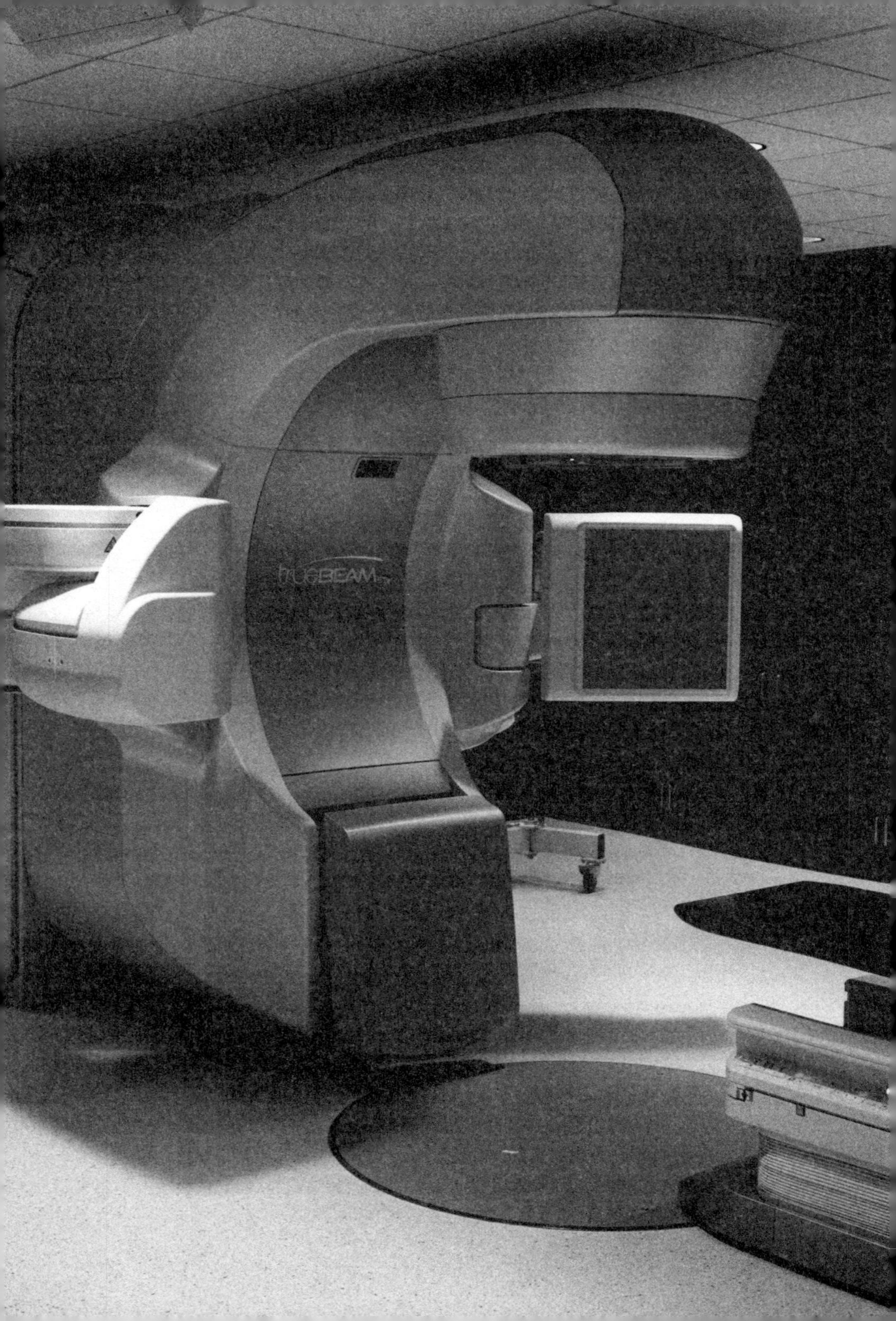

Abstracting Photography (Some Notes on the Problem of Allegorical Critique as it Relates to the Conditions of a Minor Art)

First published in Words Without Pictures, exh. cat., New York and Los Angeles: Aperture/LACMA, 2010, p. 109-125; revised, and republished in Pleated Blinds, exh. cat., Petach Tikva Museum, Tel Aviv 2010, p. 109-125.

Far from it being the object that antedates the viewpoint, it would seem that it is the viewpoint that creates the object.
—Ferdinand de Saussure

It is indeed the characteristic of the sadist that he humiliates his object and then—or thereby—satisfies it.
—Walter Benjamin

Let us begin with two images …
—Rosalind Krauss

The issue of what constitutes "Photography" as an ontological category has again gained currency, a rather surprising reinvestment in medium specificity, especially when considered in the context of contemporary art, where professional divisions between aesthetic practices are more or less a thing of the past. Despite being vaguely nostalgic, and at worst retrograde, the impulse to revive categorical boundaries signals a deeper critical dilemma facing devotees of the medium, for the drive to reconstitute a stable and practicable definition of photography is inextricable from the very real sense that the prominence of photographic discourse in contemporary art has receded. By now the charged debates of the late 1970s and 80s—between

The Museum of Modern Art's staid photography department and
"postmodernist" critics—that once lent photography and the
intellectual terrain it describes both urgency and stability,
have faded. Between the loss of photography's status as a contentious intellectual battleground, and its denaturalization via
a series of technological developments, an impenetrable fuzzi-
ness has descended over what "Photography"—as an aesthetic and
theoretical discourse—actually is, and furthermore, what might
be at stake in reopening the discussion of its identity.

In the wake of what are now decades old polemics, inert
fragments of previous formulations and aesthetic conventions
litter photography's theoretical landscape, amounting to a critical crisis for those who wish to constitute it as an epistemo-
logically coherent tradition in anything but negative terms.
To complicate matters further, the attempts to clearly identify
the contemporary status of photography often result in a ritualized indirectness from its proponents, who cast off literary
analogies and symbolist metaphors (such as the "message without
a code" or tropes like "photography and death") as though something inherent to the medium forced them to avert their eyes.
Thus "Photography" has become a Benjaminian <u>facies Hippocratica</u>,
a transformation of discursivity into dissolution, the medium
representing a disorderly field, a plane of ruins that the
historian/critic can do little more than survey. As George Baker
put it in his timely essay "Photography's Expanded Field,"
"Critical consensus would have it that the problem today is not
that just about anything image-based can now be called photographic, but rather that photography itself has been foreclosed,
cashiered, abandoned—outmoded technologically and displaced
aesthetically."[1] In other words, the Barthesian theorization of
the "this has been" contained in the photographic image, has
become the "this has been" of Photography itself.

This lack of certainty with regard to what constitutes
photography as an object of inquiry is, in all its abstractness,
a mirror of the problem of theorizing the photograph: a clash
between the apparent concreteness of the photographic referent and its slippery contextual signification. Yet the term

"Photography" and all it implies persists beyond its supposed
theoretical and practical disintegration, and with it a forlorn
pastiche of critical theorizations and aesthetic conventions
repeatedly confront a metaphor for their own failure in the
"death mask" of the photographic image. This condition is further
complicated by a commonplace confusion of the discrete tangibility of the object of inquiry for the amorphous constellation
of discourses that surround it (i.e. mistaking the tangibility
of a photograph as a discrete object for the solidity of a discourse called "Photography"), an example of what Alfred North
Whitehead referred to as "misplaced concreteness," or the con-
solidation and institutionalization of a multivalent set of discussions into a concrete object of study based on arbitrarily
discrete categories, such that the category itself becomes the
object of inquiry. Thus, in the critic's hands, the photograph
has become a metaphor for the inability to reconcile the inde-
terminacy of signification with its supposed facticity, and a
stand-in for "Photography" as a field of aesthetic and theoretical practices.[2] Before one might attempt to posit a way through
this practical and theoretical stalemate, it is important to
coax this symptom into view, because it is not so much that
photography itself is disappearing (it continues to proliferate
in most facets of daily life), but that its privileged connection
to the concrete social world, and the possibility of an ethically
viable instrumentalization of its once irrefutable political
agency (the very thing that made it such a heavily contested
subject) is at risk. Ironically, this threat is actualized as soon
as we extricate photography from its context in an attempt to
isolate it as a definable theoretical object, an operation that
at best leaves the question of its political implications debili-
tatingly abstract, and at worst, renders them inert.

PICTURING CRISIS

This contemporary conundrum is perhaps nowhere better displayed
than in Baker's aforementioned text, which, as a literary object,
simultaneously narrates and performs the dilemma. Reflecting on

the dispersal of the photographic "field" prompts Baker to
assert that "the terms involved only now become more complex,
the need to map their effects more necessary, because these
effects are both less obvious and self-evident."[3] Baker proposes
to "read" the contemporary condition of photography through
an earlier text, that of Rosalind Krauss' "Sculpture in the
Expanded Field," at times going so far as to transplant his own
terms and formulations into direct quotes from her text, inhabiting her text as much as her text prefigures his own.[4] Baker
sets out to re-picture the scene of Photography's "fragmentation,"
reconstituting it, and yet doing so with the disclaimer that
the result of this effort is destined to be tenuous and self-
defeating. The text, in its self-narrated attempt to add clarity
and order to its 'theoretical object' (a term he appropriates
from Krauss), transforms into a traumatic reenactment of
"Photography's" fragmentation (a condition emphasized by his
use of textual pastiche), that culminates in another moment of
defacement and dispersal (in its final paragraph Baker recounts
a scene where the diagram at the center of his argument is
scribbled over by one of the artists it is meant to contain).[5]
Thus, the final pages of "Photography in the Expanded Field"
serve as something of an epitaph for the short-lived theoretical
model Baker endeavors to (re)construct, and as I will argue
here, offers an exemplary instance of what has become a commonplace theoretical intrumentalization of photography as a discrete medium that serves as a metonymic representation of the
trouble facing the medium-specific comparative formal analysis
of the art historian, and for the categorical crisis facing
the historian/critic.

In other words, what is initially framed as a state of
crisis for the medium, quickly reveals itself to be a crisis of
approach (i.e. a crisis of the critic/theorist). In this respect,
Baker's text is easily read allegorically. Baker formulates
the status of the photograph by being reading it through the
urgency of critique in 1979 (and not insignificantly, Baker's
urtext was written by his mentor Krauss). Through this operation, Baker's own position as a critic within the contemporary

academy is tied metaphorically and metonymically to photography's ebb and flow as an ontological category. Here, the photographic object, in microcosm, comes not only to represent the loss of a unity between signifier and signified, its manifestations dispersed within an equally fragmented field that—for the historian/critic—requires it to be resituated and re-pictured, but also a metaphor for contemporary critique's confrontation with its own ambiguous, and evolving role.

For Baker, it is a picture, a visage of the past, that bridges the divide or rupture between discursive moments, and in this, as in many cases, it is the picture alone that signifies the wound or trauma it is meant to remedy. For pictures transform the nameless into the named, the unwieldy into the static, the sprawling into the contained, and in his quest to address the contemporary condition of photography, it is a picture that serves as Baker's point of departure, a picture that is schematized to the point of being pure geometry.

So I am going to start where Baker started: with a picture, i.e. a frame, or more exactly, a square, that serves as an emblem of a past moment in art history and photography's most contentious and heady days, and that, like the organizational impulse of all pictures, attempts to bridge a gap or cauterize a disorderly wound. Baker's text, like that of the text from which he adapted his title, represents a current historical dispersal in the quaternary field of Algirdas Julius Greimas' semiotic square (referred to by Krauss as a Piaget or Klein group, which inflects it with psychoanalytic undertones), a strategy for expanding binary oppositions into larger fields of interrelations. In 1979, Rosalind Krauss deployed this same picture when confronted with what she perceived as a crisis for the categorical language of the critic, a challenge to its mastery over its object of inquiry. Her text "Sculpture in the Expanded Field" sought to rescue a medium-based category that was "in danger of collapsing" from the sheer heterogeneity of objects it had been called upon to describe,[6] arguing that in the discussion of post-war American art, "categories like sculpture and painting have been kneaded and stretched and

twisted in an extraordinary demonstration of elasticity, a display of the way a cultural term can be extended to include
just about anything."[7] To remedy this problem, Krauss outfitted
the field with a corral, transforming an array of practices
into sequence of coordinates whose interrelations are discretely
compressed into dotted lines.

For Krauss, this was a far-reaching methodological crisis, but when redeployed by Baker (who acknowledges that the
situation for photographic discourse is radically different),
it takes on a personal dimension, for not only does he allow the
narrative of his intellectual development as a student of Krauss
to permeate the text, but he further reflects the oedipal relations of teacher and student formally through the literal
interpenetration of models and methodologies enacted within the
text. As Baker writes, "Now I have been drawing Klein groups
and semiotic squares ever since I first met Rosalind Krauss,
and the reader by this point will not be surprised to learn of
how fondly I remember sitting in her office conjugating the
semiotic neutralization of things like the terms of gender and
sexuality, some twelve years ago."[8] He then places his voice
into that of the past, and through his voice, the past speaks of
the present. The switch from Krauss' distanced and authoritative polemics, to Baker's superimposition of historical moments,
autobiography, and introspective reflexivity, further emphasizes the distance that separates their respective positions
in time and methodology while simultaneously performing a parallel critical reassessment of its contemporary context, all
of which produces a melancholic rupture that cuts laterally
through the entire text, and by implication, through the institution of critique itself. We thus have, in Baker's retrospective
reanimation of Krauss' schema, an image of critical melancholia,
and as Walter Benjamin surmises in <u>The Origin of German Tragic
Drama</u>, "the only pleasure the melancholic permits himself, and
it is a powerful one, is allegory."[9] The critic/historian, as
allegorist, displaces history with pictures, synchronic schemas
that in their attempt to "recover," "preserve," and solidify
mask a "petrified, primordial landscape."[10] For the picture,

proposed as the imago of history, is fundamentally opposed to
historical time, opting for synchronicity over diachronicity,
transforming historical time into spatial metaphor, and in res-
isting linear causal chains of development operates along the
axes of formal morphology. Baker abandons the notion of historical time, while simultaneously performing the collapse of the
organizational schema he displaces it with, and in the wake of
his argument we are left with only the rupture, the gap. In
other words, as Joel Fineman wrote, allegorical critique "must
admit to the irrecuperable distance between itself and its
object," and thereby "thematize its own responsibility for the
loss of meaning."[11] When Baker confronts this methodological
rupture, he calls it photography.

ONTOLOGICAL IMPULSES

Krauss' map was nothing if not timely, indicating both the grip
that structuralist analysis had within a certain mode of
theoretically fluent American art criticism, and the attraction
of artist of the time to structuralist theory's usefulness in
denaturalizing received meanings. It was, in other words, deeply
embedded in its cultural moment; one need only think of Robert
Smithson's "non-sites," Martha Rosler's The Bowery in Two
Inadequate Descriptive Systems (1974-75) (or more explicitly,
her Semiotics of the Kitchen [1975]), or the writings of Robert
Morris, Dan Graham, Mel Bochner, or Allan Sekula to see the
wide effect of Structuralist formulations on the American artistic landscape. Semiotic considerations seemed equally well
entrenched, making Krauss' use of Greimas' semiotic square and
its modular geometric form all the more resonant with the aesthetic conventions of the time (Hanne Darboven, Lawrence Weiner,
Joseph Kosuth, Robert Morris, Sol LeWitt, et al.). Not to mention
that this was a moment when the art historian did not limit
themselves to looking backward on an arrangement of artists'
practices, but often directly participated in an active debate
with their objects of inquiry at the very moment in which their
work was developing (a precedent set by Clement Greenberg,

and his deep influence on this generation of critics).[12] If there
was any singular insight that structuralist theory offered artists of the seventies, it was the understanding of the arbitrary
nature of signification. Perhaps no group of artists took this
understanding to its logical conclusion more decisively than the
Pictures Generation whose work, generally speaking, exploited
the fracture between sign and referent that structuralist and
deconstructive procedures laid bare. According to the reception
of the work at the time, their work argued that the image was
like that of the Kraussian understanding of modernist sculpture, a homeless, free-floating signifier whose meaning derived
solely from a context to which it had once, at some lost moment,
been inextricably tied, but now found itself separate from.[13]
In their hands, when an image spoke, it spoke of this distance.

     Thus, it seems no coincidence that, in response to the
dual rise of institutional critique and appropriation art, the
conceptual dimensions of allegory would become a potent cata-
lyst for some of the most vocal and ambitious critics of the
time (whose formulations are particularly indebted to the writing of Peter Bürger, and his application of Benjamin's theorization of an "allegorical vision" in the <u>The Origins of German
Tragic Drama</u> to the works of the early twentieth century avant-
garde). This interest produced two major texts published just
two years apart: Craig Owens' "The Allegorical Impulse: Toward
a Theory of Postmodernism (Parts 1 & 2)" (1980), and Benjamin
Buchloh's "Allegorical Procedures: Appropriation and Montage
in Contemporary Art" (1982).[14] In its most basic sense, allegory
is when one text is read through another. In the allegorical
formulation of institutional critique, the artwork re-examines
the condition of exhibition, usually along the axes of its physical, economic, or architectonic properties, proposing that
selected aspects, activated by artistic "intervention," be read
in tandem with the institution that contains them. In contrast,
the critical action of appropriation, following the pathway of
Pop art back to its roots in the readymade, was targeted at the
instrumental use of images and the repressive categorizations
they tacitly asserted.

Both Buchloh's and Owens' texts provide ample disclaimers regarding the potential political agency of their chosen subjects. Buchloh maintains that at least some of the artists within his text run the risk of merely replicating alienation (here writing specifically of Sherrie Levine and Dara Birnbaum), producing works whose "ultimate triumph is to repeat and anticipate in a single gesture the abstraction and alienation from the historical context to which the work is subjected in the process of commodification and acculturation."[15] Owens acknowledges an even more bleak state of affairs when first observing that Robert Rauschenberg (offered as a paternal figure to the Pictures Generation within Owens' text[16]) "enacts a deconstruction of the museum, then his own deconstructive discourse [that]—like Daniel Buren's—can take place only within the museum itself. It must therefore provisionally accept the terms and conditions it sets out to expose."[17] Owens then concludes, "We thus encounter once again the unavoidable necessity of participating in the very activity that is being denounced precisely in order to denounce it. All of the work discussed in this essay is marked by a similar complicity, which is the result of its fundamentally deconstructive impulse." This point is reiterated by Buchloh some twenty years later in the preface of his anthology <u>Neo-Avantgarde and the Culture Industry</u> (2000), in which he surmises that the panoply of artistic challenges to the culture industry, which "range from mimetic affirmation (e.g. Andy Warhol) to an ostentatious asceticism (e.g. Michael Asher) that—in its condemnation to a radical purity of means—more often than not in the last decade had to risk losing the very ground of the real upon which critical opposition could be inscribed."[18] Conscribed by the arguments laid out for them, the practices positioned to overturn institutionalized structures (be they in the form of cultural or economic authority), and constituted within the critical reading of allegory, offer only further evidence of the invulnerability of the institutions they identify, if only by their inability to exist without them. It is no coincidence that a similar implication of "critical failure" (Owens' term) is applicable to the work of

these critics. In their deconstruction of the institutionalized
rhetoric of validation, they rely on the authority granted to
them through processes of accreditation, peer review, etc.,
in order to present their critique of those very procedures by
which legitimacy (and thus power) is naturalized. Despite the
nearly three decades that separate us from these ideas (more
still if we credit Bürger, who clearly outlined this methodological problem), this paradox of aesthetic critique persists,
as it was succinctly put by Luc Boltanski and Eve Chiapello in
The New Spirit of Capitalism (2006)[19], "Artistic critique is currently paralysed by what, depending on one's viewpoint, may
be regarded as its success or its failure."[20] Or to put a finer
point on it, these critical models transpose their own limitations on their objects of study, embodying and enacting melancholic resignation, while claiming these to be qualities which
they are simply observing.

Yet, the proposition of materialist artistic or aesthetic
critique carries with it a seductive promise: not only that
the world of appearances can be punctured, shedding light into
its darkened recesses, but also that there is something to be
found lurking behind the curtain, a repressed "truth" that lies
dormant within all things that, and once revealed, has liberatory potential. In Structuralism-inflected writing on the
photographic image, this attempt repeatedly confronts an un-
representable rupture in signification, where laying things
bare often leaves nothing but an abyss. Here, again, it is
the "the real upon which critical opposition could be inscribed"
which is sacrificed through the operation of the image.
Writing on the work of Troy Brauntuch in his seminal 1977 essay
"Pictures," Douglas Crimp observed that "the result is only
to make pictures more picture-like, to fix forever in an elegant
object our distance from the history that produced these images.
That distance is all these pictures signify."[21] This appraisal
was not uncommon among his contemporaries. In "Photography en
abyme," Owens went further, arguing that doubling, and reproducibility was not just "a property of … photograph(y) itself,"
but that the repeated (re)depiction of this quality within the

pictorial form of photographs was an instance of photography
speaking from the abyss, in other words that its identity
was in the reflexive narration of its own reproducibility.[22]
Using Smithson as an example, Owens writes, "In a photograph,
Smithson casts a shadow over the presumed transparency of
photographs; he raises serious doubts about their capacity to
convey anything but a sense of loss, of absence."[23] The absence
Owens finds at the root of the ontological condition of
photography is theorized as death for Roland Barthes, for as
Barthes wrote, "however 'lifelike' we strive to make it (and
this frenzy to be lifelike can only be our mythic denial of the
apprehension of death), Photography is a kind of primitive the-
atre, a kind of Tableau Vivant, a figuration of the motionless
and made-up face beneath which we see the dead."[24] This argument
echoes Sigfried Kracauer, who in his 1927 essay "Photography,"
wrote: "That the world devours [photographs] is a sign of the
fear of death. What photographs by their sheer accumulation
attempt to banish is the recollection of death, which is part
and parcel of every memory image. In the illustrated magazines
the world has become a photographable present, and the photographed present has been entirely eternalized. Seemingly ripped
from the clutch of death, in reality it has succumbed to it."[25]
Kracauer saw photography as demolishing memory (the real),
the core of a liberated consciousness (the very mnemonic real
that Barthes saw as the redemptive punctum, a wound that
opened up in the surface of the banal studium, or the social
history that the photograph was a part of), the historical
real that critique itself proposed to preserve.

But this commonplace opposition between the photograph,
which embraces the illusory depiction of the "real," and a
critique that seeks to preserve material reality (where "real"
politics occur) is imbedded in photography's origins. Since its
inception, the photographic image has been strongly associated
with displacement, destruction, and erasure; a triumph of
images over the material world it purports to describe. Writing
in 1859, Oliver Wendell Holmes claimed that with the advent
of photography (for him distilled in the verisimilitude of the

stereograph), "form is henceforth divorced from matter. In fact
matter as a visible object is of no great use any longer, except
as the mould on which form is shaped. Give us a few negatives
of a thing worth seeing, taken from different points of view,
and that is all we want of it. Pull it down or burn it up, if
you please."[26] This destruction is totalizing; in Vilém Flusser's
multivalent study of photography, this conundrum of the photographic image is inescapable:

> Nothing can resist the force of this current of technical
> images—there is no artistic, scientific or political activ-
> ity which is not aimed at it, there is no everyday activity
> which does not aspire to be photographed, filmed, video-
> taped… In this way, however, every action simultaneously
> loses its historical character and turns into a magical
> ritual and an endlessly repeatable movement. The universe
> of technical images, emerging all around us, represents
> the fulfillment of the ages, in which action and agony go
> endlessly round in circles. Only from this apocalyptic
> perspective, it seems, does the problem of photography
> assume the importance it deserves.[27]

This is the apocalyptic becoming of the technological image in
the form of the photograph, an inescapable conflation of the
concrete with the likeness, an abstract gleaming dystopia where
the real is a priori an image, and vice versa. It is the photographic act that comes to stand for this transformation of
object into image, and it is the photograph as image, which renders this abstract transformation tautologically, and traumati-
cally complete. But this requires reassessment, because taken
to its extreme this pathway leads all to easily to a complete
collapse of any attempt to theorize the real world implications
of aesthetics. This transformation of objects into images as
the apocalyptic endpoint of the photographic episteme, tautologically requires that this transformation is an a priori fact.

SPECTRAL OBJECTS

As signifying surfaces, images are abstractions. The logic of its
abstraction is the reduction of four dimensions to a two dimen-
sional field. In this formulation, the photograph, as image and
an "imaged" object, exemplifies total dissolution, the simulation
of the real that diverts direct political struggle from its location in the tangible world, and into that of phantasmagoria.
Paradoxically, the only experience of the world that is accessible is the world of images. As Baker cites in his aforementioned
text, Barthes argued "(t)he goal of all Structuralist activity,
whether reflexive or poetic, is to reconstruct an 'object' in
such a way as to manifest thereby the rules of functioning
(the 'functions') of this object. Structure is therefore actually
a simulacrum of the object, but a directed, interested simulacrum, since the imitated object makes something appear which
remained invisible … "[28] To put it another way, Structuralism is
primarily concerned with images—the chain of imagistic abstractions that we encounter in the world, but only insofar as they
lead to the source ("real") from which the chosen chains of
abstractions has developed and must be thus reconstituted back-
wards from (because, of course, this "real" is obscured by
the abstractions it generated, suppressed under their weight).
Thus, for the Structuralist, another image is necessitated to
make the invisible forces at work behind images visible again.
To this end, when Structuralism confronts an object, it adds
another layer of abstraction, and another image is placed on
the conceptual heap. Built on this foundation, the discourses
around ideology critique and critiques of representation, identity, etc., insofar as they are concerned with images, do not
seek to simply reconstruct the object or origin point of the
abstraction (source text, or "real") in the physical or temporal
circumstance of the creation of the image (people, places,
things, times), because this reality is inconsequential, a matter
of minutiae, but look to reveal the sociopolitical origin of the
abstraction, unveiling its ideological formulation. In essence,
this is a shift from what an image or picture is "of" to the

identity of the transformative process of imaging itself, an
image of imaging, which distils some form of power that instru-
mentalizes the image and the symbolic order it is invariably
an expression of, giving it a name, be it that of a capitalist,
colonialist, racist, heterosexist, sexist, etc., episteme (each
of these being an ideological force that seeks to maintain
the relations between dominant and subordinate forces). The
Structuralist critique thus becomes a competition of images,
a matter of competing faiths. When confronted with a world
of appearances, the irony is that the only tool left to combat
the tyranny of images, is yet more.

But this is somewhat beside the point, for to confuse
a photograph (or any object, theoretical or otherwise) for
an image is to subject the concrete world (the real relations
between things) to another in a sequence of abstractions, and
while it is impossible to discard this cultural imagination,
it is important to look to the usefulness of the images/abstrac-
tions we employ and seek new tools when those at our fingertips
have become unserviceable. Louis Althusser saw just such an
instance with regard to the common Marxian architectonic metaphors of "infrastructure" and "superstructure," for him a debil-
itating methodological problem because the terms are purely
metaphorical, not the actual operations at work, and by "picturing" class conflict through an architectural metaphor, the
dynamics of the actual machinery of dominance and subordination they attempt to address is obscured. In short, the work
of radical politics is directed at the analogy rather than the
state of affairs that analogy was meant to describe. When photographs are treated as images, a parallel confusion occurs,
for photographs are, after all, present in four space-time
dimensions, not simply two (as images are), and are constructed
of worldly material having definite size and shape. In other
words, it is quite a leap to reduce a photograph to an immaterial imago/likeness. The term "image" is not an ontological
umbrella under which a photograph can be classified, but a conceptual tool that functions in a particular way and ceases to
function if applied in a circumstance in which it is asked to do

something other than what it was designed for. To confuse this
is to turn a relational idea into an ontological one. Perhaps
this confusion of photographic theory for the analysis of
images is why the discourse on photography shifted from a focus
on its instrumentality to a concern that photography no longer
truly exists, a rather perverse endpoint brought about by the
collision of competing metaphors for photography. Of course,
this shift occurs only after photography as a concept had been
fully imagined (imaged). Subsumed in a digital or ideological
dispersal at the whim of a multitude of discursive intrumentali-
zations, its supposed dissolution has become so utterly complete
that whatever photography once was, it no longer is (if it "is"
at all), becoming a "void" or the site of "death." It is comfort-
ing to propose that something is "behind" images in a meta-
physical sense, even if this something is an absence (death,
as Barthes and Kracauer, among others, have proposed).

The result, in practical terms, is that "art" photography has become dominated by anachronism, as though the solution
to this paradox might be in re-enacting the pictorial rhetoric
of the late 1800s (consider the aesthetic parallels between the
work of Timothy H. O'Sullivan, Carleton Watkins, Eugène Atget,
Charles Marville, or the physiognomic typologies of Francis
Galton and Alphonse Bertillon with contemporary photographic
tropes). In sharp contrast to the most prominent tactics
of non-photographic aesthetic programs of the late 1980s and
1990s—approaches that showed renewed interest in bricolage,
social networking, and rough-hewn or vernacular aesthetics—
photography of the era seemed to codify around a diametrically
opposed array of concerns. The photography of that moment
favored the staid genre forms of the pre-modern Beaux-Arts,
exemplified in an almost obsessive adherence to Renaissance pictorial formulae. Making use of art's own reflexive theatrical
death mask (the institution), architectural tropes—ubiquitous
in both contemporary photography's presentational affect and
its subject of choice—performed a tautological affirmation of
the cold geometries of the white cube within monolithic prosce-
nia, as if reassuring spectators of their ontological place in

the museum's hallowed halls. The depopulated city scenes and
emptied serial structures of seventies art photography grew
into Plexiglas monoliths, an odd hybrid of architecture's industrialized materiality and painting's scale. Photography not
only adapted itself to the wall of the museum, but in adopting
aluminum backframes and reflective Plexiglas encasements,
became materially continuous with the architecture that surrounded it, both casting an image of its site of reception back
at its surrounds through its slippery surfaces, and obsessively
depicting Cartesian arrangements in pictorial tableaux. In
short, photography became the wall of the institution _en abyme_,
signifying nothing more than its adherence to museological
convention. Its photographic alternative embraced the notion
of the archive, a reiteration of organizational power, or as
Buchloh put it with regard to Conceptual Art, "[an] aesthetics
of administration." It was as if, in the wake of the troubling
recognition of photography's malleability in the hands of
instrumental use and its critical reappraisal by artists and
critics in the sixties and seventies, the contemporary production of photographs required turning back to a time before
avant-gardist debates or postmodernist dismantling—back to
something akin to the Pictorialism of salon painting and
the hearth of the Natural History Museum. Such works become
metaphors for the instrumentalization of the photograph;
a negative parody of this foreclosure, in short, they are little
more than an image of the photograph's base social condition
in the art world, that evasive quality that Krauss termed
"exhibitionality,"[29]—a concept that again points to the nineteenth century, and the term exhibition itself, which always
indicated the dominion of the state.[30]

But perhaps this is a promising turn for photography as
an artistic practice. As photographs are increasingly produced
with an internalized awareness of the circumstances of their
display, specifically within the rhetoric of architecture and its
pastiche of art historical tropes that reiterate the circumstance of the museum, they become accountable to the social and
political realities that their treatment as free-floating images

held at bay. It is the particularities of the object that govern
the specific implications of work of art, a comprehension that
is suspended when the question becomes that of imaging. With the
image, the question is always of distance, the distance we are
placed at in relation to what is represented, the absence of the
origin of its likeness, while the material of the image, how it
comes to present itself, its "exhibitionality," is commensurately
excused. For the task at hand is to reinsert and re-politicize
photographic discourse if we are to recover some semblance of
its originary impulse rather than simply lamenting it's loss ad
infinitum, and in so doing it is necessary to abandon the foreclosed models of dominance and subordination offered by the
historian/critic-cum-allegorist, which dead end in the melancholia of symmetrical totalizing metaphors for political opposition.
The fatal flaw of this schematic is that the location of, to use
Buchloh's phrasing again, the "real upon which critical opposition could be inscribed" is situated at the level of depiction,
a turn from the politics _of_ representation to the absurdity
that politics _is_ representation. In short, the proposition of a
photograph as image, operating solely at the level of depiction,
is part and parcel of the obfuscation of the political, or in
Althusserian terms, "the real conditions of existence."

This error is underscored by the image being synonymous
with ideology, with abstraction, i.e. as representation. In
the Althusserian formulation "it is not the real conditions of
existence, their real world, that 'men' represent to themselves
in ideology, but above all it is their relation to those conditions of existence which is represented to them there. It is
this relation which is at the center of every ideological, i.e.
imaginary, representation of the real world."[31] This on its own,
is commensurate with the structuralist formulations of the
image's relation to the "real" thus far outlined, but in
Althusser's rejection of metaphor in his theorization of the
political sphere lies the insight that this imaginary not
only has a material existence, but beyond this, that it _is_ its
material existence. In other words, "ideology always exists in
an apparatus, and its practice or practices. This existence is

material."[32] The importance of the Althusserian construction is
that it moves past the struggle of just versus unjust ideologies
(and in parallel, ethical versus unethical depictions, or true
and untrue images), but locates the site of struggle in the micro-
circumstance of individual actions, or to use Althusser's more
precise language, in the "material actions, inserted into material practices governed by material rituals which are themselves
defined by the material ideological apparatuses from which
derive the ideas of that subject."[33] This also posits that opposition, like the ideology it works against, is not located at the
level of competing depictions, but at the level of actions, habits,
i.e. daily life, where the meaning of depiction is given form.

Within this formulation, a photograph can be understood
as an object and as an image, but more importantly, the production of images can be understood as containing a democratic
possibility, representing a daily ritual of compromise enacted
with various levels of awareness, but present nonetheless as
a lingering force. No longer a spectral entity, we find we are
both inside and outside of the picture, one of its parts and
one of its producers; a stratified hierarchy is not needed in
our relationship to aesthetics. Through considering the material specificity of photographs it is possible to bring the
images that alienate down to earth, give them bodily form, and
it is on this point that the developments in seventies photographic practices dovetails with the critical armatures that
were applied to it. The truth of the matter is that all images
require a material existence, and we must resist the urge to
transform the material world into an image world. This is not
an either/or choice, but a realization that images are indistinguishable from their material supports; one cannot exist without the other. And as Althusser points out our actions are a
material effect, and those rituals, behaviors, and pathways of
distribution are an extension of the object itself, and once
we acknowledge the objecthood of images these very real effects
have the possibility of being rescued from the placeless,
immaterial world of images. The embedded compromises and
negotiations present in any production and their subsequent

lack of instrumental solidity need not be seen as dirty secrets.
This would not be an absolutist proclamation of the loss of the
"real" that images represent for vulgar materialists, but rather
an assertion that the production of meaning is a communal one;
located in the public sphere, in commonplace contexts, and is
embodied in the forms of the everyday. In this a middle ground
of negotiation appears: that all production—even that of monolithic power—is comprised of myriad transit points and competing forces that deceptively assume the appearance of solidity,
but are in fact porous.

In the debris of such battles (and their ritualized reenactment), one is prompted to ask where the ground of the real
that these struggles are supposedly in the service of actually
lies. The question most urgent for photography is no longer what
inherent meaning it may contain (whether it be the interminable
presence of the aesthetic formalists, or the essentialized condition of contingency and ideological instrumentalization of
the social critics) but how specific photographs construct and
organize social space in a concrete and immediate way; how individual producers constantly restage, narrate, and recombine
these histories, ontologies, and conventions, and by doing so
open up contradictions within their seeming coherency, presenting a provisional and potentially liberatory ulterior assertion
of the conditions of the medium.

It was this quality of provisionality, what Gilles Deleuze
and Félix Guattari called the "minor"—"that which a minority
constructs within a major language"—that one would locate here,
specifically a "minor photography" one that refuses an essen-
tializing discourse on identity or its lack there of.[34] As Deleuze
and Guattari argue, "Minor languages are characterized not
by overload and poverty in relation to a standard or major language, but by a sobriety and variation that are like a minor
treatment of a major language … deterritorializing the major
language."[35] The minor language is comprised of sliding meanings
and innuendo that operates within the "cramped space" of the
mother tongue, it never attempts to assert an oppositional language, it does not seek to "acquire the majority,"[36] but rather

it insinuates itself within totalizing structures, turning them
to the service of the transitory and contingent. This form of
production sets up camp within the infrastructural, interstitial
zones of the institutionalized systems and can be considered
on both concrete and abstract levels, yet such negotiations are
obscured by broad generalizations about the culture industry,
institutions, or class. The locations they identify, conceptually
speaking, are material bridges between the concrete and the ideological, and in the expanded entertainment/cultural complex
in which aesthetic management has become global, such a reassessment seems all the more necessary. Images are accumulations of
compromise and negotiation that in truth have material solidity, and with which interaction is a two way street. The answer
to the current stagnation is not to satisfy the impulse to reorganize a seemingly chaotic field in abstract terms, or to reenact
nihilistic self-effacement by depicting a methodological rupture
ad infinitum, rather than to allow a discourse's "crisis" to
open up what were seemingly foreclosed possibilities, and focus
on the micro-operations of individual producers rather than
a totalizing framework for an arbitrarily delineated "medium."
The repeated confrontation with the absence at the core of the
photographic image is simply evidence that the language games
enacted around the photograph have ceased being useful in their
current form. It is the questions that are in need of revision,
the supposed absence they deliver merely an invitation to
formulate different methodological approaches. These momentary
openings—the pockets between, their ruins, their transitory
spaces, their ignored seams and forgotten vistas—promise a site
from which the either/or of utopian and apocalyptic thinking
or the political/formalist opposition can be dismantled, and
production can be understood as a common process, enacted in
every moment of daily life, even at the level of viewership.
A process which cuts through the juridical language of medium
distinctions and the false ontologies at the level of the commonplace and mundane, undoing the displacement of life from
us to our objects, and instead seeing the fluid negotiations
of daily life as the animating force behind the meaning of

objects and theorizing it as an active, rather than passive matter accordingly.

NOTES

1. George Baker, "Photography's Expanded Field," <u>October</u>, vol. 114 (Fall 2005): p. 122.

2. For example: the recurring theme that what is missing from a photograph constitutes what it is truly about—an approach most notoriously deployed by Walter Benjamin, in his "Short (Small) History of Photography," when he wrote that the work of Atget derived its meaning from its appearing like a "recently evacuated scene of a crime."

3. Baker, "Photography's Expanded Field," p. 138.

4. For example, on page 127, Baker writes/quotes, "'That is,' to really paraphrase Krauss, 'the [not-narrative] is, according to the logic of a certain kind of expansion, just another way of expressing the term [stasis], and the [not-stasis] is, simply, [narrative].'" Baker's insertions are represented within the text as brackets, or "breaches" in the continuity of Krauss' voice through which Baker's formulations bubble up.

5. "At any rate, when I first sketched my graph for the artist with which I began, Nancy Davenport, she quickly grabbed my pen and paper and began to swirl lines in every direction, circling around my oppositions and squares, with a look that seemed to say, 'What about these possibilities?' My graph was a mess. But the photographer's lines, though revolving around the field, had no center, and they extended in every direction." Ibid., p. 140.

6. Rosalind Krauss, "Sculpture in the Expanded Field," October, vol. 8 (Spring 1979): p. 30.

7. Ibid., p. 33.

8. Baker, "Photography's Expanded Field," p. 128.

9. Walter Benjamin, The Origin of German Tragic Drama, trans. John Osborne, Verso, London 1998, p. 185.

10. Ibid., p. 166.

11. Joel Fineman, "The Structure of Allegorical Desire", October, vol. 12 (Spring 1980): p. 390.

12. Not to put too fine a point on it, but the radicality of Krauss' text was that the diagram was centered on was constructed analogously to the work she described.

13. Rosalind Krauss, "Sculpture in the Expanded Field," October, vol. 8 (Spring 1979): p. 30.

14. Neither Owens nor Buchloh mentions the other's work despite various similarities in reference and argumentation, and the assumed awareness the two authors had of each other's work. Especially noteworthy since both were students of Krauss at CUNY, and were directly involved with the journal October from early on.

15. Benjamin H. D. Buchloh, "Allegorical Procedures: Appropriation and Montage in Contemporary Art," Artforum, September 1982, p. 56.

16. Pictures is the title of an exhibition curated by Douglas Crimp that opened at Artists Space, New York, in September 1977, including works by Troy Brauntuch, Jack Goldstein, Sherrie Levine, Robert Longo, and Philip Smith. An essay of the same title was published by Crimp in October, vol. 8 (Spring 1979): p. 75-88, which was an expansion of Crimp's essay that accompanied the exhibition.

17. Craig Owens, "The Allegorical Impulse: Toward a Theory of Postmodernism (Part 2)," October, vol. 13 (Summer 1980): p. 71.

18. Buchloh, Neo-Avantgarde and the Culture Industry: Essays on European and American Art from 1955 to 1975 (October Books, Cambridge 2001).

19. Luc Boltanski and Eve Chiapello, The New Spirit of Capitalism, trans. Gregory Elliot Verso, New York 2006, p. 466.

20. Ibid., p. 466.

21. Douglas Crimp, "Pictures," <u>October</u>, vol. 8 (Spring 1979): p. 85.

22. Owens, "Photography en abyme," <u>October</u>, vol. 5 (Summer 1978): p. 78.

23. Ibid., p. 88.

24. Roland Barthes, <u>Camera Lucida</u>, trans. Richard Howard (Hill and Wang, New York 1981), p. 31-32.

25. Sigfried Kracauer, "Photography," in <u>The Mass Ornament: Weimar Essays</u>, ed./ trans. Thomas Y. Levin, Harvard University Press, Cambridge 1995, p. 59.

26. Oliver Wendell Holmes, "The Stereoscope and Stereograph," in <u>Classic Essays on Photography</u>, ed. Alan Trachtenberg, Leete's Island Books, New Haven 1980, p. 80.

27. Vilém Flusser, <u>Towards a Philosophy of Photography</u>, Reaktion Books, London 2000, p. 20.

28. Baker, "Photography's Expanded Field," p. 124.

29. Rosalind Krauss, "Photography's Discursive Spaces," <u>The Originality of the Avant-Garde and Other Modernist Myths</u>, The MIT Press, Cambridge 1985, p. 131-50.

30. From the late 1500s through to its popularization by the Great Exhibition of 1851 and the "World Exhibitions" which followed, the term exhibition was a specialized legal term, i.e. a "holding out" or testimony presented under oath before the sovereign power of the state. Thus the application of the term to the context of the museum, implied a shift from the locus of the state proper, to the decentralized realm of the autonomous public institution, or what Althusser termed, the "Ideological State Apparatus."

31. Louis Althusser, "Ideology and Ideological State Apparatuses (Notes towards an Investigation)," in <u>Mapping Ideology</u>, ed. Slvoj Zizek, Verso, New York, 1998, p. 124.

32. Ibid., p. 126

33. Ibid., p. 127

34. Gilles Deleuze and Félix Guattari, <u>Kafka: Toward a Minor Literature</u>, trans. Dana Polan, University of Minnesota Press, Minneapolis 1986, p. 16.

35. Gilles Deleuze and Félix Guattari, <u>A Thousand Plateaus: Capitalism and Schizophrenia</u>, trans. Bernard Massumi, University of Minnesota Press, Minneapolis 1987, p. 104.

36. Ibid., p. 106.

Untitled Response, "Forum on Contemporary Photography," The Museum of Modern Art

First delivered as response to prompt on the occasion of "Forum on Contemporary Photography," The Museum of Modern Art, New York, May 26, 2011.

1)   What, if anything, is to be gained by approaching photography as a discrete medium? Is there truly any solidity to a category that links together everything from the gelatin silver print to the magazine page, the computer screen, the billboard etc. all of which have distinctly different modes of address, access to audience, and distributive networks? Do they all require the same or similar questions? Even if the "same" image occurs in each of these instances, does it make them, for all intents and purposes, equivalent? Or is this just a vernacular misuse of the term "photograph," a use of the word "photograph" as though it was synonymous with "picture" or "image," a confusion of a schematic formal similarity for material/epistemological/ideological continuity? Does it make as much sense to describe a reproduction of a photograph of a painting in a magazine as a "photograph"? Or should our approach to how to discuss that material shift be different, and if so, exactly how should it be different, since the material transformation from a painting to the printed page is akin to the transformation of the photographic print or digital file to the printed page? Does it have to do with what qualities we assume are germane to the photograph, and which are not? What qualities are these? And finally, what tacit assumptions are being made when we link these, or the multitude of other distributive forms of the photograph together?

2)   Are we speaking of conventions, or in other words, is it
more useful to speak of conventions rather than objects when
we speak of things under the umbrella term "photography"? And
if so, when we talk about photography in an art museum, are we
really speaking of the current status of the "Western pictorial
tradition" (as Jeff Wall, and others, have, with varied levels
of explicitness, asserted), and by extension, should we be speaking of "pictures" and not "photographs"? Are the conversations
about photography simply a speed bump in our ongoing negotiation
with what is a transhistorical package of concerns related
to pictorial conventions, and thus is it appropriate that questions pertaining to representation, semantic proximity, identification with, or degree of fidelity to an original object
or moment in time persist in governing the discussion of photographs? Or is this anachronistic, and should we instead turn
to questions pertaining to distribution systems, technology,
function, and application, not what a photograph is "of" but
how it circulates, structures its points of reception, and finds
form through that circulation? Is the current state of the
discussion of photographs (still caught between the language
of aesthetic formalism, the politics of representation, and a
certain brand of deterministic social art history) and their
meaning, their modes of signification, compatible with the
conversations about this larger distributed field?

3)   Returning to question 1, if we speak of each of these
instances as, for the most part, discursive, what qualities do
they in fact share? How do we speak of the distinct aesthetic,
political, and social implications of each, while acknowledging
the link between them? Are these questions, ones pertaining
to the interpretation and analysis of photographic images that
might be significant for an artist or critic, even similar to
those that concern the institutions that maintain the histories
and traditions of aesthetics? In other words, do these questions
arise from the same fundamental place? Are they even allied
in their respective goals? When we speak of the medium in the
abstract, are we not glossing over the bureaucratic details

and internal negotiations that govern the perception, or the
identity of record, of the public role photography has within
an art context? When one of the hundreds of thousands of viewers enters the galleries at The Museum of Modern Art, how are
the divisions between departments understood? Are these divisions, those between photography, prints and drawings, video
and film, sculpture, painting, design, helpful for a viewer, and
if so, in what way? What do they imply? How do the minute spe-
cificities of the departmental dynamics of a museum affect
the mass reception of the history of art? And beyond this, how
helpful are these departmental distinctions for the institution
itself; how do they enable the institution to maintain itself,
its object of study, and its mission?

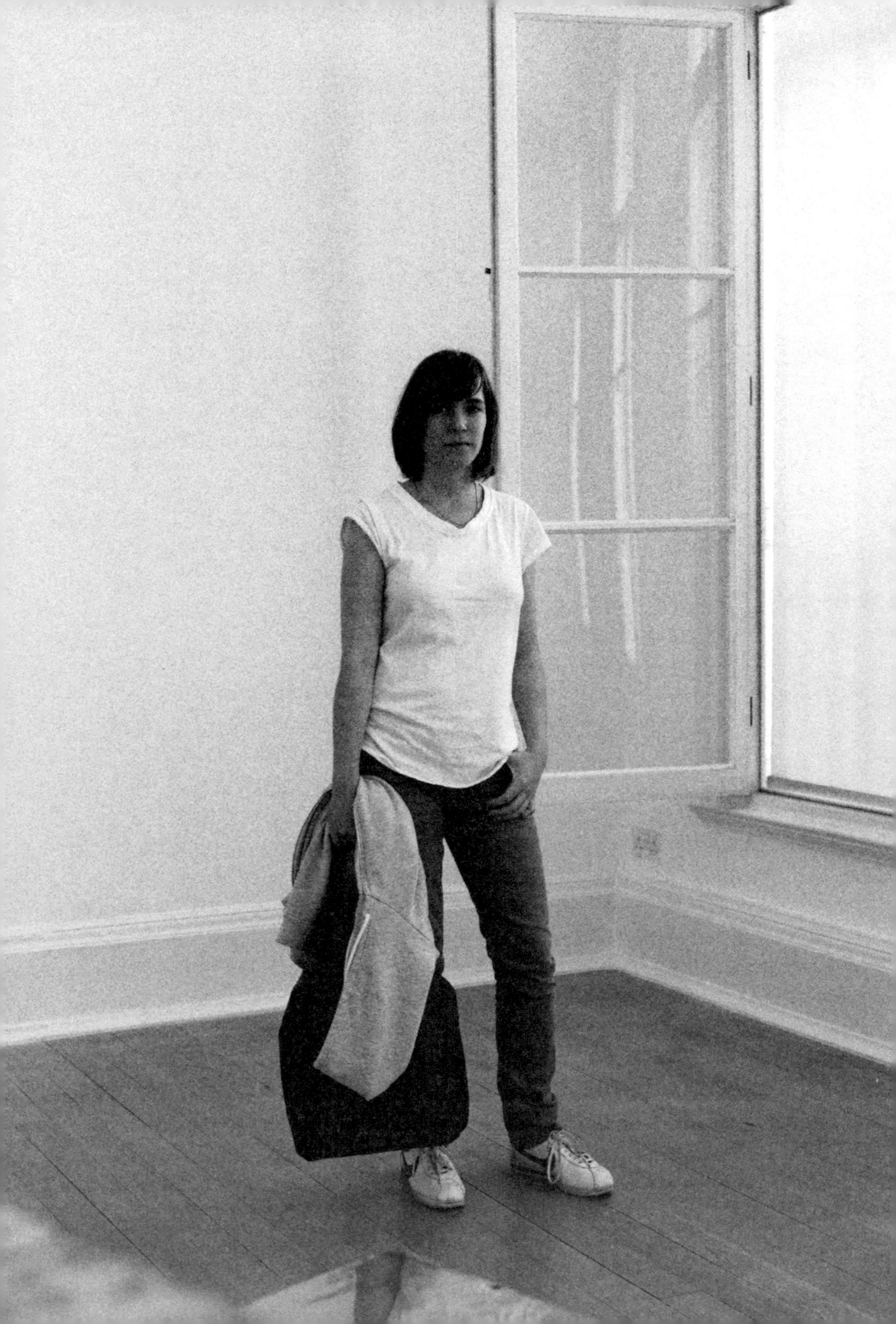

Toward a Minor Photography: Annette Kelm's Discrete Cosmologies

First published as "Annette Kelm's Discrete Cosmologies," Stipendium, exh. cat., Hamburg Kunstverein, Hamburg 2005, English/German, p. 56-58; revised and expanded in Parkett, no. 87 (February 2010), p. 158-169.

Each act of depiction is the taming of an unruly past, a condensation of conventions, histories, and processes into a singular surface that is subsequently apprehended in a flash. And herein lies the double bind of the depictive in art: depiction is the most conservative of gestures—naturalized, instrumental, idiomatic—and simultaneously the most contentious artistic act. Its sheer ubiquity and legibility place it squarely at the intersection of art and daily life, the very terrain that represented art's greatest revolutionary potential. Since the turn of the 20th century, no medium has embodied the conflict over the depictive like photography: as the most widely disseminated popular medium and the most conventionalized representational form, it has been the subject of both ritualized scrutiny and nostalgic re-entrenchment.

Yet it would be a mistake to claim that photography has been restrained by convention; rather it has no identity outside of convention, and no history that is not equally a history of convention. The identity of photography is situated in the inverse relationship between materiality and convention: as its material solidity has receded, dispersed technologically (a process initiated soon after its invention), convention has come to define photography fully. This condition is not unique among objects of theoretical discourse; it is a state shared by all media identified and isolated as a tradition. Yet the

photographic has undergone an even more extreme alchemical
transformation that encompasses both art and the public sphere:
not simply becoming a discursive collection of conventions—for
this is what it always was—but its conventions becoming subsumed within those of depiction, becoming inextricable from and
unidentifiable outside the language of the depictive. The best
evidence of this is the commonplace understanding that repro-
ductions of photographs on billboards, in books, in magazines,
on computer screens, and on gelatin silver paper are equally
a part of the photographic episteme despite their vastly differ-
entiated materiality and modes of distribution. In short,
they are argued to be equivalent because they serve as nothing
more than the depictive.

By the late 1970s, this peculiar circumstance made photography a wholly polarized artistic field. The practitioners
and critics who noticed the tide changing diligently lined
up on one side or the other of the ideological divide, arguing
either for the redeployment of the instrumental force of the
photographic to counter institutional ends—a belief that the
dominant language of the depictive might be redeemed—or for
a deconstruction of its naturalized conventions, as though negation was not simply a perverse form of preservation.

Anachronistic as they may seem today, these polarities
continued well into the following decade, and by now the
urgency once ascribed to photography in the discussion of the
politics of art has waned, swept under the rug with other
unfinished business. In the wake of this stalemate, the production of photographs in art appears to have suffered from
a curious bout of self-inflicted amnesia: rather than being
instrumental, it parodies the instrumental, abandoning any
aspiration to a revolutionary project for the pictorialism of
a premodern Beaux-Arts, retroactively inserting itself into
the tradition of the autonomous art object or the taxonomies
of the archival document and its thoroughly disassembled
instrumentality. Its contingent conventions and its elasticity
of distribution and reception have become concretized, inert,
and stagnant, accepting the mute museum wall as its foregone

conclusion, or, as George Baker surmised in his 2003 essay "Photography's Expanded Field," "Critical consensus would have it that the problem today is not that just about anything image-based can now be called photographic, but rather that photography itself has been foreclosed, cashiered, abandoned—outmoded technologically and displaced aesthetically."[1]

Thus we have a photographic discourse, theoretical or otherwise, that has become a moody precipitate of its headier days—a hermetic, over-crowded, over-theorized, and stifling field comprised of tired idioms; a discourse-driven example of what Theodor Adorno termed "late style," which he likened to an aged piece of fruit whose surface is "furrowed, even ravaged," showing "more traces of history than of growth."[2] As Adorno wrote, late style "leaves only fragments behind, and communicates itself, like a cipher, only through the blank spaces from which it has disengaged itself … its tears and fissures, witnesses to … finite powerlessness."[3] It is where "conventions find expression as the naked representation of themselves," producing "expressionless, distanced works" that turn "emptiness outward."[4]

Emerging in the early 2000s, Annette Kelm came to photography in its late moment, yet her work did not fit neatly into any of its entrenched modalities, nor did it propose a radical break with tradition. Instead, her unassuming images seem to curl up in the heart of the conflict, adapting photography's dominant tongue—its propensity for symbolism and historiography, and its pictorial and taxonomic proclivities—to provisional ends. Her deadpan, frontal image of a fallen sequoia, Mil Arrugas (A Thousand Wrinkles, 2005), with its undulating root system splayed out like an open wound and compressed against the picture's surface, offers an iconographic key to Kelm's oeuvre. Mil Arrugas was made on a trip to the same forest where Alfred Hitchcock, in his film Vertigo (1958), represented the conflation of time and space through a dismembered section of redwood. It was here that Hitchcock's protagonist, the hard-nosed detective-turned-private eye, Scottie (James Stewart), fell victim to schizophrenic time, with his muse, Judy (Kim Novak)—masquerading as the psychically tortured Madeleine—pointing

to one of the tree's annual rings and declaring it the moment of
her death. For Scottie—his grip on reality loosened by his love
for the imposter—this was the moment when the fragile barrier
between past and present evaporated, and thus, the beginning of
his phantasmagoric descent into madness.

Reflecting on this scene some 20 years later in Sans
Soleil (1983), Chris Marker mused on Hitchcock's anti-hero as
a portrait of the archetypical filmmaker, an archeologist of
images intoxicated by the fragments of the past and unable to
resist falling victim to temporal aphasia. We follow Marker
following Scottie's trail, just as Scottie followed his elusive
object of desire, and with Marker we see time and space, present
and past, reality and fantasy conflated in the synthetic tem-
porality of cinematic time, Scottie's delirium representing
Marker's filmic journey en abyme. The dizzying spiral encompassing Vertigo's opening credits served as Marker's ideogrammatic
key, his narrator commenting, "time cover[ed] a field ever wider
as it moved away, a cyclone whose present moment contains
motionless the eye"—or the "I," the seeing subject, ensnared
within its vortex.

In Mil Arrugas Kelm stalks the eye and time to the
mythical grounds of their conflation, the roots of the sequoia
becoming the striations of an iris, giving us time again
rendered as a static field. Yet unlike the tidy geometry of
Hitchcock's spiral, or the smooth cylindrical section before
which Scottie and Madeleine/Judy are seen standing, Kelm's
image is unruly: the dark center of the upended tree ensnared
in the interlocking tendrils of its root system. Kelm delivers
us an invaginated arrow of time (akin to Georges Bataille's pin-
eal eye, whose conical form echoes the tip of an arrow and the
piercing vision of the phallocentric camera), split and inverted
into an undulating pucker, an upended phallus revealing a darkened void enveloped in folds that retreat from its center like
the rays of a sunburst in negative. Time is no longer depicted
as the orderly sedimentations of the past, but as an interwoven
knotted field that defies neat dissection and has literally
been uprooted, arrested in a state of decay. Most tellingly,

we are given a monocular double of the camera lens in the
arrested spiral of the wounded tree, an eye that stares back
like a clenched fist.

Like Marker's narrator, Kelm scavenges the historical
and material world for totems, repeatedly revisiting the image
of the eye and of time, symbols for which the technological
image has always had almost religious reverence. In her untitled series of targets, we are presented with a sequence of ocu-
lar forms marred by the literal piercing of arrows that inject
pulsations of color through their blank surfaces. Again a flat
field—an orderly terrain—is shot through with incidences that
appear like an unnamed constellation. In the sequence of images
that comprise her Untitled (2007)—a depiction of a woman flattened against a blue background, her eyes, in deep shadow, seemingly glancing back and forth—the camera's eye is transformed
into a lurking, unseen stalker, yet the photographs are clearly
staged, the forebodingly distanced precision of the lens performed rather than enacted. Another series, Backstage (2004),
which shows an eye cropped tight, bracketed by false eyelashes,
and darting about as though trapped inside the frame, evokes
the infamous scene in Un Chien andalou (1929) where the empirical gaze of the camera literally dissects its object with a single slash of a razorblade, an instance where the symbolic and
the depictive, the metaphoric and metonymic, are consummated
in one horrific gesture.

Yet the violent taxonomies of the anonymous camera are
never fully exploited by Kelm. The eye is never cut, the examination is left incomplete, and the sequence never resolves. The
typological and serial turn from a monotonous drum roll into a
circumstantial cadence. It is a quality of provisionality, what
Gilles Deleuze and Félix Guattari called the "minor"—"that
which a minority constructs within a major language"—that Kelm
here deploys.[5] No series lasts more than a few iterations, and
their subjects—from a seated woman to a man at a thinly orches-
trated Italian restaurant or a palm tree blowing in the wind—
could not be confused for the subject matter of the taxonomist
or the allegorical detritus of a social realist, yet the tools

of their trades persist. As Deleuze and Guattari argue, "Minor
languages are characterized not by overload and poverty in
relation to a standard or major language, but by a sobriety and
variation that are like a minor treatment of a major language …
deterritorializing the major language."[6] The minor language is
comprised of sliding meanings and innuendo that operate within
the "cramped space" of the mother tongue. It never attempts
to assert an oppositional language, it does not seek to "acquire
the majority," but rather insinuates itself within totalizing
structures, turning them to the service of the transitory and
contingent.[7]

Channeling Walter Benjamin, Eduardo Cadava wrote,
"The history of photography can be said to begin with an interpretation of the stars."[8] In Kelm's hands, photographs, like
stars, are polysemic figures; they slyly shift meanings, slipping easily into a multitude of provisional patterns, allowing
both symbolic inference and empiricist speculation to coexist.
Her photographs embrace loose formal associations, tenuous historical linkages, and personal remembrances. The photograph
<u>After Lunch, Trying to Build Railway Ties</u> (2005) is exemplary in
this respect. The vaguely Hawaiian motif of the fabric backdrop
seen in the image evokes the anthropological uses of photography as much as it does the trope of botanical specimen documentation. Yet the mass-produced fabric never achieves the appearance of anthropological authenticity; instead it is a perversion
that parallels the absurd prevalence of the eucalyptus tree in
Southern California, which is seen here demurely displayed in
a common drinking glass. Native to Australia and imported in
the early 19th century to the West Coast of the United States,
it was not until the late 1860s that the eucalyptus was planted
on a grand scale to support the massive need for wood in the
railroad and shipbuilding industries. The fast-growing trees
came to dominate the landscape, forcing out the native oaks,
yet the eucalyptus was a poor building material, wet and sappy,
with a spiraling grain, and it had a natural tendency to curl
as it dried, slowly tearing apart any structure it was used to
build. In Kelm's image, these historical connections assume the

character of the incidental—the plant clippings and cheap
fabric infuse the larger narrative with a sense of whimsy—
while the lunch encounter is imbued with poetic significance.

Mythic conflations between the grand and the mundane
are not uncommon in Kelm's vision. The same sensitivities draw
her to the Angelino cowboy who enacts his personal fantasy
in a neighborhood park, regally trotting among power lines
and playing with children, and to Albert Frey's sci-fi inflected
restaurant-cum-spaceship, which sits in disrepair, peppered
with graffiti, a rotting futurism moored on the edge of an
equally dead, man-made sea. But the elliptical conflation of
past and present, history and image, is perhaps nowhere better
on display than in Kelm's <u>House on Haunted Hill I</u> and <u>II</u> (2005).
Both images depict Frank Lloyd Wright's Ennis House, whose
structure has been slowly disintegrating into the hill on
which it is perched. The culmination of Wright's pre-Columbian
"textile block" houses, the Ennis, unlike its antecedents,
went so far as to emulate pre-Columbian engineering, employing
a high sand content concrete drawn directly from its grounds.
While this decision literalized a very modern materialist
interdependence of architecture and site, it also made the
house particularly susceptible to erosion. The resulting piece
of modern architecture, inspired by the timeless aura of ruins,
has quickly become a ruin itself. A favorite of the Hollywood
picture industry, the Ennis has served as the backdrop for
several films (including the B-movie Kelm titles her photographs
after). But its most famous role was in Ridley Scott's <u>Blade
Runner</u> (1982), a noirish imagining of a future populated by
discursive fragments, simulations, and false figures: in short,
the future presented as a ruin of the past, a material reality
crushed under the weight of its images that ironically foretold
the fate of Wright's structure.

It would be a mistake to assume that Kelm's is a photography that proposes to remember for us; neither does it
simulate or prescribe a historical narrative, nor linger in
the hermetic realm of the personal. Instead, it resides in the
precarious position between worlds, between the personal and

the public, the fleeting and the eternal, holding within each
picture the potential for memory without prescription. It is
this photography—not constructed to undermine totalizing or
divisive potentials, but a provisional photography, grafted
onto history's interior, a photography of minor proportions—
that grows like a parasite within the dormant body of its
host and, as such, outlives its confines, drawing new life from
its dead flesh.

NOTES

1. George Baker, "Photography's Expanded Field," <u>October</u>, vol. 114 (Fall 2005),
p. 122.

2. Theodor W. Adorno, "Late Style in Beethoven," <u>Essays on Music</u>, ed. Richard
Leppert, trans. Susan H. Gillespie, University of California Press, Berkeley
and Los Angeles 2002, p. 564.

3. Ibid., p. 566.

4. Ibid., p. 566-567.

5. Gilles Deleuze and Félix Guattari, <u>Kafka: Toward a Minor Literature</u>, trans.
Dana Polan, University of Minnesota Press, Minneapolis 1986, p. 16.

6. Gilles Deleuze and Félix Guattari, <u>A Thousand Plateaus: Capitalism and
Schizophrenia</u>, trans. Bernard Massumi, University of Minnesota Press, Minneapolis
1987, p. 104.

7. Ibid., p. 106.

8. Eduardo Cadava, <u>Words of Light: Theses on the Photography of History</u>, Princeton
University Press, Princeton 1997, p. 26.

In Camera: On Luisa Lambri's Haptic Eye

First published in <u>Luisa Lambri: Interiors</u>, exh. cat., Ivory
Press, Madrid 2011, n.p.

That architecture became the subject matter <u>par excellence</u> for
those artists using photography (or, perhaps more accurately,
photographers using art) who rose to international notoriety in
the late 1990s is common knowledge. While the most prominent
emerging art practices of the time took on a dismissive, if not
antagonistic, attitude toward traditional exhibition conventions—deploying rough hewn and immersive bricolage environments, messy faux-naive paintings, or amorphous gallery experiences associated with relational aesthetics—photographic work
of the era seemed more concerned with appearing at home in the
contemplative solitude of the museum than it did in intervening
within it. Art photography was for the first time coming to
terms with the expanded parameters of institutional approval
in the domain of art, manifested not only in its expanded scale,
but in the internalization of dusty Beaux-Arts categories like
pictorial tableaux, still lifes, portraits, and landscapes, lending these anachronistic genres the air of aesthetic currency.
This reflexive obsession both unified these works stylistically,
and underscored their shared fascination with modernist
architecture, a proclivity that was evident in both what they
depicted (i.e., the sharp angularity of modern architecture
within which most art is displayed) and in the widespread use
of Plexiglas glazing and aluminum backframes, which not only
reflected the International Style palaces surrounding them

on their surfaces, but made them materially continuous with
their intended sites of exhibition. Be they the brand name or
designer imposters, these grand photographic testaments to
order, detail, and expansive perspective became so common that
by the time the new millennium arrived it seemed one could not
spend a day visiting museums or galleries without being dwarfed
by numerous hefty Plexiglas-encased monoliths wearing images
of grand avenues, geometrically sublime glass towers, or scenes
of an ant-like populous flittering about a gridded cityscape.
At its best this was a time when the medium truly came into its
own, accepted as part of a tradition that seemed, until then,
incompatible with contemporary art, while drawing forward
the still powerful hold of the pictorial on collective aesthetic
experience. At its worst, the work embraced an arid and vacant
grandiosity, inspiring feeble apologias that employed terms
like "globalization," "consumerism," and countless other theory-
lite watchwords of the late 1990s. Beyond the credibility that
stellar auction prices or museum retrospectives conferred, this
rebirth of photography, the latest of its many reintroductions
into conventional art contexts, stood out because in the hands
of these practitioners the medium achieved a self-consciousness
emblematic of serious art while maintaining a formal continuity
with the ghettoized and debased arena of art photography.
So complete was this transformation of a traditionally minor
and supplementary medium to an exemplar of the Western pictorial tradition that despite the appellation "photographer"
affixed to their producers, the works were still unquestionably
admitted to contemporary art's main stage. Here photography
in art achieved a broadly accepted default style, one that was
never ghosted by the question of whether or not it was legiti-
mately art, or whether or not it could stand up among its
more entrenched aesthetic cousins. Photography had achieved
the status of the "picture," which, as Baudelaire suggested,
is "only what it wants to be; there is no way to look at it
other than on its own terms … [It] is exclusive and absolute."[1]
In other words, photography, as picture, was no longer confined
to instrumentality, it could unquestionably claim an autonomy

and an art historical genealogy that had until then been out
of reach.

PHOTOGRAPHY AND THE FINESTRA APERTA

This was a peculiar position for a medium that had been used
by artists to undermine the very characteristics it now seemed
to sustain. Photography was now not only identified with the
dominance of the Western pictorial tradition but, more explicitly, championed as its last remaining steward. Photography
proved to be particularly convenient for these purposes. Just
as Leon Battista Alberti looked to architectural metaphors to
describe his science of perspective in 15th-century Italy, settling on the _finestra aperta_ (the open window), architectural
metaphors similarly pervaded photographic jargon, from aperture to frame, making the _camera_—itself a Latin word meaning
chamber or enclosed room—a symbolically resonant site for the
recovery of the Western pictorial tradition in contemporary art.
Moreover, the term _camera_ referred not just to any room, but
signified a cloistered and detached position of power, literally
a seat of judgment, in legal terms, from which an authority
could apply abstract form upon the chaos of daily life.

    So dominant was this link between perspective, the
built environment, and rational order that by the early 20th
century it came to transform the way architecture viewed
itself. After all, one cannot understand the history of architecture in its modernist phase without noting its obsession
with picture making: its mirrored facades, steel frames,
and expansive glass curtain walls all operated as an industrial
materialization of the Cartesian model of vision Alberti set
loose, one characterized by geometric regularity and objective
detachment. So, when Le Corbusier described his excitement for
his office's new home high above Paris, writing "From our offices
we will get the feeling of being lookouts dominating a world
in order," he performed an inversion of Alberti's ontological
metaphor for perspective: the picture was now the _ursprung_
of architecture's power, rather than the other way around.[2]

Le Corbusier established a link that would become commonplace, likening the ability of architecture to frame not only its interior, but also its surroundings creating a sensation of detached control, a transformation of the vulgar materiality into the tidy geometries of the picture, and one's body into a disembodied eye, understanding that, as Friedrich Kittler would later argue, "Alberti's real trick was to make even this activity of the eye as virtual as the concept of the window."[3]

It was this virtuality that has so convincingly been put into practice in the photographic work of the 1990s. In inhabiting this role, photography was simultaneously positing and allegorizing both its place in the lineage of high art through its reflexive examination of perspectival form and the links between architecture and vision—the thematics of which governed its technical and intellectual development—as well as its aspiration to adorn the walls of buildings, to occupy the catbird seat of high art and architecture, cleaving its last tangible connection to the readily disposable conditions of print media. The synonymy of photography with the picture, and by extension the solidity of architecture, made the transformational power of the photographic frame central to the identity of the medium, positing it as a bracket that turned the vicissitudes of daily life into an ordered field that the camera alone could still achieve, ambitious painting having abandoned this form of "realism" completely by the early 20th century. This network of reflexive reduplications—of photography's imaging of the orderly field of the built environment (itself premised on Albertian perspective), and the camera lens' synonymy with authority over its chosen object—made the photographic art of this time a formidable, if conservative, force in contemporary art.

INHABITING THE PICTURE

At first glance, Luisa Lambri simply seems to have been one of many late to this conversation, a member of a second generation working in the shadow of the Düsseldorf School (itself a

reexamination of the American New Topographics movement,
some two decades earlier). And while accounts of her work often
begin here, if only to brush these associations to the side like
impolitic dinner conversation, it seems integral to note that
not only was this the milieu within which her work developed
and in which it was first received and understood, but that her
work's proximity to those dominant styles, and even its ability
to seem continuous with them, is the very source its most profound implications. As (mostly male) photographers heaved their
large cameras about, pointing their big boxes at even larger
ones by (mostly male) architects, and then producing their own
large-scale iconic picture boxes to be one day placed within
buildings like those they depicted, like prosthetic windows,
Lambri instead created serialized, partial, and ethereal images
of architectural spaces, sequences that repeat like a stutter
or flinch, emphasizing stochastic cadence and incidental effects
rather than totalizing fields of order. As Lambri herself
observed, "My work arises from the condition of being a female
in a male-created world. I try to inject a female point of view
into my photographs of buildings designed mainly by men, and
in that way I distance myself from the dominance of modernism
in the architecture and aesthetic of 20th-century Western
culture."[4]

In Lambri's photographs we are presented with serial
images of incidents, like a ray of light grazing the topography
of Frank Lloyd Wright's Hollyhock House, the dizzying effect
of the layers of glass of Mies Van der Rohe's Barcelona Pavilion,
or the condensation on the atrium windows of Philip Johnson's
Menil House that turns the plants beyond into a haze of green
shadow. In her work there are no singular iconic views, but a
series of provisional, fragmentary vignettes that mine the
refractions and opacity of the architectural frame and the camera alike; the shared synonymy of architecture and the virtual
eye of the camera with total order is fractured, made conditional, subject to light, moisture, and incident. What we see
is not the monumentality of the buildings she photographs, but
their susceptibility to chance, their occupation by incidents.

In short, she presents the building's occupation by external forces, and among these one must count the transformative potential of the photograph itself. As Beatriz Colomina writes, architectural photography "suggest[s] that it is intended that these spaces be comprehended by occupation … by 'entering' the photograph, by inhabiting it," and, she continues in the adjoined footnote, "in this sense, built space has no more authority than do drawings, photographs, or descriptions."[5] If one accepts Colomina's proposition of inhabitation, that the photograph disrupts the autonomy of its object (i.e., our ability to experience the depicted object "on its own terms") through a kind of optical inhabitation, then the photograph is more than simply another occupational force, but the most significant one. For the photograph claims both a purchase over the "reality" of what it displays, and distributes its "reality" far beyond the parameters of the building itself. In other words, the photographic/pictorial is an a priori logic that structures, distributes, and in the end radically alters the conditions of "direct" experience, even when we are standing in front of what it depicts.

With this as its premise, Lambri's work offers us another, more subtle layer of inhabitation, not only of architecture, but likewise of the prescribed pictorial style in which it is so often depicted, occupying and rendering contingent the conventions of the dominant mode of contemporary photography her work developed within. Just as her photographs depict the inhabitation of architecture by seemingly innocuous effects that transform our perceptions of space, they simultaneously disrupt the authority that photography achieves—by allying itself symbolically with the solidity of architecture—through their inhabitation and deformation of the conventions of pictorial photography.

It is this quality of inhabitation, what Gilles Deleuze and Félix Guattari have called the "minor"—"that which a minority constructs within a major language"—that Lambri here deploys.[6] As Deleuze and Guattari posit, "Minor languages are characterized not by overload and poverty in relation to a

standard or major language, but by a sobriety and variation
that are like a minor treatment of a major language … deterritorializing the major language."[7] The minor language is comprised of meanings and innuendo that operate within the "cramped
space" of the mother tongue. It never attempts to assert an
oppositional language, it does not seek to "acquire the majority,"
but rather it insinuates itself within totalizing structures,
turning them to the service of the transitory and contingent,
emphasizing their provisionality.[8] Through this inhabitation,
dominant structures become porous, perverted, and, where they
once asserted their unassailable power to organize and frame
their chosen subject matter, they become one of many mediations,
no more solid than the passing effects of light and atmosphere
on architecture. When Lambri's camera stares into modernity's
vast picture windows, it does not confront transparency, but
opacity, interference, reflection, and with this, she rescripts
the entrenched understandings of both the solidity of architecture and the supposed transparency of pictorial depiction.
Lambri's photographs clear away the dominant compositional
logic of the pictorial and instead draw forward Alberti's equally
important, although less discussed, dialectical antipode to the
frame, what he called the veil, which is set up "between the
eye and the object to be represented, so that the visual pyramid
passes through (its) loose weave."[9] What Alberti was describing
is a screen, a membrane that separates us from the world the
picture's frame is meant to allow us to pass into.

FROM FRAME TO SCREEN

As Albrecht Dürer famously noted, "Perspective is a Latin word
meaning seeing through," and this seeing-through is a seeing-
through-a-frame, a transformation of the object at which we are
looking into its imaginary other (i.e., an image).[10] Just as
the frame is something to look through, to put around a set of
elements, it also implies a surface that cannot be broken and
cannot be touched, a Brechtian fourth wall, and this surface is
always invisible. It has no presence except as an imaginary

border, and it depends on the suspension of disbelief, on the
viewer's faith in the order it presents. It depends on our ability to see "into" objects. In this sense, the frame's effect is
a dematerialization of surface. It forces us to work from the
outside in (i.e., from its edges), and we slip into its depths as
we reach the center. It allows us to leave our bodies and the
material world behind, held at bay by the frame's edge. That is,
in order to see into a picture, to understand its logic, we too
must dissolve into its surface.

While the frame defines the epic detachment of the picture, codifying it as an organizational tool and situating its
contents in formal morphological relationships to one another,
the screen brings us back to earth, puts us back in the site
of viewership and back into the corporeal world. When acknowledged, it is palpable and is everywhere present in the picture,
its surface never disappears, no matter how we might try to
make it do so; it is always present right before us. While the
screen also implies the infinite, its infinitude does not extend
into its center, but along its surface; its visible edges are
always provisional and indefinite. The screen speaks less of
composition than of interference, of mediation, presenting us
with a membrane that lies in-between the observer and his/her
object. Rather than optical detachment, screens emphasize touching, points of contact between itself and its object. Pictorial
concepts such as "in front" and "behind" no longer exist: it is
only moments of <u>contact</u>, of <u>touching</u>, that organize the pictorial field; everything not on this plane recedes from clarity
as a smooth undulation of form and color. Consider the scanner,
which sees only on a single plane, which charts what touches
its surface, and that which does not.

Optical images, technical images, operate as screens,
and are comprised of intersecting planes. The photographer is
given the plane of focus, and the plane of the film to work
with. Photographers manipulate depth of field to simulate perspective, but in fact they are simply trying to cheat the screen
by emphasizing the frame, synthetically linking this optical
picture to that of the pre-optical synthetic picture, much as

the _paysagistes_ attempted to cheat paint with their brand of
"realism." Yet unlike the canvas, the camera's multiple surfaces,
its planes of attention, are regularized and industrial in origin, and when they produce interference, it cannot not be taken
as evidence of "artistic style," as an errant brushstroke might
be. Thus the camera-based photograph is caught between the opacity of the industrial screen and the transparency of the frame,
and each photograph is a negotiation between these. All of this
is to say that while we look _through_ frames, we look _at_ screens;
we scan the screen for incidents, for points of contact. This
emphasis on contact constitutes a distinctly bodily oppositional
term to the detached transparency of the photographic frame
and the virtuality of the eye. As Roland Barthes wrote, "A sort
of umbilical cord links the body of the photographed thing to
my gaze: light, though impalpable, is here a carnal medium, a
skin I share with anyone who has been photographed." And this
"skin" is what Barthes postulates as the medium through which
the emotional effect of the _punctum_ occurs, literally a "piercing," through which we experience a direct connection with what
has been photographed.[11] Most importantly, it is this understanding of photography as a "skin" or screen that accounts for
the photograph's empathic power, its ability to create a coun-
ter-intuitive sense of connection across time and space through
the proposition of a shared material intermediary that links
the body of the viewer to that which is viewed.

Lambri gives us screens rather than frames, a collective
"skin" rather than a detached floating eye, as is visible in
her views of the Sheats Goldstein Residence, shot through the
bathroom skylight, the tree branches grazing its cloudy panes,
the contours of the skylight acting like the camera's ground
glass, at once opaque and transparent. This emphasis is carried
through to her approach to the site of exhibition, where her
work operates like a sequence of punctuations in the walls of
the white cube, rather than as iconic monolithic forms that loom
over the viewer.

Lambri's is a photography predicated on embodiment
rather than detachment, on contingency rather than solidity.

It is comprised of translucent screens and momentary "piercings"
of incident through mute facades. Here Lambri delivers us
from the authoritative frame of the pictorial to the diaphanous
"veil" of the screen, that palpable dividing line between seer
and seen. Her work inhabits the cloistered authority of vision,
affirming its transformative capacities without reifying its
propensity for declarative order. Her photographs create a
sequence of provisional worlds, linked together through the
agency of an individual "occupant," not the arbitrary authority
of a de facto style. In this, the political implications of
Lambri's work are felt as a revision of naturalized photographic
conventions, reconceived through the lens of the minor or marginal, which posits a multitude of possible vantage points from
which any individual may reorganize and occupy the dominant
or repressive, splaying it out, and transforming its singular
order into an ongoing procession of possible ones.

NOTES

1. Charles Baudelaire, "The Salon of 1846: XVI: Why Sculpture is Tiresome,"
in Charles Baudelaire: Art in Paris, 1845-1862: Salons and Other Exhibitions,
trans. and ed. Jonathan Mayne, Phaidon, London 1965, p. 111.

2. Le Corbusier, Urbanisme, G. Crès et Cie, Paris 1925, p. 186.

3. Friedrich Kittler, Optical Media, Polity Press, Cambridge and New York 2010,
p. 62.

4. "The Poetics of Space: A Conversation between Matthew Drutt and Luisa Lambri,"
in Luisa Lambri: Locations, Menil Foundation, Inc., Houston 2004, p. 61.

5. Beatriz Colomina, Privacy and Publicity: Modern Architecture as Mass Media,
MIT Press, Cambridge 1998, p. 234.

6. Gilles Deleuze and Félix Guattari, Kafka: Toward a Minor Literature,
trans. Dana Polan, University of Minnesota Press, Minneapolis 1986, p. 16.

7. Gilles Deleuze and Félix Guattari, A Thousand Plateaus: Capitalism and
Schizophrenia, trans. Bernard Massumi, University of Minnesota Press,
Minneapolis 1997, p. 26.

8. Ibid., p. 106.

9. Leon Battista Alberti, On Painting, trans. Martin Kemp, Penguin Classics,
New York 1991, p. 30.

10. As cited in Erwin Panofsky, Perspective as Symbolic Form,
trans. Christopher S. Woods, Zone Books, New York 1991, p. 27.

11. Roland Barthes, Camera Lucida, trans. Richard Howard, Hill and Wang,
New York 1981, p. 81.

The Whiteness of the Whale
(On the Work of Kelley Walker)

First printed as exhibition poster text on the occasion of the exhibition
<u>Kelley Walker, Untitled, 2012</u>, Redling Fine Art, Los Angeles 2011;
revised and republished in <u>The Painting Factory: Abstraction after Warhol</u>,
exh. cat., Skira Rizzoli, New York 2012, p. 150-163.

> The American vanguard painter took to the white expanse
> of the canvas as Melville's Ishmael took to the sea.
> —Harold Rosenberg[1]

Twentieth-century debates over the politics of representation,
the autonomy of art, and art's capacity for critique still linger like disgruntled spirits on the hunt for living bodies to
inhabit. At first contemporary art seemed like a suitable host:
appropriated/pop imagery, collage, the monochrome, automatism,
the aleatory, and so on are no less common now than they were
when such ideas had an air of currency about them. But today
the meanings of these strategies are less certain, less overt,
as though much contemporary art beckons to these anachronisms
only to misdirect them. How better to display indifference for
such battles than to welcome them in, only to step gently to
the side, behaving, in the terminology of language acquisition,
like a <u>false friend</u>?

Rather than dismiss these evasions and layers of reference as cynical, it would serve us to remember that the key
artistic subplot of the 20th century was the development of an
art that operates in spite of instrumentality rather than through
it, a circumstance that has put both representation and the
status of the image under constant scrutiny. Certainly this is
merited, for the peculiar instability of an image's meaning

has lead many on a fool's errand, leaving the history of art
criticism and aesthetic theory littered with false ontologies
and misplaced certainties, diverting attention from the political implications of aesthetics to the phantasmagoric world of
likenesses. Just consider how quickly the early 1980s obsession
with a politics of representation led to the perversity that
politics _is_ representation, as though we had collectively transcended the world of objects and bodies, while images had become
concrete. Subjected to these interpretive schemas, the critical
or political dimensions of contemporary art were reduced to
exercises in negation, with artists left to scavenge the world
for false images to undermine, heaving metaphoric bricks at
symbolic authorities while remaining complicit with the concrete
institutional mechanisms that they depended on for support,
and wielded for effect.

As works of art have increasingly embraced the polysemy
of images—almost to the point where the question of what a
particular image depicts has become irrelevant—critical writing
continues to see art as primarily depictive, a compulsion that
has made commonplace the absurd assertion that the absence
of representational forms is in fact the representational act
par excellence—as if aesthetics functioned exclusively by
hermeneutic repression. Of course this is only a symptom. The
true culprit here seems to be the assumption that material and
image are mutually exclusive, and rather than wasting any
more time by tracking this phenomenon to its origins, one has
to wonder if it is possible to simply ignore it and start anew.
At the very least, when approaching a contemporary work, we
would do well to avoid beginning with anachronistic questions
pertaining to what an artwork might be "about" or "represent,"
and instead start by trying to address what an artwork does—
or more precisely, what we make it do, and what we do around
it. In short, is it possible to simply let the art work?

One way to do this might be to imagine ourselves in a
time when the divide between image and material was less expansive. We could then begin with flatness as an essential quality
of painting, a mid-century argument that saw picture making

and materiality cohere in the unity of a "medium." As Clement
Greenberg noted, "flatness alone was unique and exclusive
to that art," a "limiting condition" that could "be pushed back
indefinitely before a picture stops being a picture and turns
into an arbitrary object." Such a story begins (or ends) with
the whiteness of the canvas, the point where a painting flirts
with its own disappearance into the world of objects. Modifying
the Greenbergian trajectory, Kazimir Malevich's <u>Suprematist
Composition: White on White</u> (1918) could usher in this tradition,
behind which follows Robert Ryman's caked surfaces, Robert
Rauschenberg's "dust-breeding" blanks, and so on. In telling
this story one could mention László Moholy-Nagy's famous quote
about Malevich: that the monochrome would be impossible without
the open field of the cinema screen, a location for fleeting
impressions and incidental effects. An ambitious contemporary
painting would likely make this kind of lineage for itself,
as a descendant of those who first turned away from the picture
window and the salon and toward flatness and the worker in the
factory, then looked toward an objecthood, and finally posited
the flatbed as a response to flatness, and with it embraced
the slipperiness of images—a process that culminated in an art
obsessed with the immateriality of images and the instability
of meaning. We know the long version, there's no need to
waste time lingering here. But knowing that all systems gravi-
tate toward equilibrium, what might cause the pendulum to
swing back?

"MARCEL, NO MORE PAINTING; GO GET A JOB"

Bricks offer us a tidy reminder of what all paintings require.
Rather than airy and seamless, rather than denatured and
ephemeral, we are instead presented with images made heavy,
first as grounds, then as additive layers, and then as the
tedious work of manually screening and rescreening, of cutting,
pasting, and collaging. The paintings are as much depictions
of labor as they are of bricks. From building material to optical image and back again, returning the digital to its analog

origins as an accumulation of ink, back into the world of
mortar, a layering of adhesive tars that stick to the image and
fix it against time. So we have a Fordist version of the digital,
then a handmade version of the industrial, until we find ourselves back with the artisanal—a wink, perhaps, to the collective
anonymity of craft, rather than the anomic world of images.

But are these historical resonances a misdirection,
a false path forward that the momentum of history seems to
necessitate? Do we really need to think in terms of eternal
returns, or is it possible to accept the work without a nod to
its affiliations, shared attributes, and historical resonances?
We have to entertain the thought that this ground of references
may simply be flat, a picture we know, a history flimsy to the
touch, just another empty apparition we need not contend with
lest we allow ourselves to be distracted from the work in front
of us by genealogies and taxonomies. It is a picture as much
imported as any other appropriated image—slid across the Xerox
machine, handed out to students, only to be Xeroxed over again
until it is stained by an oddly brackish halo that only intensi-
fies with each generation; or now, slid across the scanner
and emailed as a PDF, to be printed out and subsequently marred
by late-night studying. Does this history land with the
stultifying thud of a textbook, or does it ring out with the
enthusiastic chime of an e-mail successfully sent?

The PDF exemplifies an important turn in the course
of our story. Unlike the Xerox, the PDF is no longer part of a
chain of reproduction that takes on its own specific contours
through a sequence of progressively degraded optical duplications. Rather, once disseminated, the PDF is a singular point
from which all subsequent copies arise. It is a new original,
and its progeny are stillborn: they are not passed from one
set of hands to another but are simply reprinted anew for each
reader. It is not so much that materiality has been lost, but
that we dispose of it freely, and so all things merge back into
the earth as compost, only to return in new forms, as new
things to be recycled. Painting itself has died several times,
only to come back again in even more muscular forms.

Speaking of zombies, when staring up at the Marlboro
Man one still feels the queasy thrill of an artistic gesture har-
nessing the power accrued by a pop image over time. The Marlboro
Man slipped into the art world on the back of familiarity,
and one can still feel echoes of the buzz that hijacking so large
a system of resonances first offered. Now he has become more
the icon for the Americanness of the appropriative act, more exemplary of a certain robust and unapologetic Pop, than for the
cigarettes we no longer smoke. As for the gumption required to
use such an image in the first place, certainly such an extreme
wager could only have been made by a young artist toiling in
obscurity—even better that this toiling was performed as just
another deck hand in the flagship of Condé Nast. The stakes
of his gamble came from how loaded the images were, and the
possibility of refocusing them on some new purpose with their
momentum intact. The payoff was clear, but the risk was that
any semblance of an artistic voice would simply be subsumed
within the image's powerful currents. It was an act of survival,
perhaps; the young artist was already drowning, not in the
image world, but in the "lottery of the sea" that is contemporary art. But for the artist appropriating now, there does not
seem to be much of a gamble. Rather, appropriation has become
something of a reliable convention, a way to get one's foot in
the door, just raw enough to have presence, just commonplace
enough that one need not be worried about being misunderstood.

The original problem of appropriation must have been
akin to the weight a painter feels in front of a blank canvas,
the heft of the medium and its long and furrowed history bearing down. Whereas appropriation now only runs the risk of
glib cheapness, jumping into the morass of painting can result
in pretension and boredom, or worse, bland tastefulness. The
canvas is no less a cheat than was appropriation, but this time
in the opposite direction, for painting is, itself, quintessen-
tially art: it already has a place reserved above the fray,
its history deflecting any concern that a gesture upon its surface might not aspire to seriousness. Once the decision to make
a painting is committed to, this history floods into the room.

Whatever graces the canvas' surface appears as a foregone
conclusion, good or bad. It is hard to imagine an appropriated
image that makes such demands, that sets in motion such headiness, threatening to smother any gesture in the weight of
history. The canvas is a force both too easy to exploit and
too difficult to improve upon. What found image has this sort
of momentum behind it? What could provide an equally potent
threat of unearned self-importance?

From the brick-filled windows of urban renewal to the
Castello di Rivoli's planked-up alcoves of missing frescoes,
or the gaps left in the Isabella Stewart Gardner Museum by
the theft of its Vermeers, Rembrandts, and Degas—another act
of appropriation, another homeless picture drifting in the flow
of the black market. As many like to comment, art is an un-
regulated market, a Wild West of handshake deals and precocious
speculation subject to extreme bubbles and total implosions.
Or instead, we could think more art historically, of Leon
Battista Alberti's "finestra aperta" filled not by real bricks
but by the industrial screen, itself based upon Alberti's veil—
that intermediary scrim that was, for Alberti, painting's limiting condition, which reminds us that the flatness and the flat-
bedness of painting had already arrived by the 15th century.
As soon as the painterly window had been imagined, something
was needed to stand in its way, to buttress the flood of light,
to make a picture possible. Perhaps we ought to think of avant-
garde painting as an industrial ghetto waiting to be gentri-
fied. Boarded up or bricked over for a new purpose, its past
offering little more than atmosphere for new inhabitants,
historical gaps and false starts smoothed out and papered over,
like the pages of the periodical that wrap the canvas as they
otherwise would a dead fish. Bricks printed as though dollar
bills, canvases wrapped in hard currency. Yet nothing is really
being obscured. Nothing is missing from behind these frames
or lurking within them, except the displaced cover of the periodical itself, a footnote that threatens to unsettle the abrupt
stop of the work's Untitled by pointing toward an outside
source.[2] Negation would seem an easy route to making these works

fit in an evolutionary narrative, but they present themselves
as more of a palimpsest than as a covering up or crossing out.
Perhaps they signify just another round of aesthetic renovation,
the bricking over of the towering windows of the industrial
warehouse of painting to make way for shiny new condos, to be
cloaked in white and occupied by new tenants (and tenets) who
care little for materialist painting's ideology of factories
and smokestacks, or the anomic graffiti of a certain early 1980s
critique of pictures through the assertion of slick surface
and disjointed narrative, but who are instead concerned with the
ambiance both provide as a backdrop, as accoutrements of contemporary life. And on the coffee table, no doubt, there would
be a tastefully placed magazine for visitors to flip through.[3]
"Would you care for _Domus_ or _Interview_?" This is loft living.

"I'll take _Interfunktionen_. By the way, did you know
they used to make things here?"

… and what to do with the oddness of their shape, their
rejection of more conventional painting ratios for the narrow-
ness of beams and the dumbness of planks? Not windows but
ten-by-eights? Is it McCracken and his UFOs, or a one-ton prop
held up by drywall screws? Lawrence Weiner's wall removal made
portable? Lifted from a moment when being in situ was like
moral armor, a defense against the vulgar opulence of painting,
like shooting grainy bohemian porn in a SoHo loft that was
itself once a warehouse, only to have it refurbished, swabbed
clean, and turned into a design studio that churns out digital
pictures by the score, digital pictures freed from the weight
of printing presses and copy film, free from bricks and mortar,
images that caress so many screens and were born from the slow
crawl of the scanner's lens, or better, from algorithms alone.
Pictures that slip around the world like financial transfers,
just another sequence of numerals beamed from one place to
another. Colorless, odorless, like rays of light. Frictionless
horrors repeated, reprinted, rotated, and disseminated.

Our images are no longer tied to just one event,
but seem to resonate as eternal, and the arrangement of bodies
presented here seems academic, a Caravaggian knot of tensed

muscles, both energetic and formally balanced. Is the original
photograph from Birmingham still affecting, or is it so distant
from our lived experience that it is only available as an allegory? Maybe it is nothing more than numb shapes, as chillingly
blank as the riot cop's Aviators. For its violence is less
surprising than its tastefulness—the black, white, and red,
the milky browns and yellowing creams, the faint sweet smell
that still lingers even after the chocolate has gone chalky.[4]
That ghastly whiteness, which imparts such an abhorrent mild-
ness, even more loathsome than terrific, the discreet tastes
of the bourgeoisie reproduced in the modernity of our lofts
and lobbies, in the contemplative solitude of our museums and
airports—from the whiteness of things to the horrible thing-
ness of whiteness. Andy Warhol, perhaps, was the first to make
this horror vacui tangible. Blankness, alienation, boredom,
and disembodiment: white people love this shit.

This is not yet the end of the story. We still have
the press, we have the book, the magazine, the painting, and
the poster as hard currency; the scanner itself hums with
the factories that delivered it. All those hands: the trucks,
the labor, the oil derricks that give us the plastics, the store
clerks who shelve and reshelve the units in the networks of
chain stores. Then it arrives here, its glass creaking under the
weight of brick, its ephemeral output brought back down to
earth by the weight of the screen print, the inking, the layering, the buildup, the stench of turpentine, the high-pressure
washers, the emulsion. We still print out the PDF we fancy for
its portability; we still must contend with the bodies we fantasize about abandoning in the age of the digital. And so, the
painting crawls slowly around the room, caught between these
worlds, hung and rehung with sweat, drills, plaster, and screws;
it does not move with the ease we might expect of the digital,
it is not just drag and drop. It is a canvas made heavy, not
from the stories we tell about it, or the context from which it
has been wrenched, but from the hands it has passed through.
A picture as heavy as the bricks it contains are light.

NOTES

1. Harold Rosenberg, "The American Action Painters," <u>Art News</u> 51/8, December 1952, p. 22.

2. Although Walker makes use of many different magazines, all have a common urban, liberal, upper-middle-class audience (or, in the case of <u>Playboy,</u> once did).

3. Walker's various <u>Black Star Press</u> canvases feature a screen printed photograph of a white riot police officer and dog attacking a young black man. The image belongs to the same series of photographs of the 1963 Birmingham riots that Andy Warhol used for his "Race Riot" paintings. In Walker's work, layers of white, milk, and dark chocolate are screen printed over the image. The artist begins by scanning drips and smears of chocolate on his scanner, turning those scans into silk screens, and then using actual chocolate to print the enlarged chocolate splatters onto the paintings: in short, they are paintings of chocolate in chocolate. Over the course of the series the orientation and colors of the photographs, and the configuration of the chocolate drips change.

4. Many (but not all) of Walker's "brick" paintings have no natural orientation and thus can be hung in any direction. For the 2011 exhibition <u>Kelley Walker: Untitled, 2011</u> at Redling Fine Art, Los Angeles, the title work was moved periodically throughout the gallery space.

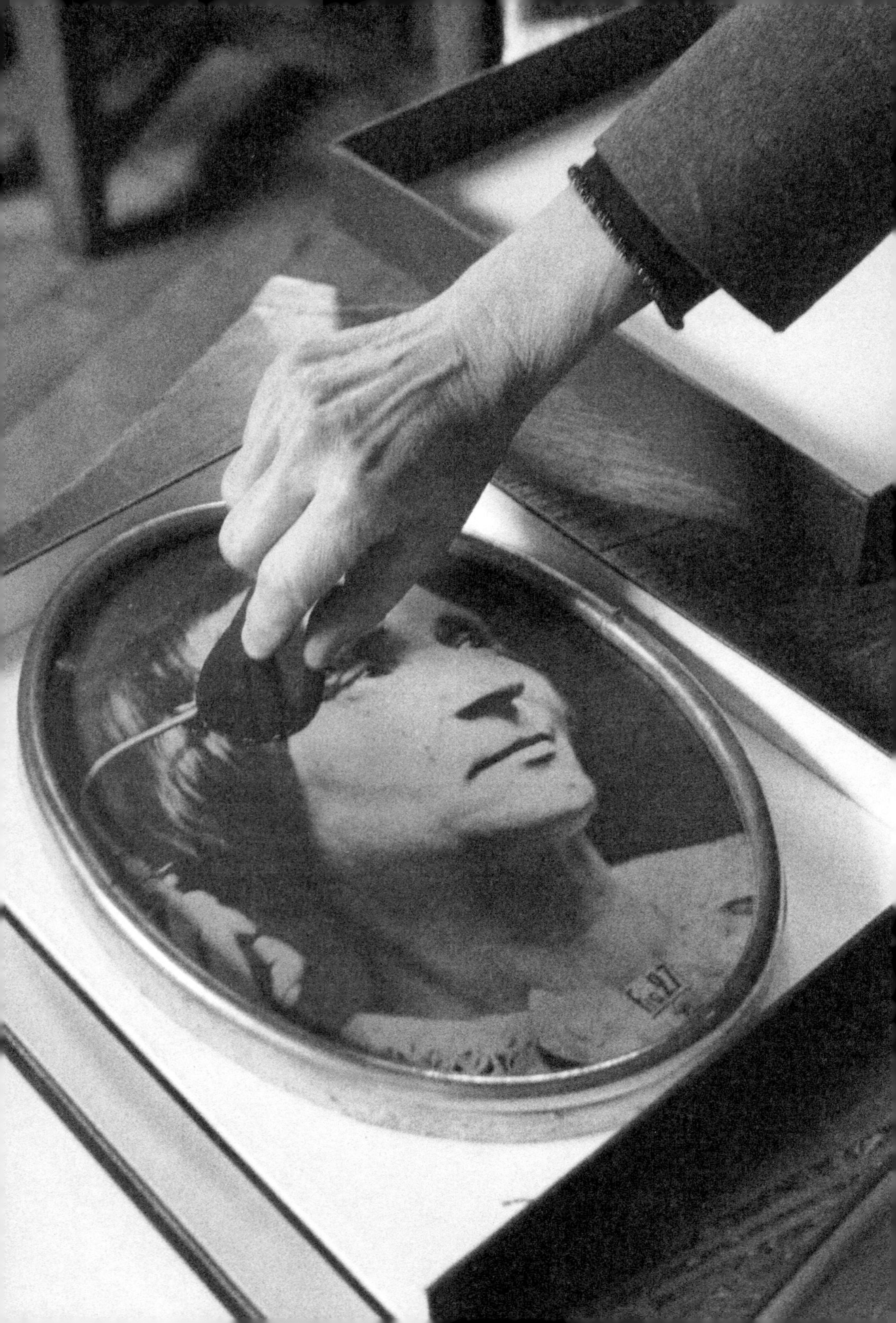

In Medias Res
(On the Work of Sharon Lockhart)

First published in <u>Sharon Lockhart | Noa Eshkol</u>, Sternberg Press/TBA21, Berlin/Vienna 2012, p. 30–36.

What is at stake here, I believe, is the close tie between cinema and history.
—Giorgio Agamben

<u>Achat … shtayim … shalosh … arba' …</u>

The countdown initiates synchronized movements, which are punctuated by the ticking of a metronome. The dancers' bodies, moving in unison, seem to pivot and turn on an invisible armature as though linked together by dowels and gears. The projectors are silent and out of view, yet their machinic presence, their position between our bodies and those we are watching, resonates in the tapping out of time at 120 beats per minute. The sound directs us back to the camera shutter, which too vivisects bodies in time, slicing them into manageable units. The movements themselves are full of stiff radial actions, like rack-and-pinion swaying, which at times veer close to the motions of the everyday and at others appear almost overwrought, brooding, and expressive. Yet in each instance they announce their avoidance of anything so blatant by retreating from citation or signification at the moment when meaning might be consummated. An almost militant fist pump turns into a lunge; what appears to be a glance over the shoulder is extended into a protracted lean. The movements appear commonplace, but in contrast to

the routines associated with the Judson Dance Theater, which
reframed quotidian actions within the aesthetics of dance in
a more strictly Duchampian manner, these gestures seem indifferent to the boundary between art and daily life, focused
instead on the transitory act of signifying itself, which by
necessity transcends such distinctions. They are movements
that announce themselves as gestures by repetition and synchro-
nization in much the same way that Roman Jakobson noted that
"/pa/ is a noise and /papa/ is a word."[1] And yet the gestures
remain unattached to a specific referent, as if "papa" had never
achieved its status as a word and was instead suspended just
before the point where meaning becomes defined—an utterance
caught in a moment of becoming, of approaching a limit, as
<u>meaning-in-formation</u>.

As the rhythm of the minimal dance develops, secondary
effects begin to accrue; the bodies of the dancers start to
betray their age through their varying rigidities and contours.
As our awareness of the ticking recedes, the sound of the soft
padding of feet on solid flooring, the gentle shuffling, the
rumpling of fabrics, the hush of barely audible breaths come to
the fore. The sounds of the film blur into the space of the
gallery; the noises the film emits are only intermittently dis-
tinguishable from the sounds that our own bodies produce as we
fold and unfold our arms or shift our weight from leg to leg.
As the dancers pivot in front of us, we think about how certain
movements feel and how we would sound making them. Our own
actions fall in and out of sync with those in front of us;
the noises of the dancers' bodies audibly identifying the surfaces they brush and pound against just as our own feet drag
against the floor. When we move from film to film through the
gallery, there is a consciousness of our own breathing, thud-
ding, shuffling, pausing, and it is as though we can hear others
experiencing the same awareness. We think, "If I can hear,
they can hear; if they are making noises, I am making noises."
And even as we turn away from one of the five parts of the film
to another, the metronome follows us, turning even our movements between the films into an extension of the projection.

The segments start again. Each of the five parts of Sharon Lockhart's <u>Five Dances and Nine Wall Carpets by Noa Eshkol</u> begins with the same countdown, each is synchronized to the same metronome, and each segment's looping keeps time with the others. Our eyes wander: rather than being in a dance studio, it looks like the dancers are in an exhibition space not unlike the one we are currently in, their bodies flanked by large rectangular volumes much as we are at this moment. As the metronome metes out time for the dancers, it metes out time for us, governing our movements, pacing them. A fellow viewer is tapping her thigh; another is bobbing gently. Are these self-conscious acts, or are they unaware of their movements? <u>Was I the one who was fidgeting?</u> One is gradually co-opted into being a participant in the prolonged dance (and does that mean we were/ are <u>always</u> dancing?), drawn into it simply by being aware of one's body while simultaneously standing apart from it in contemplation. Simply by being in the room, simply by noticing oneself, one is either in sync or out of sync with the metronome (there's no other option) and thus with the bodies of the dancers and the bodies of other visitors.

This is a moment of being-in-relation to all of the bodies, of producing relations through mutual sensitivities, the site of reception turning into the site of production, and vice versa. The image bleeds into the corporeal space. This is not to say that we are experiencing a waking dream; that would be image as illusion. No, we are here, aware, and present. This is not fantasy; it is simply a moment when it is possible to absorb stimuli from all bodies in the same way. This is experienced as an indifference, an indifference to the separation of the images of bodies from actual bodies in space while being fully aware of the constructedness of the context. It is a giving over to the image while retaining a sense of the real; here the image does not supplant the corporeal but coexists with it.

By definition, an image is not what it is <u>of</u>; this is its singular certainty. In order to be an <u>imago</u> (likeness) of something, it is by definition not that thing. It is an approach toward that thing, and its referent acts as its limit, performing as an adjacency that it cannot be. Thus, identifying with an image means approaching this boundary as well. It requires a moment of misrecognition, a moment when the clinical distance we feel when shielded by the image screen recedes, and boundaries between the now and the "this has been" disperse into the immediacy of experience. This is what it is to be in the throes of what Walter Benjamin referred to as the dialectical image, "constellated between alienated things and disappearing meaning … instantiated in the moment of indifference."[2] It is this "indifference" to the boundaries between experiences that the work engenders, an indifference toward a position inside or outside the flow (and thus being enthralled in both at once), an indifference to frames of reference, placing us in a zone of counterintuitive continuities—it is fluidity where before there were only partitions. It is an indifference to the separation that lies between <u>Sharon Lockhart | Noa Eshkol</u>, not a disavowal of it, nor a making indistinct, but an allowance for a thought or action or gesture to move through that boundary between them. It is an indifference to the distinction between film and dance, between the optic and the haptic, as our sense of vision and sense of touch confound, conflate, and circulate through each other.[3] It is an indifference to the division between then and now, between production and reception, between bodies in space and bodies in pixels. In short, it is an indifference that breeds other indifferences, that removes obstacles to the flow from one locus to another, that is affirmative, and that allows connections rather than destroys structures; it simply allows an alternate path of cursivity and fluidity to coexist within the taxonomic. It leaves it to bureaucrats and filing cabinets to police bodies and separate them; it removes the burden of our having to act as functionaries of that program.

This quality of indifference, or being positioned in-between and through—as in being in-between genres, in-between mediums, in-between bodies, in-between moments—marks much of Lockhart's work. The in-between is always in a state of

disappearing or diffusion, only to appear in another location.
This in-betweenness disperses when signification becomes locked
in, and this is why Lockhart has been so strongly identified
with disappearances: disappearing cultures, disappearing crafts,
disappearing groups. She is drawn to practices that operate
in the margins: Japanese girls playing American basketball, an
artist performing ikebana with agriculture, the eroding culture
of American skilled labor, children carving out their own private spaces in the world. When Lockhart comes close (some might
argue dangerously close) to certain genres—say ethnography
or structuralist cinema—she similarly pulls back and away,
inserting a deviation, a wrinkle in the smooth trajectory toward
instrumentality. It appears like a search for what Gilles Deleuze
and Félix Guattari posit occurs when "language stops being
representative in order to now move toward its extremities or
its limits."[4] This capacity is something that Lockhart shares with
Eshkol (or at least it is this quality that she draws out of
Eshkol's work), an ability to approach clear and defined expression fearlessly, and then, at its limit, the emphatic retreat
from the definitive, a retreat from signification in order to
display it <u>as signification</u>, asserting the communal nature
of discourse, what Giorgio Agamben has called the "being-in-
language of human beings,"[5] or what we could call here the
"being-in-mediation of human beings."

This in-betweenness could be understood as a form of
inhabitation and deformation, a mixing of genres whose meanings
are overdetermined, overloaded, and dominant. It appears at
times in Lockhart's work as a creolization of conventions, a
kind of patois or hybrid language: for example, her conflations
of German romanticism and structuralism (<u>Pine Flat</u>, 2005 and
<u>Podwórka</u>, 2009), of documentary and performativity (<u>NO</u>, 2003),
between orchestrations for the camera and events the camera
records (<u>Goshogaoka</u>, 1997), of serialization and still life (<u>Lunch
Break</u>, 2008), of social experimentation and contemplative meditation (<u>Teatro Amazonas</u>, 1999). It is a deterritorializing of
the dominant mode, what Deleuze and Guattari have described as
the <u>minor</u>, or "that which a minority constructs within a major

language": a minorization, if you will. They note, "minor languages are characterized … by a sobriety and variation that
are like a minor treatment of a major language … deterritorializing the major language."[6] The minor language consists of
meanings and innuendo that operate within the "cramped space"
of the mother tongue; it never attempts to assert an oppositional language and does not seek to "acquire the majority,
even in order to install a new constant"; rather it occupies the
majority, perverting it, détourning it, putting it to different
ends while emphasizing provisionality.[7] Most importantly,
it does not establish itself as the "true" condition, a real that
lurks behind the scrim of false consciousness, but rather one
reality of many. It stops just short of becoming the dominant,
of replicating that which it sought to dethrone. Through this
inhabitation, dominant structures become porous, and where they
once asserted their naturalized authority to organize the perceptual world and to frame their chosen subject matter, they
become one of many mediations, as fleeting as a passing gesture.

In Lockhart's work, these disruptions often occur as the
aestheticization of instrumental forms—the work's acknowledgment of itself as an aesthetic object—turning on the awareness
of the actions portrayed as being presented exclusively for
the camera, and the camera being present for the sole purpose
of bearing witness to those actions. For example, in one sequence
in Goshogaoka, the young Japanese basketball players terminate
their sprints at the edge of the film frame rather than at
the edge of the court. The initial sense of naturalness of these
actions is met with the realization of their picturehood; the
participants were not only performing for the camera but also
modifying their actions for it, adapting to its frame as much
as the actions were adapted to their own bodies and the relations between them. The activities vacillate between mapping
the field of vision and the field of action, and each location—
the rectangular screen and the rectangular court—acts as a
scrim or boundary delimiting and defining the other.

Mark Godfrey, in his essay "The Flatness of Pine Flat,"
noted a similar instance in NO, in which the performance of

the activity again draws attention to the pictorial qualities
of landscape and thus film, while at the same time the activity
provides a legible metric, a kind of pictorial time stamp indicating the duration of the film through the relative "fullness"
of the frame.[8] As James Benning describes, Lockhart "designed
the haystacks to appear relatively equal in size … by making the
stacks smaller as they were placed closer to the camera, while
their locus was chosen to describe a trapezoidal field, making
it easier to map them into the rectangle of the camera frame."[9]
In short, the performed action acknowledges the synchronic
and diachronic constructions of the filmic, both in duration
and as pictorial form. Thus the filmic and the performative
engage in a dual modeling, the filmic splaying out the actions
presented for the camera as pictures conveyed in sequence,
the performative mapping out the filmic visual field as it also
circumscribes its temporal axis. It should go without saying
that while the former is a description of the conventional
use of images and of film (and really all instrumental mediums),
the latter is the truly remarkable aspect of Lockhart's work.
Thus, the collapse of the distinction between performance and
film, along with the intertwining of the documentary and the
phenomenological made explicit in the Eshkol films, had already
occurred in Lockhart's work by the mid-1990s.

    In the internal dialectic between film and performance,
the conventions of authenticity and instrumentality, of genre
and convention, become as malleable as any other stylistic
conceit in the cinematic repertoire. This serves as an assertion
that the film is not, as it might have originally seemed, simply
a recording of a phenomenon. Nor is it being essentialized as an
autonomous art form; rather, its status is poised between the
two, as a "medium" or agent that acts between agendas or forces
and is defined by the tensions between those forces. There is
no function to the activity other than its being shown, and
no function to the depiction other than the activity conveyed
by it. Instead the work situates itself between these valences,
opening up a site from which the question of fact or fiction,
real or staged, is abandoned as literally immaterial. Here the

camera-based operations of cropping and flattening, and even
the duration of a roll of film, become social mechanisms, structures that mediate and organize the relations between viewers
and images as much as those between viewers. Thus, technological
mediation can (or even must) be understood as wholly continuous
if not indistinguishable from the social field as part of the
structures through which the generation, production, and reproduction of sociality are here made manifest.

This condition of mediality extends to the subject matter Lockhart concentrates on, such as the drills of the young
women in Goshogaoka. In the film we see only the drill, itself
a preparatory act, structuring an approach to a limit without
becoming that limit. Furthermore, these drills are modified and
established in conjunction with the young basketball players,
as were their uniforms, akin to but apart from the conventional
forms of each; they are minor adjustments and revisions of the
conventional, distinct from, yet embedded within, the standard
from which they deviate. Despite their independence from the
established or standardized, these activities are pursued with
an earnest determination, what Giorgio Agamben, channeling
Immanuel Kant, calls a "purposive purposelessness," attaining
a significance that is specific to the context within which
the activities developed.[10] Yet they are no more intrinsic to
their circumstance than they are autonomous from it; instead,
the activities are embodied within and exist in relation to
the communities in which they originate, and the broader world.

Or consider the film Lunch Break, which consists of
a ten-minute take of a 1,200-foot hallway at Bath Iron Works,
where workers spend their time during their mandated midday
respite. In real time the film would last only ten minutes,
but Lockhart extended it to some 83 and then looped it. We
never reach the end of the hallway; nor do we approach it from
the outside. It is in itself a full world, a world as "break"
or "cut." Lunch Break is projected in a construction that forms
a light baffle with an adjacent wall and appears like a long
hallway from the outside. In other words, the spatiality of
film is mapped onto the architectural armature, which creates

a phenomenological sensation of looking down an expansive
hallway, proposing this not as an illusion but as a provisional
continuity (this aspect recurs in Five Dances and Nine Wall
Carpets by Noa Eshkol, in which the films are projected on
forms that sit on the floor and create a spatial continuity
between the architectural site and the space depicted in the
projection). When one is watching the film, the hallway appears
endless, and one settles into its indeterminate length. The
incidental movements are drawn out to the point of being durational, and then rise to the fore as gestural; they exist
as part of the continuity of the film but also as autonomous
events that are isolated and stand apart from the arc of the
film. In essence, the film behaves as an extended interruption,
a cut drawn out to occupy an almost endless event, its medial
nature extended and stretched until it is mediality alone,
an in-between with no external edge. Actions that could be seen
as subordinate to the motivated behaviors of work, that could
be understood from the perspective of the workday as insignificant (i.e., without meaning), ascend, expand, and gain
momentum, transcending the managerial regime that initially
gave them shape.

The exhibition of Lunch Break at the Colby College Museum
of Art in 2010 prefigured the approach Lockhart took to the
exhibition Sharon Lockhart | Noa Eshkol. Lunch Break included
the craft works of the skilled laborers at Bath Iron Works,
displayed alongside art objects from the museum's collection,
one of several instances in which Lockhart's work provided
a context and occasion for a broader inclusion of cultural practices; in short, the authorial gesture is opened up as a passage
for alternate agendas and independent flows, becoming a site
of exchange within a group rather than a unidirectional message
from producer to receiver. As Lockhart put it with regard
to the Colby exhibition, "People were coming to see what they
did as much as they were coming to see what I did."[11] While
in the Eshkol work Lockhart similarly uses the frame of her
own practice to support and distribute the work of another,
again allowing her work to act as a vessel (this also occurs

in the photographs that accompanied the film <u>NO</u>, in which she
presented the practice of Haruko Takeichi, an Ikebana artist),
the <u>Sharon Lockhart | Noa Eshkol</u> exhibition is a markedly more
radical step, in which Lockhart's authorial presence begins
to dissipate, transforming a solo exhibition into a two-person
show. This was a deliberate effect, a process that Lockhart
herself implies was a necessary result: "That my authorship
disappeared, in a way, would strengthen the viewer's perception
of my actual project and the complex relationships of authoring
and interdependencies it implied."[12] These "interdependencies"
are the instances of fluidity, of continuity despite existing
divisions that Lockhart has repeatedly managed to draw forward.

The hybridization of the conventions of exhibition
(solo show and group show, the monographic and the two-person
exhibition, the artist and curator), even the intermittent
appearance and disappearance of Lockhart as author, blows back
on the conventional solidity that naturalized forms of aesthetic
management, from curatorial practice to authorial autonomy,
assert. Just as <u>Lunch Break</u> posed the question of who produces
culture for whom and what possibilities are open to museums
as conduits for social exchange among the communities in which
they are embedded, <u>Sharon Lockhart | Noa Eshkol</u> proposes not
only the individual artist's work as a conduit for histories
lost or unacknowledged within the institution, but also that
<u>all</u> practices contain other practices embedded within them,
each telling provisional histories of art, and that these provisional histories are legible and exist in multitudes extending
in every direction, if we choose to see them.

While always careful to indicate the interdependencies
that exist between her and her subjects-cum-collaborators,
here Lockhart turns the same attention to Eshkol, devoting con-
siderable effort to interviewing her dancers and charting the
shifting conditions of their relationships and the effects they
had on Eshkol's output. Thus, Lockhart positions Eshkol's practice as a kind of platform for interpersonal exchange, a frame
for others to inhabit, and in doing so, constructs a similar
space from which the reception of Eshkol's work might develop

through an engagement with Lockhart's. Yet, Lockhart does
not claim this open territory once it is established, but simply
releases it into the cultural infrastructure (e.g. catalogs,
museum collections, galleries, etc.), and by not claiming it
under the umbrella of her practice, she refuses to define it or
give it boundaries that are circumscribed by her own work,
allowing this proposition to achieve potentials beyond the reach
of her own practice. Lockhart thus makes a cut in the museological and the historical that can expand to the entirety of
the museum or art history and that, while diffusing throughout
the structures it inhabits, upends the neat taxonomies and
evolutionary canons that permeate them.

This is the political dimension of the minor, for under
the auspices of the minor language, "everything takes on a collective value … there are no possibilities for an individuated
enunciation that would belong to this or that 'master' and that
could be separated from a collective enunciation."[13] It is just
this condition that mediality provides, for it is not a circulation of images or symbols or even things; nor is it the hierar-
chical relation between the originator of a message and its
receivers, but the spaces between things, the links, the connec-
tivities, the flows back and forth, exhibited on their own, in
states of motion. It is this that Agamben defines as constituent
of gesture, proposing it as "the exhibition of a mediality …
the process of making a means visible as such," for in gesture,
"nothing is being produced or acted, but rather something is
being endured and supported." It is the expression of a convey-
ance, an expression of a "being-in-language." This is where he
locates the impulse of cinema, because "in the cinema, a society
that has lost its gestures tries at once to reclaim what it has
lost and to record its loss."[14]

In short, while the image obstructs or banishes the
gesture in its resolute stasis and its ease of dissemination,
the cinema recovers it, reinscribing the gesture through the very
means by which it was banished, by presenting the gaps between
images where gesture reemerges as a mode of communication
that stands apart from and outside of the filmic narrative and

achieves its once central role as the connective tissue between
human beings. This is not only a theoretical argument. It has
been noted that a whole generation of Americans who first grew
up with cinema credit it with instructing them in multiple
forms of sociality as adolescents, most often those of intimacy
(the acts of gazing into a lover's eyes or grasping the back of
a lover's head are most often cited as being of cinematic origin),
which were accessible in still images previous to cinema, but
became tangible and communicable as gesture under the conditions of cinema alone. (That cinema provided a semiprivate location for the pursuit of these intimacies should not be ignored
either.)

The gestural disappears into the ticking of history
and the accumulation of images only to reemerge in the gaps
between images, for that is where the body reasserts itself
in film (both on screen and off), and that is where film under-
stands itself as a corporeal medium. Its movement, its gesturality, is not an illusion despite being a composed sequence of
stills. Quite the opposite: the movement of film is the movement
of our bodies; it is the embodiment of perception that images
so often place at a remove. This is the <u>persistence of vision</u>,
the body's suturing together of the fragments into a whole,
completing and filling the gaps at the loci of loss and absence.
Where the gesture was lost, it returns, this time in the body
of the viewer. Thus, what Lockhart reawakens here is the work
of Eshkol, inserted back into a phenomenological reality, but
also the physicality of perception; film, in her hands, allows
for the rescue of the past in the uncertainty of the present and
thus posits the possibility for a better (more ethical) future,
one where history is not opposed to the bodily but is indistinguishable from it, where the politics of perception is manifest,
and where distinctions between the collective and the individual
collapse, as do the divisions between production and reception.

The bodies of the viewers are the medium of this transformation; they are the in-between, extending it to the entire
exhibition. This is an in-betweenness that is the same as
the community, as the collective, which is always poised between

outcomes, between concrete definitions, and, in short, is always
in a state of formation or becoming. In retrospect, the invisible
mechanics between the dancers is actually their being-in-gesture
together, the constant production and reproduction of the
relations of one body to another, their shared status of being-
in-the-world together, and their assertion of this to one
another. As we watch the film, inexplicably, the invisible armature extends to us, and whether or not we move with it in time,
we feel and are connected to it. This mechanism extends outward
from the film and the bodies that immediately surround it
and expands to fill the room, the galleries, and so on, dissipating slowly over the extended topographies that the various
bodies who came into contact with it traverse. Even as the sensibility, the awareness of bodies, of one's own body, diffuses
throughout the life world, it remains inscribed within the
viewers, permeating them, and establishing possible communities
cohered around this establishment of collective sensation,
a means of understanding our status as human beings engaged
in relations with one another, a sensibility that "reveals who
can have a share in what is common to the community based on
what they do and on the time and space in which this activity
is performed."[15]

It is this notion of collectivity, of self-awareness and
awareness of others, a state of collective empathy and transfer-
ence that Agamben is describing when he writes, "Politics is
the sphere of pure means, that is, of the absolute and complete
gesturality of human beings."[16] And it is this notion of ethics
and collectivism, unencumbered by the obstructions and abstractions of images and symbols, of institutions and their managers,
that Lockhart posits and recovers simultaneously.

NOTES

Epigraph: Giorgio Agamben, "Difference and Repetition: On Guy Debord's Films,"
<u>Guy Debord and the Situationist International: Texts and Documents</u>, ed. Tom
McDonough, trans. Brian Holmes, MIT Press, Cambridge 2002, p. 313.

1. Roman Jakobson, "Why Mama and Papa?," <u>Selected Writings</u>, vol. 1, Mouton,
The Hague 1962, p. 542.

2. Walter Benjamin, <u>The Arcades Project</u>, ed. Roy Tiedemann, trans. Howard Eiland
and Kevin McLaughlin, Harvard University Press, Cambridge 1999, p. 466.

3. As Erika Fischer-Lichte observes, "in performance … public vs. private, distance
vs. proximity, fiction vs. reality … are all based on the seemingly insurmount-
able, fixed opposition between seeing and touching." Erika Fischer-Lichte, <u>The
Transformative Power of Performance: A New Aesthetics</u>, trans. Saskya Iris Jain,
Routledge, London 2008, p. 62.

4. Gilles Deleuze and Félix Guattari, <u>Kafka: Toward a Minor Literature</u>,
trans. Dana Polan, University of Minnesota Press, Minneapolis 1986, p. 23.

5. Giorgio Agamben, "Notes on Gesture," <u>Means without End: Notes on Politics</u>,
trans. Vincenzo Binetti and Cesare Casarino, University of Minnesota Press,
Minneapolis 2000, p. 60.

6. Gilles Deleuze and Félix Guattari, <u>A Thousand Plateaus: Capitalism and
Schizophrenia</u>, trans. Brian Massumi, University of Minnesota Press, Minneapolis
1997, p. 26.

7. Ibid., p. 106.

8. See Mark Godfrey, "The Flatness of Pine Flat," in <u>Sharon Lockhart: Pine Flat</u>,
ed. Chus Martínez, Sala Rekalde Erakustaretoa, Bilbao, 2006, p. 112-113. With
regard to his discussion of duration, see p. 113, n. 1, where he writes: "I wanted
to note another remarkable feature of the work. The duration of the film was determined by the space it depicted, namely by the size of the field. When you watched
the film, even if you did not know how many minutes it was, you knew it would last
as long as it took for the two farmers to fill the field. As a result, just as the
farmers went about their activity with neither haste nor slowness, the viewer had
no anxiety about the film's length."

9. "James Benning Interviews Sharon Lockhart," <u>Sharon Lockhart: Lunch Break</u>,
Mildred Lane Kemper Art Museum, St. Louis 2010, p. 100.

10. Agamben, "Notes on Gesture," p. 59.

11. Sabine Eckmann, "On Collaboration: A Conversation with Sharon Lockhart,"
<u>Sharon Lockhart | Noa Eshkol</u>, p. 108.

12. Ibid., p. 109.

13. Deleuze and Guattari, <u>Kafka</u>, p. 17.

14. Agamben, "Notes on Gesture," p. 58, 57, 53.

15. Jacques Rancière, <u>The Politics of Aesthetics</u>, trans. Gabriel Rockhill, Continuum, London 2004, p. 12.

16. Agamben, "Notes on Gesture," p. 60.

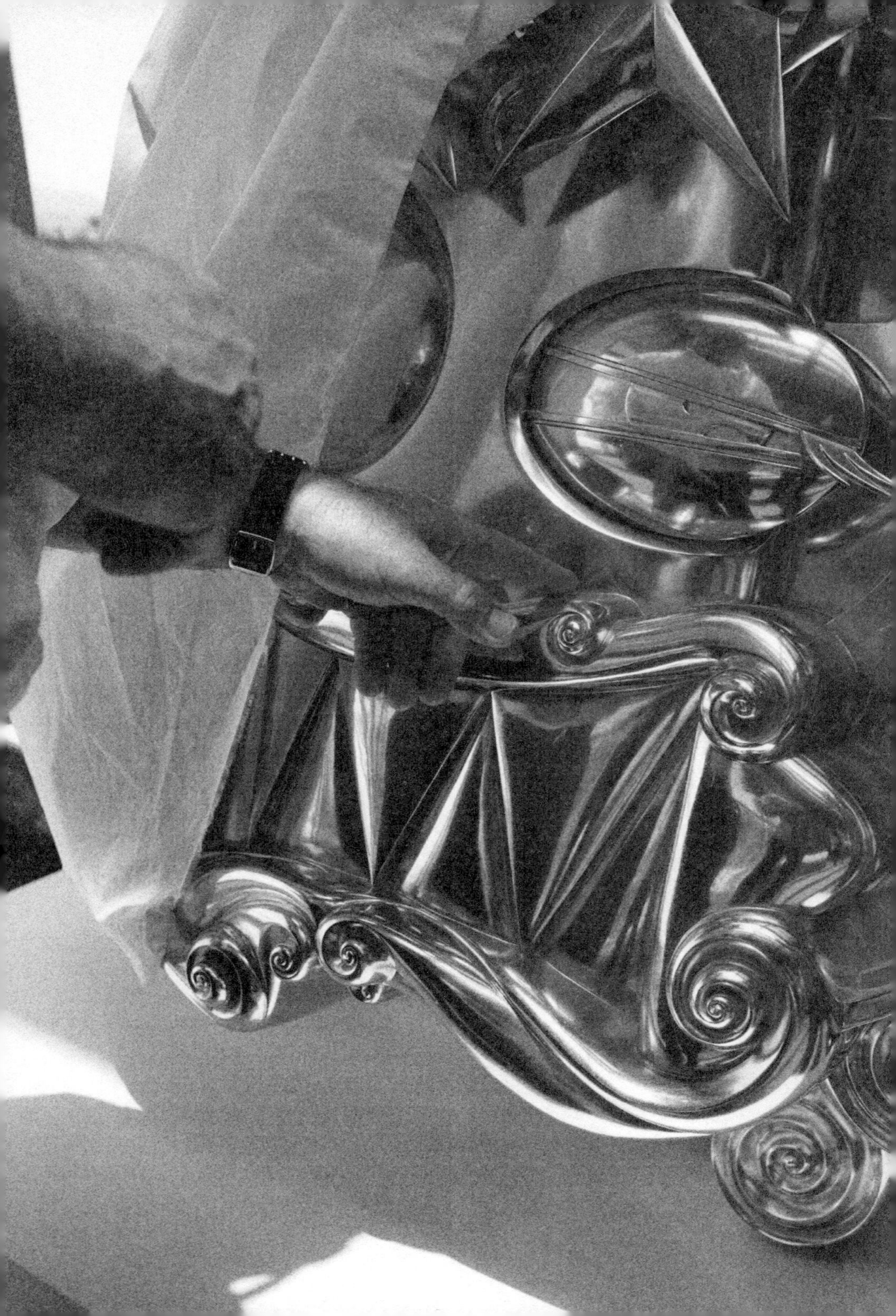

On the Matter of Abstraction ...

First published on the occasion of On the Matter of Abstraction (figs. A &
B): Parallel Exhibitions of Postwar Nonfigurative Art from the Collection,
organized by Walead Beshty and Christopher Bedford Rose Art Museum,
Brandeis University, Waltham, MA, February 12-June 9, 2013; reprinted in
Walead Beshty: Natural Histories, 2nd ed., JRP|Ringier, Zurich 2014, p. 184.

Let's begin with two examples, two versions of nonfiguration
that form a dialectical pair. Think of them as dual rejections
of the depictive held in tandem, or better, held in tension with
one another; looking-glass visions of a world liberated from
likenesses and the falseness of images. But before we get into
this, it of course bears mentioning that if we think of the origins of the modern picture, we ought to think of Leon Battista
Alberti, and his On Painting. Alberti himself was concerned
with the problem of reflection, of the image (i.e. imago, or
likeness) and how it could be given order. To begin this task,
he turned to Narcissus for his origin myth, not only of painting, but for humankind's fascination with images, to explain
why we produce them endlessly, why this desire for order was
with us at all. Is this not a rather odd pursuit of humanity's?
It does need some explanation, some ontological divination.
To produce endless reflections of the world around us, while
knowing them to be inferior to what they represent, certainly
does not go without saying, and in actuality, it seems quite
perverse. As Alberti asked, "What else can you call painting
but a similar embracing with art of what is presented on the
surface of the water in the fountain?" Alberti even gave his
own treatise an impoverished reflection of itself, first launching it on the world in Latin in 1435 as "De Pitura," then, just
a year later, a second iteration arrived in the vulgar tongue

of common Italian as "Della Pittura." They differed both in
language and in the symbolism that each contained for the masses
(the high intellectualism of Latin, the low chatter of Italian),
but also in content, for the discussion of complex mathematics,
and other headiness eagerly explored in the first version
were noticeably absent from the latter, as if to remind us that
copies always pale in comparison to the original, reducing
and schematizing their objects.

But let's keep that parallel in the back of our minds
and get back to the matter at hand. We arrive in a room bathed
in light even in winter, a shadowless jewel box of terrazzo
and glass enclosing further geometries and hard edges. A world
of frames, of frames within frames, and what we see is less
what Alberti called "finestra aperta," a world of windows to
gaze through, than "specchhio finestra," windows that give us a
reflection of the act of viewing, that tell us about the desire
to gaze. For these windows do not organize the world outside,
but reflect back on themselves, organizing themselves as though
representing the sites of their future exhibition, as though
they knew they would find their ways into the gridded expanses
of International Style palaces. They are depictions that depict
depicting, for what is depiction laid bare but the edge of
a razor, a cut or incision in the drabness of quotidian life,
a glimpse of the best of all possible worlds that leaves one
with the sensation of floating, as though watching things tran-
spire from above, untethered from the vulgarity of bodies.

But of course there are still bodies, and if we see order
and geometry above, the bodies we left behind must be down
below in the unruliness of the earth beneath our feet, in the
dirt that thwarts our best attempts to peer inside with its
resolute opacity and heterogeneity. Here discovery forces us to
dig with our hands, revelation requires getting into the muck,
and so, once we are here, we spend the majority of our time
scraping exploration from under our nails. As we move from
the cathedral to the cave, we should remember that both are the
sites of ritual and contemplation, places of reflection and
divination, but down below the zero point of the picture is

no longer Cartesian grids or tidy territories, but smears and
stains. We see bodies without the figure, or figuration. Where
else would one hide all the corpses left in the wake of a master
plan executed in precise geometries but in the basement, out
of sight. We hope they might return into the earth, so we might
deal with the cleanliness of spirits without the bodies they
are shackled to. This is what happens when we look to the other
side of Alberti's pictorial dialectic, for what is often forgotten is that the anti-pode of the frame ("fenestra aperta" or
"open window") is the screen, what he called the "veil" or "intersection," that which receives action, which is about touching,
digging into the stuff of life, it is "quello sta cosi" or "what
is so," the mundane state of affairs that is mediation, that
which both stands between us, and allows us to speak, or rather,
allows us to touch, for between us we need some "thing," some
"thing" that can touch for us, link us, no?

    But is it not time to collapse these ideas into one?
These notions are, after all, almost six hundred years old.
Rather than an object being what it is not, rather than being
non-figurative, could we imagine this coming together as a
new form, one that describes disfiguration, one that neither
separates itself from the world nor crawls its way through it,
subservient and prone. Is this opposition not false anyway,
an extension of religious ritual, a false penance for the bodies
we are indistinguishable from? We could imagine a way to
describe things that neither requires art to stand apart or
below the world, but within it. Would this be a trade of nonfigurative painting for a new category—disfigurative painting?
Because what better than to disfgure this world, or simply
acknowledge our ability to disfigure it. Is this not the way out
of this limiting trade off? Bodies or ideals? But more on this
later …

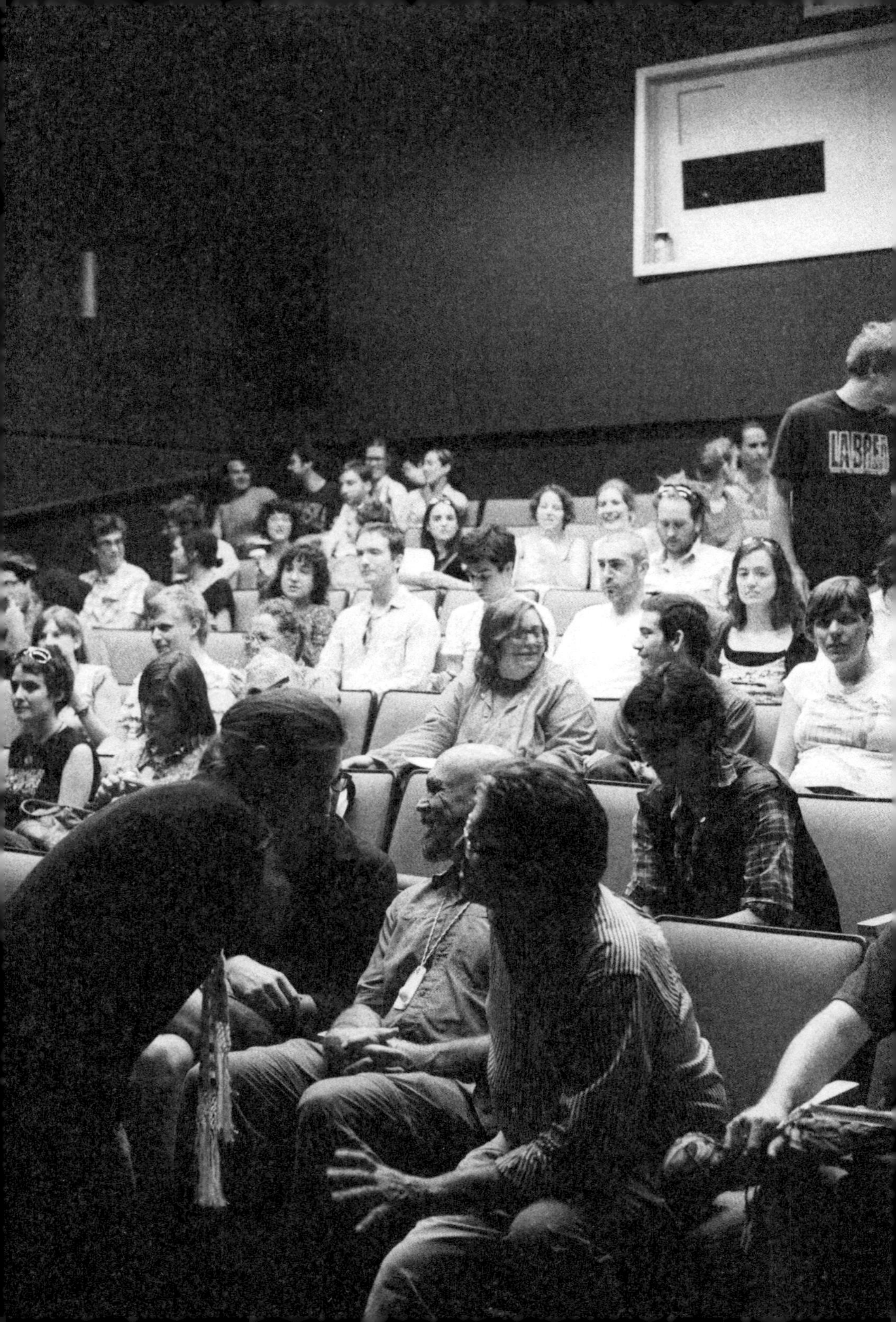

Aesthetics and Distribution Case (1), Preliminary Notes on Art's Ability to Radicalize Academia

First published in <u>Still Searching: An Online Discourse on Photography</u>, http://blog.fotomuseum.ch, Fotomuseum Winterthur, May 7, 2012.

If we start with the idea that a medium is constituted by a dialectic of applied use and technological development, and that it is further defined by the conventionalization of the relationship between the two (a process that occurs over time and is in a state of constant revision), it follows that a medium is never freed from its use, nor is it freed from its position between some agents in a transaction, meaning that it can never stand apart from these conditions. It also follows that a medium is always steeped in the inertia of its conventions, for this is how, by comparison, each new relation between shifting technologies and new applications is self-historicizing and legible, i.e. able to be understood as an expression of that medium. The rhetorical transformation of a series of disconnected relations between technology and use into a singular entity is the becoming of a "medium." In short, the institutionalization of these instances of negotiation is completed by the use of a name in an abstract transhistorical sense, as when a name is invoked in and of itself as a stable entity. The identification of a medium is an act of institutional reification; in fact, it is <u>the</u> institutional act, that which makes the institution concrete, like air made solid.

This institutionalization is the medium's "memory." As the collective understanding of a medium (not to mention its practice) is transformed by how it is recorded (we should think

of these various institutionalizations as a form of material
tracing of the history of a medium), we should likewise remember
that the medium also changes existing institutions, altering
its methodologies and transforming its conditions as they are
molded around one another. A comparable example is the development of recording devices and music: music adapted to the
conditions available for its recording as much as recording
technology was adapted to the conditions of music; it would be
pointless to discuss the relationship between the two without
acknowledging that they developed in parallel. Not only does
each inform the other dialectically, but they are in actuality
impossible to separate from one another. The seeming stability
of the terms we use for each conceal these interdependencies
by claiming a delimitation between them that in fact does not
exist. In short, institutions by nature create their objects as
much as they adapt to their contours, by both explicitly and
tacitly asserting a framework for the analysis, display, and
collection, as they are reactive to those objects. This applies
as much to the term "photography" as it does to "art," the
"museum," or for that matter "art history." The solidity of the
terms conceals the active negotiations that arise around their
borders and the constant ongoing renegotiations of these borders. Regardless, we could say that one site of institutionalization is the museum and another is the educational complex,
or academia, which is an extremely powerful vehicle for the
distribution and maintenance of aesthetic discourse (whether
via practical/vocational, or meta-critical/disciplinary means).
I might offer that the widespread attribution of the term
"critique" as an action of art objects, rather than "use,"
occurred as a result of currents in the academy, more specifically, the cultural turn and the adoption of theory in the
art school (for how can an object "critique"? Is this not a
rather perverse anthropomorphism?).

   In the case of art, higher education has taken the form,
at least in the US, of the master of fine arts degree. Within
the university, the MFA is what one would call a "professional"
degree. What this usually means is that the majority of those

with these degrees are destined for work outside of academia
(i.e., the world of instrumental use), and the degree qualifies
the recipient for the professional demands of that system.
For example, be they business degrees, medical degrees, architecture degrees, law degrees, etc. Into this mix, art is a particularly strange addition, specifically because the MFA is a
required degree to become a teacher, and many art students cite
teaching as their reason for obtaining the degree. Rather than
qualifying one to make art, it qualifies one to teach art. But
this is beside the point. The study of art qualifies as a professional degree because the artistic profession has direct points
of sale at which the general public might participate. Like law
or medicine, individuals can get access to art directly through
acquisition. This is unlike science, mathematics, or the humani-
ties, where the market products are several steps removed from
the discipline itself. Each of these fields requires intermediary
producers (say book publishers or pharmaceutical firms or car
manufacturers, etc.) to bring them to market. For example, in
the art world, the relationship between a "client," or one seeking to obtain services and the venue they acquire these services
from, is more similar to law, or medicine, than it is to say philosophy (where a publishing house must make the discourse concrete, i.e. an object), or mathematics (where another must apply
the math to a circumstance before the public can directly engage
with it). Architecture is an interesting hybrid, for architecture must be built for the public to directly experience it,
but architects operate out of firms that can be directly hired,
while the material building occurs through another entity that
does not mediate the financial transaction between the client
and the service provider, but instead mediates the "publicness"
of the services that the architect sells.

Yet the inclusion of art under the umbrella term
"professional degree" is not a natural fit either. Art objects,
unlike other disciplines for which professional degrees are
granted, are separate from the world of instrumental use.
In other words, art is a reflexive discourse, a discourse about
aesthetics staged through aesthetics, and thus is more like

philosophy (a discourse on language through language or thought
qua thought) than they are like law (a discourse on social
interaction through language, which is tested by its ability
to be applied to social interaction and is subject to bodies
which police the activities of the discipline). In the case of
professional degrees, the criterion of success or failure is not
abstract; rather it is established by professional cadres (such
as the state medical board or the state bar, which govern the
ability to practice) and is based on its efficacy in relation to
daily life (the ability of a medical procedure to extend life or
improve the quality of life) and the potential harm associated
with its malpractice from which the public must be protected.
This is not the case for art, where the criterion of success or
failure is constantly being disputed on a fundamental level and
is wholly abstract, contained neither in the market response,
nor in critical or academic accolades. What is more, art is meant
to stand apart from the direct function of aesthetics. If one
doubts this, one need only think of the meaning a stop sign has
on the street versus the meaning it might have in the museum
or gallery. On the street, we look for messages and instantane-
ously act accordingly. But in the museum or gallery we ask,
"How does it create meaning?" Of course, this is for good reason,
because if we stopped to ask this question on the street, we
would likely injure ourselves or others. In most instances, in
daily life, aesthetics function habitually and without thought,
and that is a necessity.

The political implications of art lie in the second
question (the "how does it create meaning?" question), for art
creates a transparency about how aesthetics elicit meaning,
which can, after examination, be extrapolated and applied to
daily life. This possibility of making transparent the habitual
function of aesthetics not only holds the potential to upend
power relationships, but also makes art wholly separate from
daily life, for it requires this separation in order to ask
how aesthetics produce meaning (meaning being less a message
and more the production of subject relations, i.e., that of
dominance and subordination, or communality, etc.).

This questioning of meaning is inextricable from a
concrete material object. So unlike philosophical discourse,
where the mode and form of distribution is treated as being
"outside" of the content of the discourse (one would not discuss
the font, paper stock, or cover design of a philosophy book
when assessing its value), the form of distribution (medium)
is inextricable from art's meaning, and moreover, that form
of distribution is always object-based or accountable to objecthood, and objects are never freed from exchange. Art thus
offers a way to comprehend the transactive elements of intellectual thought, a reality of all modes of discourse (for economic
transaction is a ubiquitous form of simple communication) that
art is uniquely capable of drawing forward.

Rather than be too exhaustive here, I'll clearly state
a few ideas:

1) There is no such thing as an art that is untainted
by the market economy. That in no way means that art
either supports or rejects the notion of a market transaction; it is simply, by definition, based in market
transaction.

2) Despite its dependence on the marketplace for part
of its circulation, this does not disqualify if of being
capable of progressive political change. For there is
no place "outside" of economic transaction. Places
that present themselves as outside are simply concealing
their implication within exchange. Yet art's radical
proposition is its greater capacity for transparency
(as transparency is a core artistic value) and its
ability to articulate its own implication within such
a system of exchange. Very few other disciplines are
capable of this. Political change here is realized in
the form of a viewer's understanding, as an expansion
of the parameters of what can be known or knowable
through aesthetics, thus expanding access to the commons.

3) This proximity or "coming to terms with the exchange
rate of objects" is in essence one of art's most radical
potentials. It contains the possibility to force the
world of progressive philosophical, intellectual, and
political thought into the sphere of daily life, and
collapse the idea of "meta" discourse or critique, to
make all discourse continuous with the world it is meant
to describe. It is the destruction of the fantasy of an
outside.

To conclude, theoretical discourse always avoids confronting
its own monetization, its own instrumentality, and in those rare
moments when it does, it fails to fully comprehend the stakes
of the conflict. Art must confront this, in order to operate
as art (i.e., as a reflexive discourse about aesthetics through
aesthetics), nor can it eschew its own monetization, or exchange
value, as inextricable from its meaning or message and its history. Art, after all, has thankfully abandoned the content/form
divide, whereas other disciplines have been unable to do so
(for example, literature rarely examines its circulation in the
mass-produced book form), and because of this inability, they
cannot fully embrace their own material condition and their
role in the monetization of thought, a role that it is urgent
for all discourses to reflect upon because this structures our
relationship to thought, our very ability to participate in
dialogue with others. The inclusion of art in the institutions
of higher education is a first step to this engagement, and
as the boundaries between these disciplines are rendered more
porous (simply thinking of the number of philosophical, political, and literary texts that take aesthetics as their points
of departure), the interpenetration of intellectual discourse
and market economies will be a reality that it is increasingly
difficult to avoid, and that art brought to bear.

Introduction: Andrea Fraser, Art Center College of Design, February 19, 2013

For those of you who don't know, I'm Walead Beshty, Associate
Professor in the Graduate Art Program here at Art Center College
of Design. Tonight it is my pleasure to introduce Andrea Fraser …

Beyond a recounting of her resume, it is a difficult
task to introduce an artist, theorist, and critic who has spent
their career laying bare the social, political, and institutional
implications at work within the loose constellation of networks
we call the art world. Of course a central ritual of the art
world is the professional introduction—one of many forms that
have received incisive dismantling by Fraser. I am thinking now
of her work <u>Official Welcome</u> (2001/2003) and <u>Inaugural Speech</u>
(1997), each a meandering through appropriated moments of
sincerity, hyperbole, and grandiosity which are all part of the
pomp and circumstance common to public address. When experiencing their performance, the disjunction between the various
sources from which the text is drawn increases until the
seemingly centralized voice of the speaker becomes, in its progressive fragmentation, inconsistent and absurd. Ever since
I first experienced the work, it has been impossible for me to
speak in this capacity without recalling Fraser's fierce refuta-
tion of the possibility for direct address and her destabiliza-
tion of the self-validating authority upon which such speech is
premised. In those works, like so many others of Fraser's, one
is drawn into a set of contradictions, wedged between the desire

to speak outside of power structures, while fully confronting
one's implication within them; caught between the hope to slough
off these armatures and engage in direct address, and the realization that doing so is impossible. I am tempted to say that
what is most striking about Fraser's work is that one is never
allowed to view such moments of conflict and contradiction from
a distance, one is never allowed to observe from a safe remove,
shielded from implication, instead as a viewer—even of this lecture—one is forced to directly confront these contradictions,
even if their acknowledgement does not produce a way to evade
or solve them. Instead one is left to come to terms with their
own compromised position between seemingly irresolvable critical
and ethical mandates. As Isabelle Graw has described, in
Fraser's work "the line between 'being' and 'acting,' between
authenticity and imitation, is no longer drawn."[1] This is a
particularly caustic territory for artists and artworks to
enter, for the question of meaning in the work of art (as Marcel
Duchamp made unavoidable with the innovation of the readymade)
often relies on the strict division between art and daily life,
between instrumental and noninstrumental aesthetics. In short,
art depends on institutions and their conventions to be recognizable as art at all. Yet Fraser calls this binary into question
as just another false opposition, positing an art that functions
in the broader world, without reverting to sheer instrumentality. It is this sense of implication, and proximity, that allows
her work to draw the entire network of institutional frames
into question, or rather, it is this aspect of her work which
causes these frames to be questioned, both by making them
conscious, and by making their malleable, even fragile, nature
unmistakably clear, leaving them open for intervention, and
vulnerable to subversion. Since some of her earliest work, such
as <u>Artist's Statement</u> (1992), Fraser has opted to perform from
a position within contradiction, instead of at a remove one, a
position that is evidenced in the two texts assigned here (one
of which being her contribution to the last Whitney Biennial).
In this she opens up what is to me one of the most profound
political questions facing the artist, which is, to put it

bluntly, whether it is possible for art to propose a better
world, a more ethical world, despite it being so deeply implicated in inequity, despite it owing its very existence to
the state of inequality, and to self-validating power. It is
in Fraser's work that these questions are forced open, and
the currency that these debates now have is owed, in no small
part, to the impact her work has had on contemporary art.

Needless to say, it is an honor to be able to introduce
her here. Please join me in welcoming Andrea Fraser.

NOTE

1. Isabelle Graw, "Hamburger Kunstverein," <u>Artforum</u>, vol. 42, no. December 2003,
p. 40.

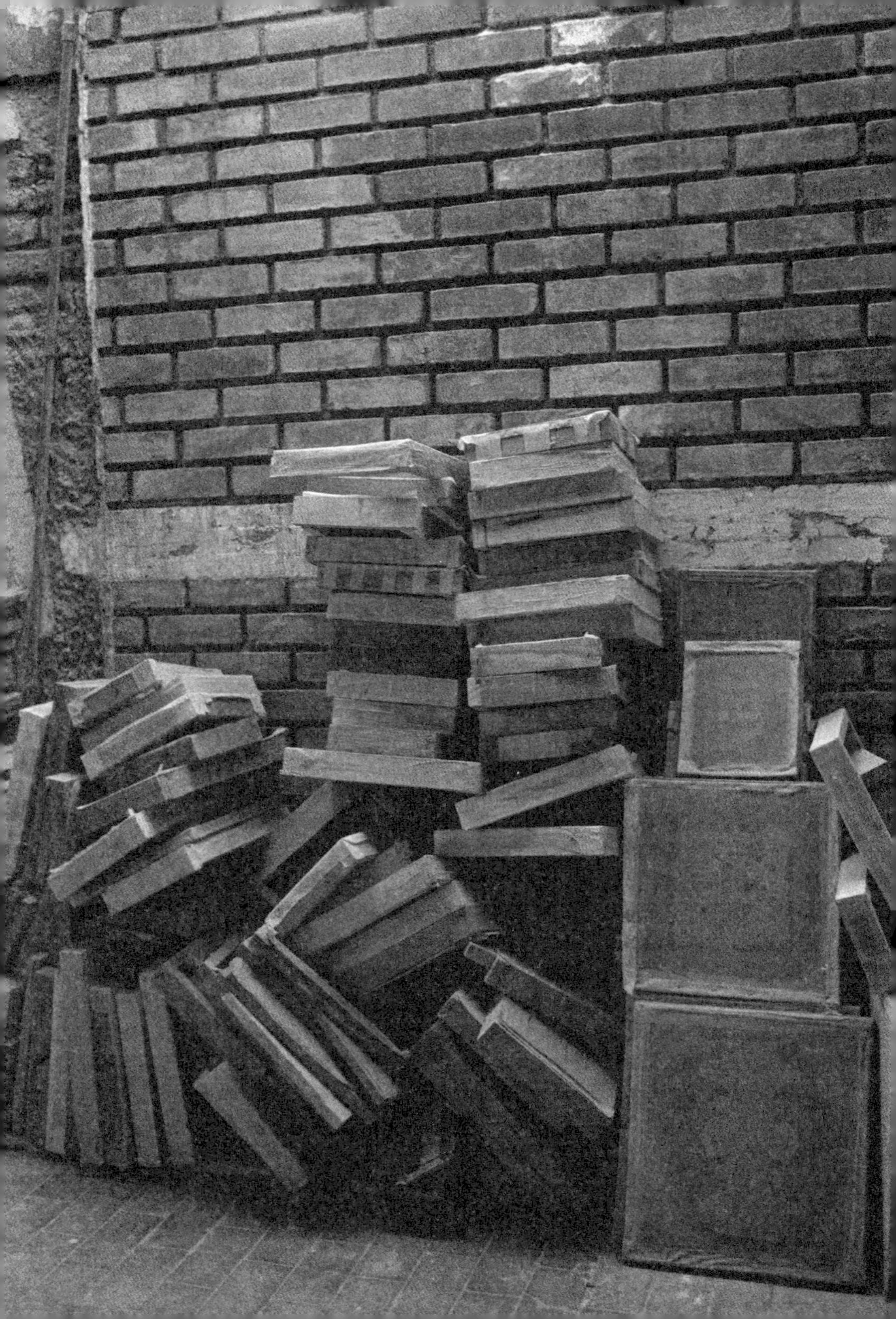

Introduction: Mark Grotjahn,
Art Center College of Design,
March 19, 2013

For those of you who don't know me, my name is Walead Beshty,
and I'm Associate Professor here in the Grad Department of Art
Center. Tonight it's my honor to introduce Mark Grotjahn …

This narrative of institutional affiliations runs
the risk of situating Grotjahn's work too neatly within a
certain rather austere trajectory of art making, an impression
that would be misleading. Since his earliest exhibitions,
the strength of Grotjahn's work has been the ease with which
it navigates both the tradition of high abstraction and the
coarseness of the common vernacular, demonstrating an indifference to the conventions and niceties which distinguish one
from the other, inflecting the imposingly weighty trajectory
of abstraction with unexpected regionalism. It is this play
with the conventions of high abstraction, and his improvisation
with gesture and form, that unifies his seemingly disparate
bodies of work. Rather than marking out distinct or discrete
attitudes, his varied approaches to the question of painting
and object making attest to the ability of a simple mark
or gesture to move fluidly between aesthetic spheres, aesthetic
spheres that are commonly held tastefully apart, and are, in
Grotjahn's work, allowed to intermingle and cross-contaminate.
This play is perhaps best illustrated by the sense of expansive
space in his "butterfly" paintings, which draws forward
the modernist conditions both of abstraction and opticality.

The geometric sunbursts inscribed on their surfaces evoke
Renaissance perspectival form as much as they do the striations
of an iris. These are stamped, or better, incised, with text in
the form of dates and signatures like phone numbers on home-
made "For Sale" signs, branded cattle, or the mechanized dates
on drug store photographic prints, undermining both their
potential preciousness, and complicating their seemingly endless
meditative depth. Thus the work speaks as eloquently of the
tradition of painterly abstraction, of flatness and the grid,
of utopianism in the mother tongue of high formalism, as it
proves itself conversant in the rough patois of the vernacular
as evidenced in the naive signs of the corner bodega, or the
makeshift crafts of primary arts education. It is this porous-
ness, this inclusive lack of preciousness that marks his work
so clearly. This intermingling not only seduces us into the
traditional experience of painterly meditative contemplation,
but opens up and out onto the aesthetic possibilities that
lie nascent in the world around us, and in this, reanimates the
democratic aspirations of abstraction that are far too often
forgotten.

Needless to say, I'm very happy he has taken out the
time to join us here. Please join me in welcoming Mark Grotjahn.

Introduction: Raymond Pettibon, Art Center College of Design, March 21, 2013

California deserves whatever it gets. Californians
invented the concept of lifestyle. This alone warrants
their doom.
—Don DeLillo

For those of you who don't know me, I'm Walead Beshty, Associate
Professor in the Graduate Art Program here at Art Center College
of Design. Tonight it is my distinct honor to introduce Raymond
Pettibon. Pettibon is one of the most significant American artists
of the late 20th century, and a singularly definitive figure of
Southern California, innovating a practice that coheres around
an unrelenting literary and aesthetic voice …

For how significant a figure he is, the irony is that
most of us likely first encountered his work without ever realizing it, on album covers, in a friend's basement, or staring at
our own bedroom walls. A prize possession of mine was a promo-
tional poster for Sonic Youth's album Goo that I had lifted from
a record shop, and which would become a bedroom fixture of my
teenage years. I bring this up not to claim punk, or even rock
and roll as the proper context for Pettibon's work, but to point
to the sheer infectiousness of his work, how it circulates with
ferocity—its ability to merge into, and course through the
contours of popular culture and lodge itself into our consciousness. I cannot drive a freeway for any length of time without

thinking of his drawing of a rumpled pile on a curb, the caption
reading, "that dead dog by the side of the road was just a pile
of rags." In this sense, his work manages to do what is truly
unusual for art, surviving outside of its native context without
losing its meaning or power. Pettibon's work not only survives,
but colonizes those territories it is exposed to, without sacrificing either its complex literary voice, nor its often caustic
aesthetic force. In so doing it brings another form of time with
it wherever it goes, one that is at once slower, and more intimate and contemplative, no matter how many viewers or how chaotic the context. It is this sensation of slowness in the middle
of tumult, a kind of focus, that I remember so clearly from my
first encounters with his work. It was the act of reading, or
more exactly, an insertion of the tempo of reading into the frenetic zones of visual experience that stands out so clearly in
retrospect, a gesture that is complimented by his insertion of
visuality into the act of reading. It is this collapse of reading
and looking that marks my first recollection of his work, the
unique feeling of having these two sensations merge, drawing
each into the other. This is unlike the kind of reading we are
used to in the form of Conceptual art, for Pettibon's text is
literary, rather than instrumental or Structuralist; by this
I mean that metaphor and poetic voice courses through his work,
opening it up to, and out onto, the world around it.

It was not until some 12 years later that I got to see
his work properly, in the middle of documenta 11 in 2002, just
after September 11, when I was living in New York. One of the
central themes of his installation at documenta was this post-
9/11 moment, in which Giuliani was depicted as a newly anointed
superman. It was this confrontation with his work at a time
when no one seemed to be speaking publicly about what the
country was attempting to justify in response to the trade
center attacks, when the climate was becoming markedly fearful
and repressive, that his installation stood out as one of the
few instances where something coherent, politically salient,
irreverent, and fearless was being said. This time it was not
only the sense of slowness amid the chaotic chatter of that

mega exhibition that held viewers in place, but the unrelenting critical nature of the work in the middle of the standard apolitical conditions of art, not to mention the nationalist atmosphere within the US, which had successfully stifled any serious questioning of the US government's domestic and international responses to the events of September 11th. Thinking back on his extraordinary work for documenta, Don DeLillo's _Mao II_ came to mind, as one of his characters says, "The state should want to kill all writers. Every government, every group that holds power or aspires to power should feel so threatened by writers that they hunt them down, everywhere." Earlier he also noted, "It's a curious knot that binds novelists and terrorists. In the West we become effigies as our books lose the power to shape and influence. Do you ask your writers about this? Years ago I used to think it was possible for an artist to alter the inner life of the culture. Now bomb-makers and gunmen have taken that territory. They make raids on human consciousness. What writers used to do before we were all incorporated."[1] DeLillo went further in a 1988 interview (_Vogue_, August 1988): "[T]he writer is the person who stands outside society, independent of affiliation and independent of influence. The writer is the man or woman who automatically takes a stance against his or her government." Concluding, "now, more than ever, we have to resist. American writers ought to stand and live in the margins, and be more dangerous." In seeing his contribution to documenta, and those since, I have come to feel as though Pettibon has, in some measure, filled the void that DeLillo outlined; that his work has reclaimed some of this space where the docile consciousness will again be assaulted, where writing can be dangerous, reclaiming the territory of writing in, of all places, the art world, and yet reimaging it with renewed intensity.

Needless to say, it is an honor to be able to have him here tonight. Please join me in welcoming Raymond Pettibon.

NOTE

1. Don DeLillo, _Mao II_, Penguin, New York 1991, p. 97, 41.

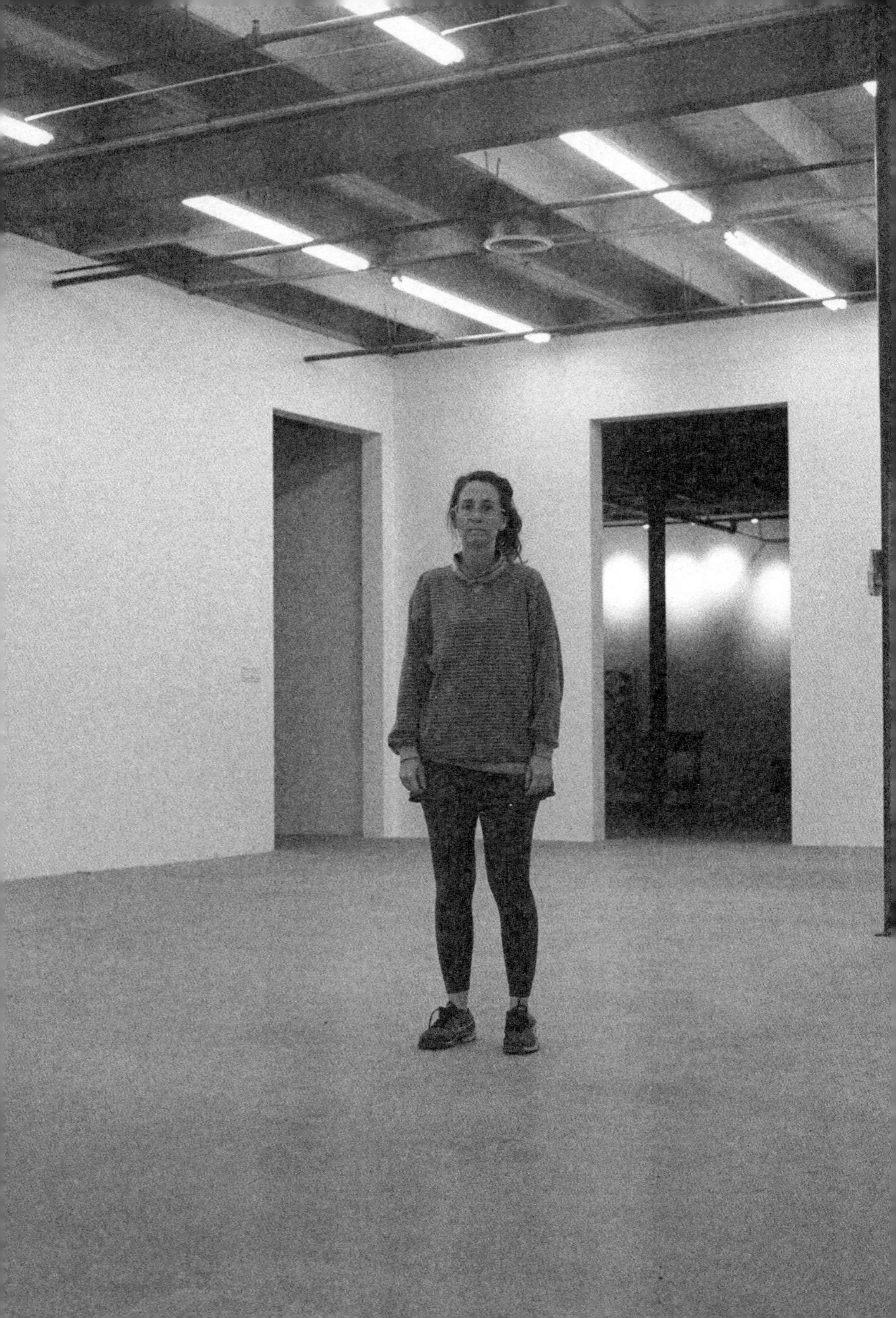

Introduction: Laura Owens,
Art Center College of Design
April 9, 2013

Hello. For those of you who don't know me, I'm Walead Beshty,
Associate Professor in the Graduate Art Program here at Art
Center College of Design. Tonight it's my honor to introduce
Laura Owens […]

Owens first came to wide attention as a standout among a
group of young artists who, in the 1990s, brought renewed energy
to the field of contemporary painting, reinvigorating and reimagining it in the wake of the polarizations left over from the
heated debates of the 1980s, when the general consensus seemed to
be that painting as a medium was outmoded stylistically, and had
grown fallow theoretically. From its onset, Owens' work exhibited
a robust and playful use of form and gesture, often infusing
traditional painterly concerns with narrative, mythos, and whimsy.
The result was an oeuvre that neither neatly rested within
the staid conventions of traditional painting, nor existed as
a rejection or refusal of those traditions; a form of painting
that was affirmative, that both said yes to the contemporary as
much as it said yes to painterly tradition, all the while avoiding being amnesiac or regressive. Owens' work carved out a
territory where the expressive and the referential, figurative
and gestural, narrative and formal, could coexist within the
confines of the canvas, where a furious gestural mark could also
serve as a monkey's tail, a drip or expressive smear could also
be a seagull, or a painting could exist as a citation or reference

without sacrificing its immediacy. Despite their seeming lightness and play, her approach was a serious challenge to both
those who wished to preserve painting's somber authority, and
those who sought to dismiss it variously as classist, heterosexist, macho, or regressive.

In so doing, Owens proposed a redefinition of the very
foundation of painting, wresting the notion of the gesture from
the bravado of traditionalists, while still producing paintings
that strove for, as she put it when we visited her in her studio
this past summer, a "penetrating" and "commanding" hold on
the viewer, one that—and I am paraphrasing here—reached out
and took you the from the other side of the room. In the recent
Artforum interview you all received in advance of tonight's
lecture (March 2013), Owens provocatively compared this reimagining of gesture to the female orgasm. As she put it:

> Is it even possible for a woman artist to be the one who
> marks? At the same time, in 2013, does anyone at all
> have this ability, or is it an antiquated or sentimental
> idea? Isn't it interesting that the male orgasm has a
> DNA imprint that will replicate itself over and over
> again, reinforcing itself the way language or naming
> might, but the female orgasm has no use, no mark, no
> locatability? … I want to think about how it can be
> the model for a new gesture.

Aside from this being an absolutely brilliant formulation of a
new set of possibilities for painterly gesture, one that I hope
we will hear her expand upon tonight, it also highlights a form
of criticality that, rather than being constituted in the notion
of negation or rejection of a certain set of tools or modes for
their negative implications, opts instead to rescript or reimagine them anew, distorting and turning them to new ends. It is
this that acts like an inhabitation or occupation of a dominant
rhetoric that seems bereft of life, an approach that draws new
life from its dead flesh.

But to limit this insight to painting alone would obscure the
fact that the same animating force is at work around her practice. Her notion of the mark, the gesture, one that, as she so
eloquently contrasts, is not consummated in a single burst, a
unified explosive moment as an event, but rather one that builds
from a rumble, permeating rather than penetrating, forms the
context for her practice, moving between works, and around its
margins. From her exhibition <u>Pavement Karaoke</u> in 2012, which
included both the Pavement paintings and an actual karaoke
session, to the current series of events being held at her Boyle
Heights temporary studio cum exhibition space and social hub
(now called 356 Mission), where everything from performances
to Scrabble Sunday take place, events that take place in the
periphery form a dull rumble that supports and lends energy to
her paintings. It is this notion of gesture, of painting, of art
practice, one that operates as an unequivocal "yes," an affirmation of the possibilities of practice, that I feel distinguishes
her and her work, that draws all that surrounds it into its flow.
As Aristotle put it, "Production [poiesis] has an end other than
itself, but action [praxis] does not: good action is itself an
end." To which Giorgio Agamben would later offer that Aristotle
had defined the very idea of gesture, that gesture, "breaks with
the false alternative between ends and means that paralyzes … "[1]
for gesture underscores, fundamentally, what it is to be "in
language," because to be in language is to be human, for to be
human is to be among humans, and in relation to them. It is
this type of presence that is so clearly evidenced in Owens' work,
one that constantly reminds us of our own being in relation
to the things around us, and to one another, and further underscores that we are always in a position to reimagine and rede-
fine the possibilities of those relations.

   Needless to say, it is great to have her here at Art
Center again. Please join me in welcoming Laura Owens.

NOTE

1. Giorgio Agamben, <u>Means Without End: Notes on Politics</u>, trans. Vincenzo Binetti
and Cesare Casarino, University of Minnesota, Minneapolis 2000, p. 56

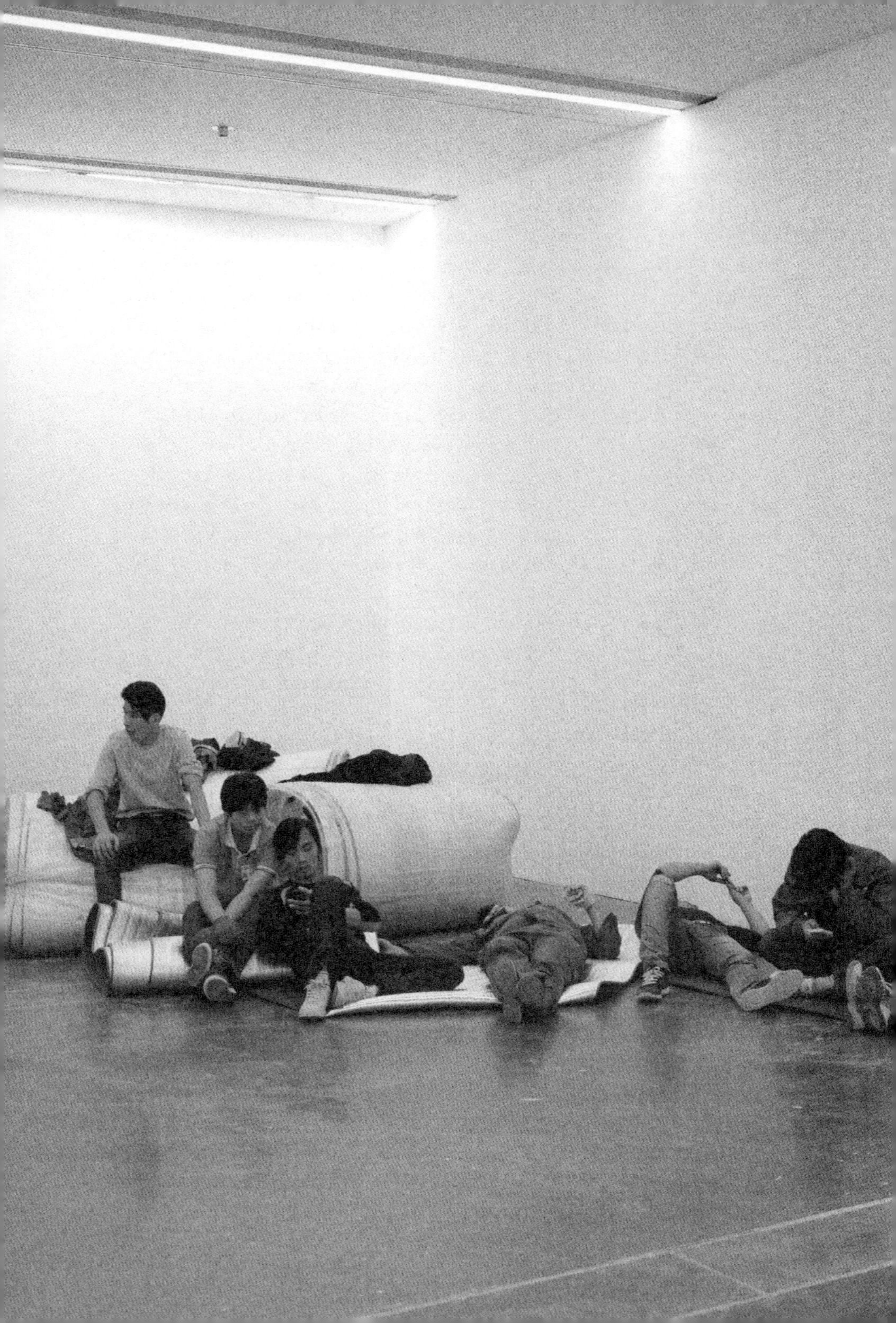

Introduction: Gabriel Kuri, Art Center College of Design, February 11, 2014

For those of you that don't know me, I'm Walead Beshty, Associate
Professor in the Graduate Department here at Art Center, and
this series is organized by Jack Bankowsky and myself. …

Our guest tonight is Gabriel Kuri. Since the early 1990s
Kuri's work has navigated the tensions between materiality
and iconography, positing a mode of sculptural production that
deploys an extensive array of heterogeneous materials in formally elegant yet precarious compositions. His often uncomforta-
ble juxtapositions of objects have both phenomenological weight
and an airy provisionality, destabilizing the classic hierarchies
of sculptural materials, while simultaneously questioning the
equivalences posited by market exchange.

Thus a receipt finds itself wedged between massive
marble blocks, as fragile as it is valueless under the obdurate
masses; or a can of energy drink is doomed to perpetual agita-
tion atop a treadmill, a consumer object used for its packaging
more than its contents, in an intermingling of classicism and
the detritus of daily life. Even the act of grocery shopping is
posited as a potential moment of artistic production, an act
he referred to as a "primordially sculptural experience," which
leads one to consider his repeated use of receipts, for example
in his work Trinity (2006), which comprises three large woven
tapestries of enlarged receipts, as yet another juxtaposition
of objects, as though he is offering us the recipe for one of his

sculptures. In this instance, it is commerce, rather than materiality, that draws these objects into relation in the form of a list. In so doing, Kuri asserts no hierarchy of objects or actions, instead positing them all as interconnected, for in his work shopping can operate as a form of production, or a telephone book can perform as a sculptural component as elegantly as a block of granite. As he put it, "all materials, no matter how raw they appear (water, stone, the wood from trees, the flow of electricity …) are socially branded and coded … the difference between a printed plastic bag and a bundle of wool is a matter of degree … and not a categorical difference." Thus all objects are products, and just as none are treated as pure or natural, none are excluded for being man-made or commercial. This gives his juxtapositions an immediate visceral impact for the sheer disparity between the things we see, which opens up into the logic of capital exchange, for the logic of exchange equates all things in the mechanations of financial transaction, for whether it is a question of a granite block, a strip of stamps, a Saab, or even, by implication, a human life, all things have a generic interchangeability from the perspective of capital. An insight that was shared by Georges Bataille, when he offered up in his journal <u>Document</u> that the value of the raw materials contained within the human body was approximately 25 francs (this was in 1935, I am not sure what it might equate to today).

While the amalgamation of objects in Kuri's work appears discordant, he supplants the total exchangeability of materials for a materialist logic of weight, balance, and form, reinscribing a fundamental distinction between things with the logic of the handmade. While a block of granite might cost as much as a television, when they come into contact with one another, they behave quite differently. This it seems is Kuri's end run around the cynical equivalences of capital, a recourse to the logic of the bricoleur, an agent who refuses the iconicity of products for the brute fact of their material existence. The anthropologist and semiotician Claude Lévi-Strauss proposed that the Bricoleur is the model aesthetic producer who "'speaks' not only

<u>with</u> things … but also through the medium of things … by the choices he makes between limited possibilities."[1] The Bricoleur, as a scavenger of everyday life, tinkers with established meanings, investigating cultural symbols whose meanings are locked up tight, and pries them open, reimagining the place of the object, and in turn, our place among objects. Kuri's work manifests an absurdity and lucidity that challenges the hierarchy of objects at work in daily life, infusing them with alternate possibilities and renewed agency, whether it be the <u>Financial Times</u> sandwiched between layers of sod, or sheets of insulation, curving and weaving with a grace that construction materials should never have, with two coconuts indelicately hanging below, each of these works making the process of art making open and available. Because they operate under clear constraints, Kuri's work presents the possibility of alternative productions that could be conceived under those very same constraints. Thus he offers us not just sculptures, but a way of working, of conceiving a point of entry into a world that usually relies on economies of scale to produce aesthetic objects, a world from which we are limited to being only consumers. Here he proposes a kind of ethics of production, an attitude toward making that democratizes the access to aesthetics, and the transparency with which they operate.

It is through this ethic that the political quotient of Kuri's work is manifest with a cogency and rigor that rejects neither beauty nor the power relations at work in aesthetics.

Please join me in welcoming, Gabriel Kuri.

NOTE

1. Claude Lévi-Strauss, <u>The Savage Mind</u>, The University of Chicago Press, Chicago 1966, p. 21.

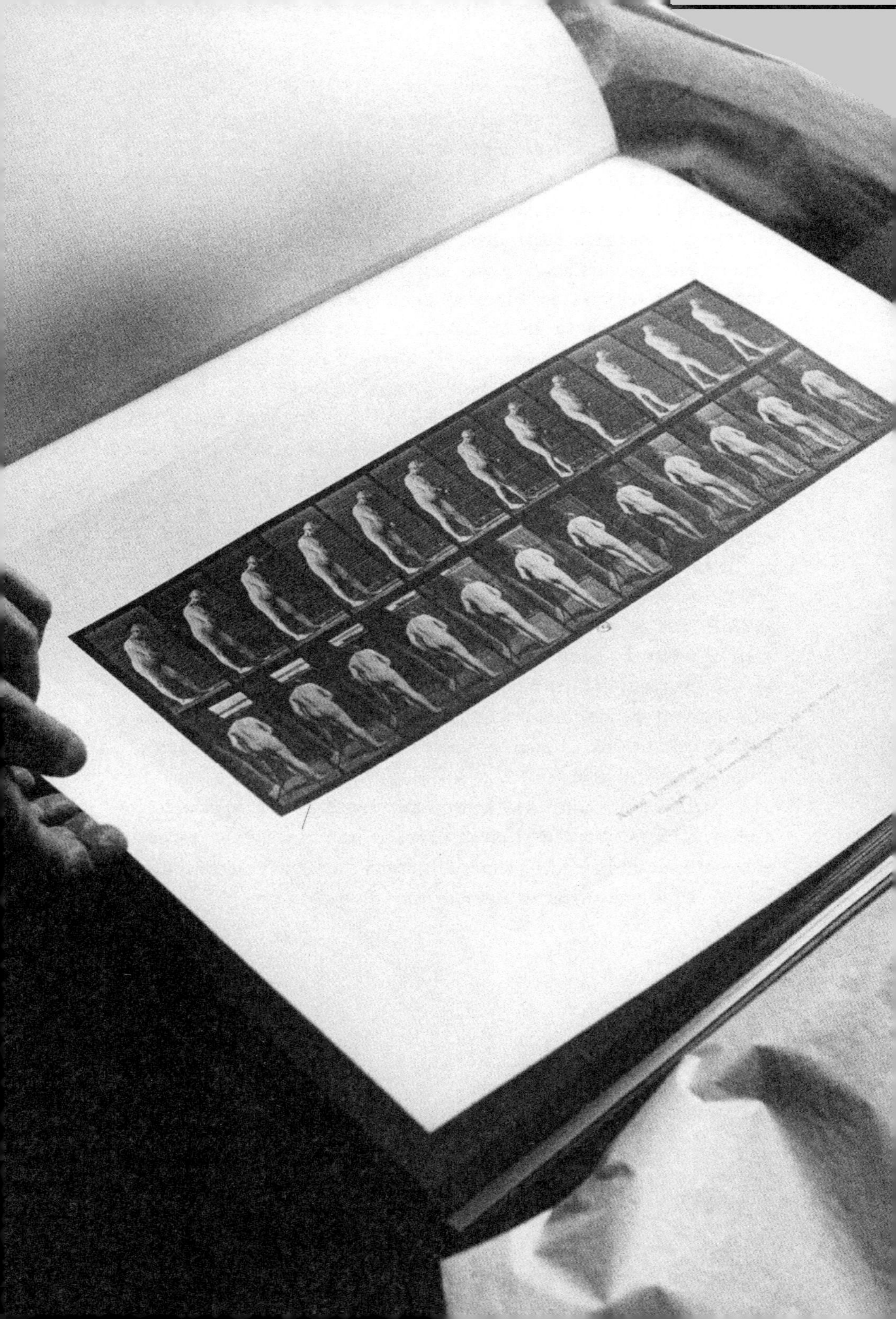

Introduction: Paul Pfeiffer, Art Center College of Design, March 11, 2014

For those of you that don't know me, I'm Walead Beshty, Associate Professor in the Graduate Art Program here at Art Center College of Design, and this series is organized by my colleague Jack Bankowsky and myself …

Our guest tonight is Paul Pfeiffer. Pfeiffer first became known for videos and photographs that draw upon popular spectacle, wresting from them moments of uncanny abstraction, where popular icons appear caught in the worlds of their making, suspended within the parameters of the image, doomed to endless repetitions. He offers us basketball player Larry Johnson in a perpetual state of screaming in horror or perhaps ecstasy; Michael Jackson becomes an inhuman blob that oozes across the stage like a sparkling animated Rorschach blot; or a member of the Backstreet Boys acts as an undulating phallus, throbbing faceless in front of a microphone. Above all, Pfeiffer's body of work unlocks the libidinal subtext of mass phenomena, whether sporting events, stadium concerts, or films emblazoned in cultural memory; it is how these objects of fascination reflect and formulate their audiences, and the uncanniness of their libidinal production that Pfeiffer so eloquently brings forward. The icons presented to us are sacrificial figures, often literally emptied out and filled with the crowds who watch them, as in his trilogy <u>The Long Count</u> (2001), where Muhammad Ali and his challengers are rendered as ghostly apparitions through which the audience who watches them is visible. Their bodies are on display, their tragedy and triumphs presented to the world for vicarious pleasure, while their interiorities are splayed out, and diffused through a multitude of screens, to be further disseminated by the fans who animated their personae.

In Pfeiffer's work, digital artifacts act as sutures in the image screen, as though his digital images had scarred over these removals and manipulations. In this sense the image reveals itself as another body, a sacrificial body offered up for inspection by the mass. And it is this insight into massification, into the unity of the crowd and the images it demands that so thoroughly animates Pfeiffer's work, the many becoming one, as when a children's chorus recites Michael Jackson's infamous 2003 press conference addressing accusations of molestation; or the intoxicating ecstasy of the crowd, as in his work The Saints (2007), where young Filipinos become wrapped up in the chanting crowds of a World Cup match from 1966. In these instances we find that we are wholly implicated in the world of images that Pfeiffer calls forward.

All of this was evident in Pfeiffer's first video Pure Products Go Crazy (1998). In it we see Tom Cruise in an iconic scene from Risky Business (1983). It is a nascent Cruise, a teenager caught in all his adolescent awkwardness, who is the focus of optically libidinal excess. In the scene Cruise is dancing around the house in his underwear, celebrating the departure of his parents. Pfeiffer catches him in a moment of ecstasy, of throwing himself onto the couch, face down, falling and thrusting, and then looped endlessly. Rather than recalling a scene of masturbation, as some have offered, his entire body seems to be enraptured, as though he were a phallus caught in the moment of climax. Cruise's body appears like a fly caught in a spider's web, undulating, twitching, and kicking in a manner that is seemingly ecstatic yet reminiscent of death throes. Pfeiffer consistently catches his subjects in a state of frenzy, of sustained anticipation of a release that is deferred indefinitely, of explosive quiver that characterizes the mass effect: the coming together of crowd and its icon, the many into one, and through this becoming we feel the undercurrent of death, of depletion, of an anti-climax that is forever forestalled. As Elias Canetti put it in his magnum opus <u>Crowds and Power</u>, "The most important occurrence within the crowd is discharge. Before it the crowd does not exist, it is the discharge which creates it. This is the moment when all who belong to the crowd get rid of their differences and become equal."[1] And it is this moment that Pfeiffer freezes, catching it in perpetuity, and it is here that the libidinal force of the crowd is felt, as Klaus Theweleit observed in his treatise <u>Male Fantasies</u>, in these moments of mass cathexis: "the mass looses its multiplicity and becomes one, a single organ at the tip of which stands … the one … the … phallus on high (which) is united with the body of the people to form a new whole."[2] When we watch our screens, we too become part of this mass effect, we become one, quivering in unison as Cruise does, pulsating along with our totems. These phenomena of the crowd, its sexuality, its violence, and its energetic pulsations that Pfeiffer exposes; our coming together to become a singularity, and how our images speak to us of this transformation, and the repressed implications of that becoming. His work catches us in this moment of losing oneself to the strangeness of the mass—on the edge of a climax that is endlessly deferred. He does this not by peering into the depths of our images, not by unmasking, nor simplistically revealing their falseness, but rather by keeping his work trained on the images' seemingly impervious surfaces, which act as elastic mirrors of our desires. He offers revelations of how we make our icons, and how they in turn, make us, positing neither critique, nor condemnation, but a distillation of the uncanniness that is everywhere around us.

Needless to say, I'm very excited to have him here today. Please join me in welcoming Paul Pfeiffer.

NOTES

1. Elias Canetti, <u>Crowds and Power</u>, Farrar, Straus and Giroux, New York 1984, p. 17.

2. Klaus Theweleit, <u>Male Fantasies, Vol. 1: Women, Floods, Bodies, History</u>, University of Minnesota, Minneapolis 1987, p. 125.

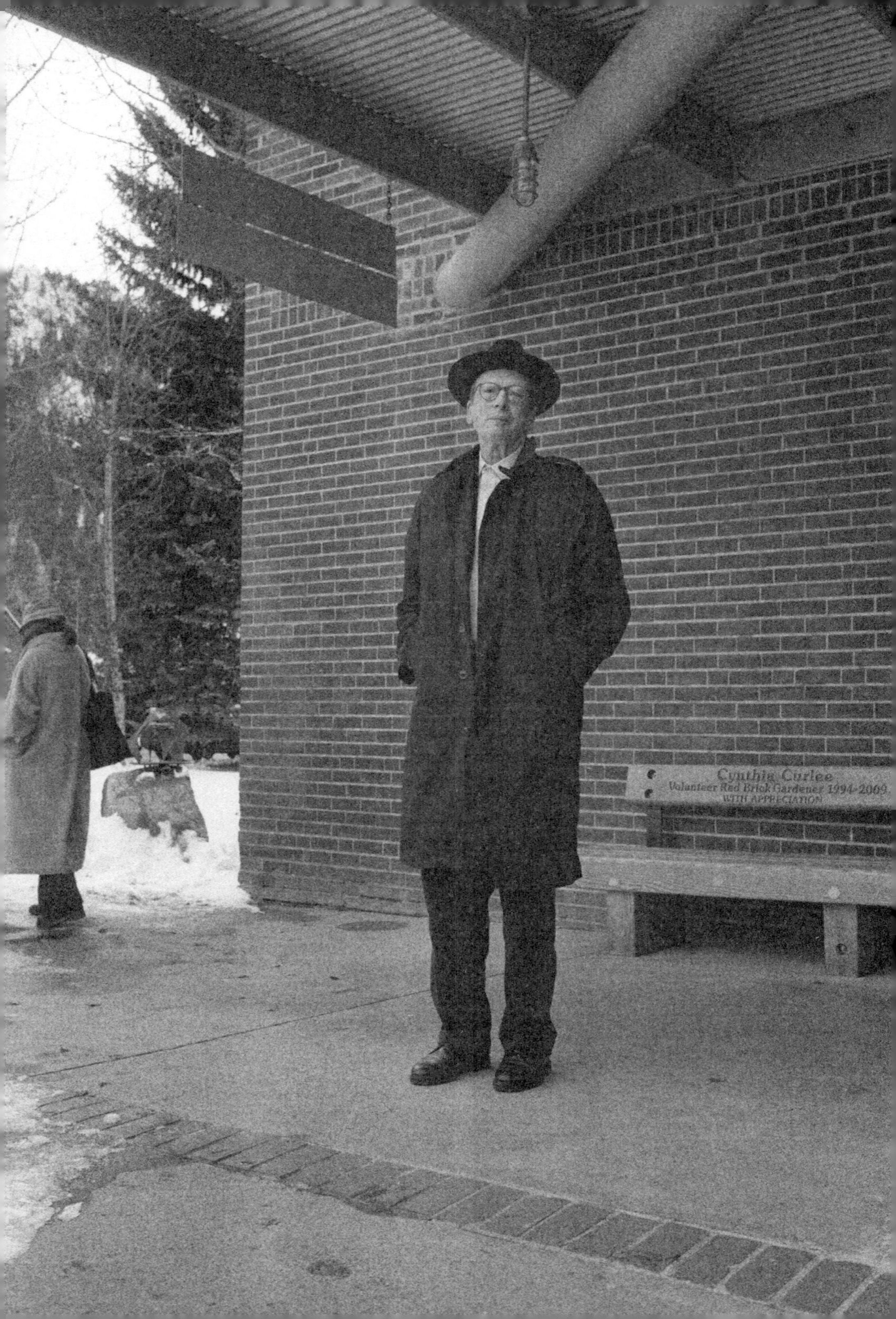
Cynthia Curlee
Volunteer Red Brick Gardener 1994-2009
WITH APPRECIATION

Introduction: Morgan Fisher, Art Center College of Design, March 25, 2014

Hello, for those of you that don't know me, I'm Walead Beshty,
Associate Professor in the Graduate Art Program here at Art
Center College of Design, and this term's lecture series is
organized by my colleague Jack Bankowsky and myself …

Our guest tonight is Morgan Fisher. As I am hesitant to
confess for I know it would annoy him to no end, I first saw
Morgan Fisher's films on a DVD borrowed from a friend, who had
in turn borrowed it from one of his European galleries, and
only agreed to lend it to me after I pestered incessantly and
with the caveat that Morgan would never know she supplied it.
Once I had the DVD in my possession, I watched Picture and
Sound Rushes (1973), Phi Phenomenon (1968), Protective Coloration
(1979), Standard Gauge (1984) and so on, devouring the films,
and they immediately became incredibly important to me, representing a materialist and conceptual rigor that I had not
encountered before. Each film managed to merge the question of
what a work was "about" with what it "was" in radically different ways; in other words, while the films performed exegeses
on their chosen subject matter, they also wholly implicated
themselves within that subject matter. In works like Cue Rolls
(1974), or Picture and Sound Rushes, it seemed like the medium
of film was speaking for itself, and out of this speaking, out
of this reflexivity, a world was opened up, and perception was
both demystified, and yet rendered uncannily alien. It was as

though the unconscious of the medium was being expressed, how
the conditions and conventions of a medium formulated what was
sensible or knowable through it, denaturalizing it. I had the
distinct sensation that a hidden drive or desire lurking within
the conventions of cinema seemed to rise to the surface. I made
my way through the works chronologically, and the last work on
the DVD was Standard Gauge, which reached beyond, or rather,
through the cinematic apparatus into the autobiographical and
the emotive, drawing the life of the filmmaker, the lives of all
those who work with and through film, and by extension, the
lives of those who watch it, into the work itself. The work made
me realize that Fisher's work was not simply about film or its
immediate surroundings, but about how lives are formulated and
lived through their relations to the moving image and, more
broadly, to technologies of perception, and he located this complicated emotional and perceptual relationship without recourse
to romanticism or nostalgia, while avoiding the air of false
objectivity.

It wasn't until I had the fortunate experience of seeing
his films in a theater that I realized that Morgan's mandate—
that his work be viewed in its intended format—was for more
than a good reason. In seeing films like Phi Phenomenon projected at his film retrospective at the Museum of Contemporary
Art, Los Angeles—a seemingly innocuous silent film of a class-
room clock with the second hand removed, the title derived from
the optical illusion of perceiving continuous motion between
separate objects viewed in rapid succession—I realized the
hugely complex relationship his work had to the site of its
display, as well as the phenomenological richness of the work,
interactions that were wholly lost when watching the films
alone and on a computer monitor. Phi Phenomenon places the
viewer in a sequence of temporal frames—the time of the clock,
and cinematic time, which push and pull upon one another—which
further opens up onto the site of reception, the awareness
of the other viewers in the room, and one's membership in this
collective. These complicated insights arose from what was seemingly so little, with no presumption of even the revelatory

gesture common to most materialist aesthetics. As Fisher wrote,
"time will pass, as you know it does in any film, and what
you see on the screen is an instrument that tells you what you
already know, that in a film time passes. There are no surprises.
There is no variety, no relaxation and increase of tension, no
comic relief, no rising action, no climax, no denouement. And,
most frustrating of all, there is no movement, at least none
that you can see." (This is because the movement of the minute
hand is too slow to be perceptible.) Yet, as Fisher goes on to
explain, the focus of <u>Phi Phenomenon</u> is not the film itself,
but the conditions surrounding it, or rather, the expansive cinematic apparatus that it is apart of. "The viewer is reminded
that he or she is sitting in a seat, and that the seat may or
may not be comfortable, and that the seat is in a theater, and
that the theater is a specific place with a specific décor." And
while, on the one hand, the film itself places the viewers in a
restrictive, if not frustratingly alienating confrontation with
the parameters of cinematic time, and its incompatiblitly with
the "time of lived experience," it also refocuses attention onto
the parameters of the audience, where the audience, through
their shuffling, sniffles, sighs, and so on restructure the
time of viewership like the ebb and flow of a tide, for as their
activities shift, the perception of the passage of time also
shifts, even as the repressive or institutional face of the
schoolroom clock stares back. Thus the audience becomes the
animator of the film, prescribing time, as much as the clock.
And it is through the film's integration into its sites of reception or distribution that one becomes aware of one's own bodily
experience of time, and the imagined similar experiences of
those that surround us—a collective sense of a "being in time"
or "times" pervading the room.

It is this sensitivity that Fisher's work repeatedly
deploys to surprising ends, revealing the mechanations of a
seemingly innocuous effect, whether it is a monochrome, or the
face of a clock, or an alarm, which opens up into the broad
conditions of viewership, of the nature of being a viewer. It is
this insight into how the mode of distribution and its site of

reception is inseparable from the object itself that he repeatedly brings to bear, and what I believe connects his film
work and his paintings of the last decade and a half. From his
<u>Door and Window Paintings</u> of 2002, or his <u>Anamorphic Pendant
Pair Paintings</u>, where the viewer, who is situated between paired
paintings that cannot be seen at the same time, becomes the fulcrum of the perceptual experience, to his spatially disorienting
mirroring of the gallery architecture at Portikus for his exhibition <u>Portikus Looks At Itself</u> (2009), each work uses the conventions of painting and architecture to exceed the tautologies
they arose from, producing arresting phenomenological effects,
which similarly create a wholly embodied understanding of being
a viewer, and of the social conditions of being an audience.
It is this awareness, this resolute understanding that materialist, and intellectual rigor is not anathema to the personal
or the affecting. Through his work we are reminded that we are
the animators and participants in these systems of art production, that their meaning and life is dependent on us, and we are
not only reminded of our implication within these systems, but
our very integration within such systems. It was this quality
that Giorgio Agamben associated so strongly with the cinematic;
an effect he referred to as a reminder of our "being in language."
I would add that Fisher's work provides us a reminder of our
"being in aesthetics" of being connected through the aesthetic,
that the aesthetic is a collective phenomenon.

    Needless to say I am thrilled he is joining us tonight.
Please join me in welcoming Morgan Fisher.

Introduction: James Welling, Art Center College of Design, April 1, 2014

Our Guest tonight is James Welling. In isolation, Welling's work
is a resuscitation of 19th- and early 20th-century traditions
of photography, brought into the contemporary discourse through
a myriad of means. While studying under John Baldessari and
Wolfgang Stoerchle at CalArts in the early 1970s, Welling engaged in the flirtations with appropriation and Conceptual art
that would structure his uncommon approach to the photographic
medium. Despite undergoing substantial change in his work,
these practices were still evident in the pieces he made just
prior to leaving Los Angeles in the late 1970s, the playful
twisting and turning of his hands in a series of photograms,
which were as much an evocation of the avant-garde's fascination
with the hand as an instrument of labor and material agency
in the works of László Moholy-Nagy or El Lissitzky, as they are
echoes of the lyrically pictorial portraits of Georgia O'Keeffe's
hands made by Alfred Stieglitz. These works by Welling stand
as an early example of the seemingly diametrically opposed attitudes toward art that could coexist in a single work. Around
the same time he produced his Los Angeles photographs, which
evoked the brooding narratives of film noir, adapting a distinctly Angelino version of street photography, one bereft of
the cast of characters who populated its New York counterpart,
as though the city were a stage set waiting to be inhabited.

This engagement with the camera, and early darkroom experiments, would evolve into a deeper negotiation with photographic
history when he first moved to New York—his early tinfoil photographs, stoic images of contrasting lights and darks that
are distinctly majestic yet of modest means, the glacial beauty
of his Gelatin photographs, or the poetically titled images of
phyllo dough spread on velvet drapes, all of which were made
in his humble Grand Street loft. It could have been asked what
projects such as these had to do with the appropriationist work
of Sherrie Levine, the loaded sexuality of David Salle, or the
high production icy smooth contours of Jack Goldstein's paintings and films, with which he would immediately be grouped.
Despite not being blatant, this kinship was definitely present.
Welling, rather than focusing on the direct appropriation of
images (aside from a brief flirtation with this strategy while
a student at CalArts), instead appropriated the historical traditions of the photographic image, all the while making use
of the basic materials surrounding him, recombining them into
his haunting images. Thus we see phyllo dough on velvet achieve
sublimity and drama in works that evoke the mundane materials
of the everyday, while also calling forward the tradition of
sublime landscape painting.

It was this duality, an understanding that appropriation
need not be a literal transcription, that his early work brought
forward. Rather, his work alluded to a stream of other images
in one's memory, no singular source being directly referenced,
an insight that would open the door to the plurality of historical styles that one sees in evidence in his works from New York
and after. A major focus became the industrialization of the
image, from his railroad photographs to the premodern buildings
of H. H. Richardson, or the Lace Factory series, which notably,
pointed both to photography's history in the all too common
photograms of lace in the 19th-century work of Anna Atkins,
Henry Fox Talbot, and others, yet also point toward the future
of photographic production in the digital, by referring to
the jacquard loom, the precursor to the computer punch card,
rendered in the tonal ranges and traditions of modernist

photography's fascination with factories and the railways
that serviced them. In this way, Welling's work uncovers both
the logic of the material and conditions of image production in
practice, while at the very same time depicting sites that are
central to its history in a type of reflexively conceptual documentary procedure. These connections to the historical conditions can be found all over his work, for example in his early
photographs of the diary of Elizabeth and James Dixon of the
mid 1800s. As Welling observed, " … my great-great grandmother's pressed flowers and feathers could be seen as proto-photo-
grams. So not only was the diary written at the beginning of
photography, but also the book contained things that resembled
the earliest photographs." Later Welling would photograph
Philip Johnson's Glass House, a favored subject of photographers,
which architectural historian Beatriz Colomina would later
observe was essentially, "a machine for making pictures," the
building itself acting as a frame for the landscape that surrounded it, as though a picture frame were placed directly into
the scene.

Regardless of these conditions, Welling's work never
settles at the point of simple depiction or the inhabitation
of historical processes, whether they are the photogram or the
view camera photograph. Rather he deploys the logic of the
tinkerer, or the bricoleur, opening up and transforming the
technologies he uses. It was this attitude that set him so strongly
apart from his contemporaries in the Pictures Generation, for
rather than reiterate, and replicate the alienating facades of
the image world, Welling actively intervened, peeling back its
layers, not in the service of some sort of revelation of its
inner workings in a didactic show and tell, but rather to give
access to its mechanics, to let them be transformed and redeployed to democratic ends. It is this logic of the bricoleur
that links together his work, and further formulates a politics
of the everyday, for it actively intervenes in what is understandable through art, modifying what can be made visible, or
perceivable. This modification is what Jacques Rancière called
the "distribution of the sensible," "the system of self-evident

facts of sense perception that simultaneously discloses the
existence of something in common and the delimitations that
define the respective parts and positions within it … determin[ing] those who have a part in the community of citizens."[1]
In other words, art signals our role as members of the polis
(the citizenry) through its organizing of that group around
sensate material, by opening up who and what can be made
sensate. It is from the vantage point outside of individual bodies of work that the intricate relations between works become
evident, where Welling marks out not only an economy of related
productions, but a set of percepts that elude direct depiction,
a broader system of understandings that outline what it means
take part in technological perception, finding within it evocative beauty, and conceptual rigor.

It was this richness that Eduardo Cadava was referring
to when he said, "the history of photography can be said to
begin with an interpretation of the stars." In short, it is
the interpretation of vast and malleable systems, systems whose
workings are only comprehensible from a distance. Welling
reminds us that photography is a medium of the everyday,
a medium whose agency lies in the mundane all around us, but
despite this, is capable of elucidating the broadest array
of possibilities. It is this dual view, of expansive terrains
of perception, and the everydayness of vision that Welling so
eloquently delivers.

Please join me in welcoming James Welling.

NOTE

1. Jacques Ranciere, The Politics of Aesthetics, La Fabrique-Éditions, Paris 2000,
p. 12.

Introduction: Stephen Prina, Art Center College of Design, January 13, 2015

For those of you who don't know me, I'm Walead Beshty, Associate
Professor here at Art Center. The lecture series for this term
is organized by myself and my colleague here, Jack Bankowsky …

It's my pleasure to introduce Stephen Prina. I'm not
going to recite his impressive CV, or the bio which graces the
announcement for this lecture … including a recent beautiful
and expansive exhibition at LACMA entitled <u>As He Remembered It</u>.
Rather, I would like to say that a deep understanding and
engagement with convention and history runs throughout Prina's
practice, his work drawing together myriad points of reference
that cohere within constellations of interrelated concerns.
As he locates and deploys various traditions he deftly torques
and perverts them, eschewing tenets of 1960s and 70s Conceptual
practice, such as site-specificity or seriality, for ever growing
recombinatory projects that react to their site of reception,
but are not married to them, that rely on cadences and citations,
without becoming simple repetitions. In addition, his works
have a complex and arresting relationship to the body and there
are several through lines evidenced in the majority of his work,
such as his "blind paintings," which are common window shades
painted in a range of colors. Here the heady avant-garde tradition of painting is connected to the space of the domestic, in
paintings that move restlessly in the occasional breeze, or the
movement of bodies through the room, and moreover call forward

the idea of painting as a "window on the world," which he
bitingly makes opaque. Or his exhibition <u>As He Remembered It</u>,
where built-ins from two no longer extant Rudolph Schindler
buildings in Los Angeles were painted honeysuckle pink, and
arranged in floor plan configurations around the exhibition
hall, implying the absent body of the building which housed
them (importantly, I would add, Prina referred to these fragments as being "amputated limbs"). As the art historian Alex
Kitnick commented, "both history and architecture appear here
less as reconstituted bodies than as a strange phalanx of phan-
tom limbs." Within his work, the notion of the body as a site
of indexing, reformation, and registration recalls what Walter
Benjamin described as "negative expressionism," offering the
analogy of "the man sitting in the seat after the chair has been
pulled away." In short, a negative expressionism realized in
a body that registers the forces and objects it has come into
contact with, and never looses those traces, but rather carries
them with him. As James Meyer put it when speaking of Prina's
Max Hetzler project, "as it unfolds, it encodes site-specificity
as memory or absence; it marks the transience, the shiftingness
of place itself." Meyer notably mentions Prina's work as a form
of mourning, but it is limiting to understand Prina's work as
a testament to loss or absence alone, which makes it seems closed
off, or sealed away from its surroundings. Rather Prina's
work also is maintains an openness to its surroundings, a kind
of acceptance of contingency and chance, and an acknowledgement
of shifting contexts as part of the life of the work of art.
In so doing, Prina's work evades the melancholy that dogs so
much of the allegorical critique he recovers, positing works
that grow through time, and that register the growth of meaning, and the accrual of significance.

I also think it is important to say, by way of context,
that not only is Prina an artist, but also a composer, a musi-
cian who also has a hauntingly beautiful singing voice, and one
in a line of great Los Angeles teachers, and I'm particularly
honored to host him here at Art Center under the auspices of
the Graduate Art Department, where he was a longtime Professor

and former Chair. On becoming involved in the art world, one
quickly hears the folklore of Los Angeles' art schools, from
John Baldessari's post-studio class at CalArts which seemed to
incubate several generations of the most important American
artists, to the inheritor of this class, Michael Asher, whose
epic 12-hour plus version became equally well known for its
duration as it was for its impact on the artists who took part
in it, to Chris Burden's locking himself in a locker at UC
Irvine, or Jason Rhoades' mini formula-one race staged around
the studios of UCLA. But within this tradition, the most curious
and provocative entry is Prina's 1994 class taught here entitled
"The Films of Keanu Reeves," whose fame reached beyond the
art world into the pages of the New Yorker, the Chicago Tribune,
People magazine, and even garnered a substantial exposure on
MTV News (which can be watched on YouTube). It was in the MTV
interview that Prina said, "I take frivolity very seriously,"
the thoughtfulness of his responses to a news program run by
a music video channel enacted his own prescription, a mise en
abyme that seemed to be lost on the giddy interviewer. What on
its first face seems bombastic or just flip, quickly reveals a
sly and subtle logic (and I think it is important to note that
Prina was a student of both Baldessari and Asher), the class
proposing a durational, serial, and comprehensive format while
acknowledging the traditions of Pop and appropriation, his own
version of the epic course as a beautiful détournement of the
durational pedagogical experiments of his teachers, a kind of
perverse revision of a Los Angeles tradition (one could describe
his class where students watched Robert Bresson's classic, The
Devil, Probably [1977] during every session in similar terms).
To this end, Prina's pedagogical contributions were as innovative
and destabilizing as his quietly subversive work. They are also
evidence of a dubious polymath, one who continues to twist the
strictures of convention, and unsettles entrenched propositions
with pop, humor, and impassioned consideration.

Needless to say, it is truly an honor to have him back
to Art Center. Please join me in welcoming Stephen Prina.

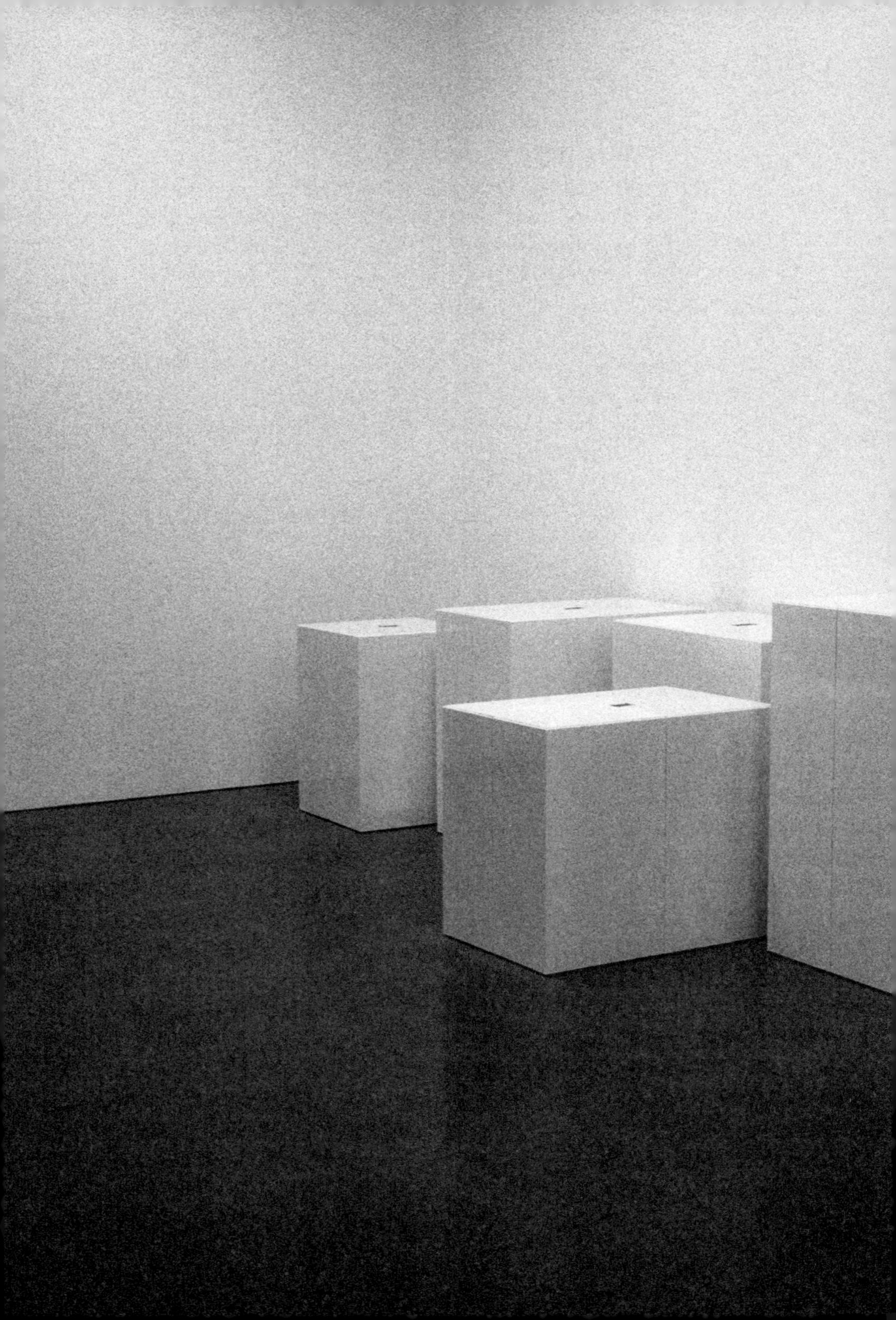

Introduction: Jorge Pardo, Art Center College of Design, January 20, 2015

Hello, I'm Walead Beshty, Associate Professor here in the Graduate Art Department, and this series is organized by my colleague Jack Bankowsky and myself.

Our guest tonight is Jorge Pardo. Pardo has not only worked in a range of media, from sculpture, to painting and installation, but also within a variety of disciplines, his practice interweaving architecture, furniture making, interior and exhibition design with conventional art practices. At times his studio operates like a commission-based design office or an architecture firm, at others it approximates the intimacy of a traditional trade craft (early on he made it a family business, collaborating with his mother). If anything is to be gleaned from the array of productions and methods he employs, it is that to reconcile the range of his practice one must adopt a holistic way of thinking and looking, one not mired in commonplace divisions, one that doesn't separate design from art, commerce from aesthetics, the personal from the professional, or presume that in order to be art, an object must be free of function or use, an attitude that often perplexes conventional art critical or museological approaches. Rather his work requires that one see the connections between all of the elements in our built environment, that one think in terms of relations between things, and that one acknowledge the intimate intertwining of our lives with the objects that surround us. From its earliest moment,

Pardo's work has sought ways to insert art into the flow of
everyday life, and by doing so, enliven it and shake it free of
its often staid and divisive social strictures, democratizing
and demystifying it at the same time. So I would offer that it
is not so much that Pardo confuses professional categories like
artist, designer, or architect, or that he situates the low forms
of design and material culture in the highbrow context of
art to critical effect, but rather that his work operates within
the conceit that these distinctions are meaningless; thus, in
his work, the home is but a modest museum, a lamp a work of art,
the museum a public meeting point, the art gallery but another
type of shop, the gallerist, just a shop keeper, and the artist
a tinkering entrepreneur. He does this by using the medium
of exchange, whether it is financial or social, to slice through
commonplace distinctions, revealing their illusory nature,
while opening up opportunities to reimagine our relation to
the world we have in common.

I want to say also, that Pardo is an alumnus of Art Center,
having received his BFA here, and it has been more than two
decades since he last gave a lecture in the school. I am very
excited that we are able to have him back; please join me in
welcoming Jorge Pardo.

Introduction: Allan McCollum, Art Center College of Design, February 3, 2015

For those of you from outside of the Graduate Art Department,
I'm Walead Beshty, Associate Professor here at Art Center.
It's my please to introduce our guest tonight, Allan McCollum.

      Nearly four decades ago, McCollum produced one of
the most significant bodies of work of the late 20th century,
works that would bring him to wide attention, and would in-
delibly mark art history. His Surrogate Paintings, modestly
scaled plaster-cast objects, drew together the longstanding
self-reflexive discourse of painting, with the then newly emergent discourses on representation, signification, and simulation; I would add that since this work, the formalist trajectory
within painting can no longer be held apart from the understanding of painting as a cultural form. Here the seemingly
discrete trajectories of Pop and materialism in the form of
appropriation and the monochrome are drawn together in one
elegant gesture. Upon seeing them, the Surrogates appear almost
plasticine, affectless, and industrially produced, often installed
swarm-like in the blank white caverns common to art exhibitions.
Yet on closer examination, it becomes clear that each of these
diminutive objects is hand-painted, its contours betraying an
unmistakably human touch. In this duality, McCollum's Surrogates
troubled the dominant notions of art in the late 1970s and 80s,
for the Surrogates were neither the slickly anomic objects
that were common to the protagonists of appropriation or the

Pictures Generation. Nor were they at home with the clumpy
monolithic expanses of their Neo-Expressionist contemporaries,
where the hand of the artist was returning in newly bombastic
form. Rather his works were both resolutely unique, yet wholly
interchangeable, affectingly hand wrought, yet impersonal,
they were a work where the hand of the artist merged seamlessly
with the hand of anonymous labor. The <u>Surrogates</u> were undeni-
ably paintings, as much as Rymans, or Mardens were paintings,
and yet, more than any that had come before, they also were
representations of painting. In other words, the <u>Surrogates</u>
were works that were simulations, intangible projections,
while remaining wholly insistent on their status as things.
They were both apparitions, and cold hard facts.

It is this this uncanny sensation of looking at an idea
made solid that I often confront in McCollum's work, as though
I have found myself surrounded by dream objects, in the middle
of the indentured productions of some sort of magical realist
sweatshop, the exhibition space itself transforming into a representation of itself, acknowledging itself as one of an endless
procession of white sterile rooms, which hold a similarly infinite procession of distinct yet wholly interchangeable objects.
In this way McCollum's work holds a memory of the industrially
serialized past, while troubling the conventions of the endlessly customizable present. It is this tension between the representation, the copy, and its material form, its place in the
concrete world, and in the lives of human beings, articulating
both the chilling alienation and the democratic potential
of mass production, that courses throughout McCollum's project.
Like all great artists, he offers no easy solutions to these
conflicts.

Please join me in welcoming Allan McCollum.

The Ritual of Everyday Life:
On the Migrating Objects of Jay DeFeo

First published in <u>Jay DeFeo</u>, Mitchell-Innes & Nash, New York 2014,
p. 5-18.

> … far from sucking the sixteen stones turn and turn
> about, I was really only sucking four, always the same,
> turn and turn about. But I shuffled them well in
> my pockets, before I began to suck, and again, while
> I sucked, before transferring them, in the hope of
> obtaining a more general circulation of the stones from
> pocket to pocket. But this was only a makeshift that
> could not long content a man like me. So I began to
> look for something else …
> —Samuel Beckett

One could imagine it being turned over and again, pinched
between her fingers as she looked at student paintings and
chatted with colleagues, then think of it intermingling with
loose change and pocket lint until it found its way to the bed
of a copy machine, where it would be pressed tightly between
her palm and the optical glass as the LED eye beam scrolled
back and forth. It would journey back from the Art Institute,
Mills College, or any of the other schools she passed through
as a teacher, to her Fillmore home, then Larkspur, or later
Oakland, just as it had beforehand, and begin the trip again
with her the next day, next week, or next month, its orbital
period as much in flux as hers. It would be photographed, pos-
sibly with its little carrying case if it had one, positioned

in raking morning light one day, washed by studio floods the
next, then later its image would be enlarged to an unnatural
scale, be cut out, laid roughly on the surface of a drawing and
haloed by an array of stray marks, without any stable ground
to give gravity proper purchase or it a sense of context. There
it would loom like a monolith over the page, before it would
be abstracted as a string of forms in thick oil on canvas, or
sketched in arcing geometries like a half-completed diagram,
shifting scale again, before reappearing in still other forms.
It would appear in photographs of her home and studio, the
images positioned uncomfortably between works of art, studies,
and simple documentation, showing the object in its mundane
existence, a nod to its modest belonging in the quotidian. Yet
the object would also perform as a compositional element, acting
in the service of a picture rather than as its focus, reduced to
schematic line and shape by the eye of the camera or the swipe
of charcoal. Its image would bounce from surface to surface,
material to material, going dormant for a period only to return
later. In some instances it was a muse just as she sometimes was
for other artists, at others a memento of those very relationships, all the while soaking up the atmosphere she was in as
it acted as her own personal satellite, circulating through the
world with her. And just as it cycled to and fro, so did its
image, moving from canvas to page to emulsion; each arrival of
its echo would see it stretching and contorting in a seemingly
endless game of telephone. Then abruptly she would abandon it,
and some other object would take its place and be animated by
her affections. It may seem fickle, perhaps, but maybe it was
the object that changed on her rather than she on it. But that
did not matter, for it would likely return later with renewed
significance, reinstated to its position as the passive recipient
of her movement through the world. One could think of this in
less absolute terms, that her object never really changed, it
simply shifted physical form, that what constituted it were her
attentions, and these attentions are what gave it shape.

Such is the nature of the ritual object. It acquires
meaning through its circulation, usually among a group, and it

can easily exhaust itself, run aground, be replaced, because it
is little more than a container for the meaning those proximate
to it fill it with. Ritual objects are above all else allegorical,
looked to for symbolic meaning while also treated as another
thing in the world (you drink the wine that symbolizes Christ's
blood just as you would any other wine). The ritual object is
literally infused with meaning just as it is infused with the
secretions of the bodies who covet it and pass it among themselves; it has no significance outside of this flow, it is a husk.
It achieves meaning through gradual investment, builds it up
as actions accrue over time in moments of habitual communion.
That is to say, when it first arrives, it is simply a vessel, a
prosthetic; its most pronounced quality is that it is something
noticeably incomplete, and this incompleteness often implies the
bodies that move it through the world. Objects are constituted
by the acts that people commit with them, and ritual objects
are exemplary in this regard, for the ritual object lays this
process bare. And from these acts meaning arises, and can arise
anew, tabula rasa, with each new group that posits an investment in that thing. This is how an epithet can turn into an
expression of camaraderie, or a torture implement can become
a symbol of salvation, from the banality of evil and the all-
too-common brutality perpetrated by the powerful on the power-
less, to its improbable metamorphosis into a symbol of brother-
hood, of belief, of atonement: a tool of exclusion transformed
into a symbol of collectivity. The torture device is well suited
for such a transformation given its intimate connection to the
body. The cross implied the body even before Christ, the empty
space at its center being a place we could all potentially occupy.
That was its initial terror and later, its affective potency.

Jay DeFeo began her engagement with the ritual object
early in her life, painting the devotional signs of the masses:
crucifixes rendered on paper in splashy reds and yellows,
some of the earliest of these containing a smeary Christ-like
figure embedded within them, as though his body were merged
with the structure of the cross. These came to her on travels
abroad, first in Paris and then with regularity in Florence,

the practice following her back to New York where the crucifix
even appeared in sculptural form. Perhaps because she had little space at her disposal, her objects were often for the hand,
able to be easily passed around, put in a suitcase, carried at
one's side. In 1953 she made a cross, two sticks wrapped in canvas administered as though it were a tourniquet, drenched in
a thick coat of plaster, which further evoked something like a
bandaged limb, a motif that would reappear some 20 years later
in her punning work Untitled (R. Mutt's Cast) (1973). The cross
appears like a body and an object, the tourniquet providing
structure and suture all at once. Rather than a cross that
might receive Christ, it appears like Christ's body merged with
the cross, its abject slouch more that of a tortured figure than
an icon, the drape of his loincloth echoed in the fabric knot
that acts as a wounded form both attached to and attaching the
trough sticks together. The object itself has achieved a patina,
a browning and fraying of the edges that betrays its passage
through the world as one among many things that moves through
anonymous hands. Instead of being a symbol of suffering, it
is as though the cross itself had suffered injury and is being
made whole again in its coming together as an object, like a
wounded limb bandaged not simply to heal, but to become more
than it was, adding that bandage to itself for perpetuity
rather than shedding it at some point when wholeness was
re-achieved, another instance of accumulation, of patchwork
expansion. More exactly, it is a stick, or fragments of a stick,
bandaged once severed, becoming a cross in its mending. It
would continue to be added to with each future moment of viewing or transport, for each of these instances would animate
it further.

Rather than continue her focus on the iconography of
the ritual object, DeFeo instead came to treat the production
of her works with ritual precision. Just as the ritual object
accrues meaning incrementally and over time through a repetitive
process of investment and stewardship, DeFeo came to favor producing paintings through a process of slow accumulation in lieu
of the explosive and loose gestural compositions that were common

at the time. This evolution was slow, but by the mid-1950s the individual mark in DeFeo's work had become incidental, insignificant. Instead, what formed on the canvas occurred gradually, first in her painting <u>Origin</u> (1956) or <u>The Verónica</u> from the following year, whose all-over compositions consist of an array of almost identical marks configured like feathers on a bird's wing. Furthermore she began employing a palette knife, which created even greater uniformity among her marks. If the gestural mark had become the sign of radical individuality in the hands of a select few postwar New York painters and their champions, hers had a distinctly communal air. Each move of the brush or palette knife was set in a sea of identical brethren, no one standing out from the others, none overlaid with added significance. Should things have continued in this vein, one could imagine a serial mark making that would link her to the likes of Agnes Martin, Lee Lozano, or Yayoi Kusama (of these three, Lozano shared the most with DeFeo, especially in her gruelingly physical <u>Wave</u> paintings from 1967–1970). But soon even those lowly marks disappeared, receding into the surface of the encrusted caked-on expanse she called <u>Incision</u>, or the more iconographic <u>The Jewel</u> (1959), an epic ten-foot-tall painting with a star-like form surrounded by deep reds and black. <u>The Jewel</u> looks like an excavation site, as though the yellows and whites of its cruciform were unearthed from the strata of oil paint using spade and pick, a fantasy that makes one speculate as to what might lie beneath the surface of <u>Incision</u> (1958–1960), as if it too had something beneath its mute topography waiting to be unearthed. The painting's very title lies precariously between the description of an act and an indication of what is hidden, patched up, sealed through the application of generous helpings of grey muddy paint like a sutured wound. By this time her work lacked any evidence of the explosive spatters of paint or brushwork that had momentarily appeared in her canvases from the early 1950s, an intermediary moment when her identification with the expressive and emotive tenets of Action painting seems to have produced a parallel inhabitation of its style. By the time <u>Incision</u> was completed in 1960, gritty

and heavily worked surfaces had replaced the indexical residues
of furious motion, light and airy compositions were sacrificed
for heavy tarlike expanses of paint, and where there were any
signs of a mark, it appeared as though it had been imprinted
into the surface by an enormous weight. Terms like "composition"
or "arrangement" no longer seemed to apply; instead the paintings appeared to be stamped with meaning, literally impressed
with iconography like some ancient rune.

The most communal mark is the impression, the simple
transcription of contact, the pressure of one thing upon another.
Faceless and nameless it betrays no virtuosity; it is a byproduct of living more than an expression of it. The imprint is
simply what happens when bodies come into contact. This trajectory reached its pinnacle with The Rose (1958-1966), whose
weight and physical presence belie comparison to any other
painting before it or since; an almost alien object that simultaneously refused both Greenbergian dogma and the Minimalist
responses it solicited. It was as though it appeared from
another evolutionary process, another history of painting all
its own, and in a sense it did. If we accept the Abstract
Expressionist mark as gendered bravado, strongly identified
with masculinity and Cold War individualist exceptionalism, we
must see DeFeo's slow accumulations as something of a response.
What existed was an aesthetic rhetoric that treated masculinity
as the default subject position of expression, that in turn,
made no place for her unless she was interested in impersonating
it. She was forced, instead, to proffer not just a model for
painting, but a painterly lineage all her own, one that gave her
the same expressive carte blanche her male colleagues were not
required to earn. This did not come from a position of resistance;
she never described her work in political terms; she refused
any appellation ascribing gender to her work, preferring gen-
der-neutral terms (it bears noting that on more than a few occa-
sions it was assumed that she was a man on the basis of her name
alone) and she had even less interest in the term "feminist."
No, she began this process because she had to in order to keep
working. In the end, she would out-scale and out-weigh her

Abstract Expressionist contemporaries in literal terms, not by
being more expressive and brash, but by rejecting the very
evolutionary model their work implied. If their sublimity was
ejaculative spatter and expanses of willowy diaphanous color,
hers would be monolithic, opaque, and solid. By the end of the
1960s, she had set herself up outside of their historical trajectory, as though her work had preexisted not only their own,
but their art history as well.

But embarking on such a mission is no small task. In the
years leading up to The Rose, DeFeo had slowly formulated a style
that was almost geologic, and a method of working that approached
the devotional. By the time its completion neared, she was less
the author of The Rose than its humble steward, passing by
to keep it whole and healthy, tending to its array of ailments,
such as its slow migration toward the floor, all the while dutifully adding layer after layer of heft to its bulk. She spoke
of the tedium and necessity of her work with the exhausted
stoic resolve of one who cares for an invalid relative for years
on end, and sees no end in sight (perhaps the painting would
never have been completed had she not been evicted from
her Fillmore Street apartment where it was housed). Rather than
Action painting, hers was a painting of accretion, a painting
where time spent was time spent. It was over this period that
her mark completely receded under the weight of paint: where
she had once brushed its surface, she now built it, and in turn
sometimes she carved at it, alternating between additive and
subtractive activities. Her act became anonymous like the slow
work of nature, achieving the imperceptible rhythm of the tides
rather than volcanic expulsions of emotive power. Looming like
an exhumed rock face in her studio, wedged in a bay window for
a period of nearly eight years, the painting had to be, as is
well known, literally cut out of her apartment and lowered by
forklift through her window, its heft having reached almost one
ton. The painting would shift and ebb with a change of season,
the force of its weight wedging it deeper into its architectural
frame. It was subject to the elements due to the enormous
amount of material it contained, experiencing these effects in

a manner no other painting would. That is to say that it ceased behaving like a painting, but instead acted like the rock faces it resembled, contracting in the winter, expanding in the summer, slowly settling into the spot made for it; when the time came, it stubbornly resisted being excised from the room that had become almost continuous with it. And then, once torn free, it was gone, off on a bizarre trajectory filled with missed opportunities and false starts, much like the one on which DeFeo herself was about to embark.

The Rose would be one of the last works that would borrow symbolic weight from established iconography; neither geology nor crosses would reappear in her paintings with the regularity or emphasis they did before, nor would the sun, not even as a negative imprint into one of her surfaces. Such motifs would be relegated to the industrial eye of the camera. But in The Rose, the sun, the earth, and the cross were one singular form, compressed together through the slow work of time, no single moment isolated out, a daily practice of service realized in unending layers of paint. Now that sort of work was finally over. After The Rose left her apartment, their lives together would be untangled, the painting going first to the Pasadena Museum and later the Bay Area, where it would be hidden away beneath strata of plaster in a conference room of the San Francisco Art Institute. It would take years for her to return to working, or, rather, to call what she was doing since the completion of The Rose, work. Instead, for this period, she simply did things, made drawings, took photographs, but with little idea that this was a continuation of her practice. She lamented not being able to work, as she put it, she "needed some time to mend," engaging in what she referred to as "a six-year dropout." When she did find a way forward, she kept things relatively small, mostly works on paper: photographs, collages, slight drawings. Displacing the grandeur of crosses and the stoicism of the geologic were symbols of her daily existence in works derived from the commonplace around her. All of which seemed the opposite of the processes she deployed in The Rose in every way. For the new works tended to be fast if not

instantaneous, as it was with the photographs and the Xeroxes,
which can be thought of as exemplary objects of this period:
ephemeral, multiple, serial. They were as light as The Rose was
heavy, as quick as The Rose was slow, as playful as The Rose
was stoic. Small objects would now receive her devotion, offering her a less demanding muse, and giving her work a quickness
it had not had for over a decade. To start out, she began with
her body and its increasingly fragile boundaries, and in this,
another story is told, one of her body subjected to the conditions of being an artist, its stresses, its toxins, its financial
distress, and the foraging around necessary to simply keep
working. If her life and career momentarily disappeared into
the granite surface of The Rose, they reappeared in the fragments and debris it left in its wake.

The first of her object muses were the teeth out of her
own head, a removal from her body that was as violent as the
extraction of The Rose from her apartment. Banded together in
gold, they fit into a hole in her skull, a combination of her
actual teeth and porcelain ones molded for her. This ghastly
hybrid object, both of her and alien to her, would act as a kind
of codex for the work that would continue until the end of her
life. The teeth were a part of her body that were no longer just
part of her body; they were a fusion of her body and the outside world. They were something that would fit into her body,
all the while reminding her of their foreignness. Even in death,
they would be independent, remaining behind to continue circulating through the world. Her obsessions with future muses grew
from this prosthesis. They would all be things close to her: a
cup, her goggles, a fragment of a piece of jewelry, her tripod,
her kneaded erasers, a tissue box, and so on, and so forth. They
would all share this quality of proximity to the body, as bodies
that were not one, a synthetic appendage, incomplete without
her, something that at once fit her without being her. DeFeo's
was a ritual object as prosthesis, which literally only had meaning by interfacing with the body, and in particular, her body.

Regardless of what the object happened to be—many would
be palm-sized, for the hand, others could comfortably fit in a

suitcase as if mobility were her chief concern after producing
a work that so stubbornly kept its place, and all were alien
to the mass and weight that exemplified her practice up until
that point. From the small stature of these slight things, grand
forms arose whose theatricality and iconographic weight rivaled
her pre-<u>Rose</u> canvases. Hovering obelisks, a ghostly, truncated
sphere, a gaping void with an angular zag emerging from it,
all seemed to levitate from the haloes of white she crowned them
in. But unlike her early canvases, which seemed exercises of
prolonged investment in a singular monumental work, these privileged multiplicity, and together formed a constellation. Out
of one slight object, so many others would appear that would
convey its sides, its silhouette, one distended detail or another
making up an entire work. Each of these resulting works acted
as fragments as well, manifestations of passing instances of
contemplation and confrontation with her muses. She would give
them equally mysterious and oblique titles, <u>White Shadow</u> (1972),
<u>Lotus Eater No. 1</u> (1974), <u>Reflections of Africa II</u> (1988), none
of which betrayed their modest origins in the quotidian, or the
intentions behind the work. Like the objects they were based
on, they are partial figures, flattened, skewed, fragmented.
Sometimes these echoes would appear face-like, twisted into
expressions by the Xerox machine; at other times they seemed
unremarkably ordinary, occupying a tabletop or shelf in a
photograph; or they would appear starkly graphic, schematized,
and abstract. Each work that resulted was a point in a cycle
of formations and deformations that would manifest in a singular object, each operating like a star in a constellation,
as nodes that are autonomous when observed in isolation, but
when viewed from afar arrange themselves in a logic that spans
great distances.

From the diminutive pink cup given to DeFeo by Ron
Nagle, a friend and colleague at Mills College, a monolithic
black silhouetted form would end up on a series of drawings,
haloed in white, hovering like a shroud and given the title
<u>Seven Pillars of Wisdom</u>, but this occurred only after it had
been silhouetted by hand or turned over and again on the copy

machine. Or it could have been the other way around, the drawings initiating a reexamination of the object in the eye of the
copier. It makes little difference, because it is not the order
of things that matters, but the pathways between them that are
of import. It would be misleading to draw too sharp of a distinction between her Xeroxes and her canvases, the qualities
of each infecting and echoing the other. For example, in a Xerox
of her pink cup, she merged smudgy graphite with the plastic
layers of industrial pigment if only to make this continuity
between her mark, and that of the machine unmistakable. In
another of these one can just make out DeFeo's hand lurking in
the inky distance of thick toner, putting the copy machine in
equivalence to the brush, and further offering a reimagining
of her mark in collaboration with industry; the machinic accumulations of toner reminiscent of the thick layers of <u>The Rose</u>
she had applied by hand. In these gestures, the Xerox would
transcend its ephemerality and become another picture made by
accrual, her hand literally applying pressure onto the picture
plane. This is how she would locate the gaping maw of a tissue
box, compressing it onto the glass of the Xerox machine, turning it into a swollen industrial orifice shrouded in the dark
accumulations of toner on paper, and yet find in it the looping
regularity that animates her <u>Reflections of Africa II</u>, where it
would appear as almost Constructivist, with light chalk markings and dull whites giving it a hazy, sketch-like quality, the
painting seeming like both an industrial diagram and some sort
of alien piece of architecture. It would flatten and turn again,
coming back as another black-and-white Xerox, this time belch-
ing forth a Kleenex, turning and twisting in the coarse light of
the photocopier, as though writhing, its contents spilling out
this way and that, until a final image shows the box with a
black void in the center, empty and hollow, prefiguring her own
body's consumption from the inside.

     We would do well to remember that to see a constellation
one has to stand back and look to the gaps and spaces between
points. DeFeo makes us do the same, training our eye on the movement between works, concentrating our attentions on the invisible

lines between them from which an expansive figure can be dis-
cerned. We wonder how a 1972 photograph of a table in a shop
window could find its way into the center of a drawing from
1989 as a photocopy, as in her Seven Pillars of Wisdom No. 10.
But there it sits, as though gestating within it, a materially
and compositionally alien form plunked down at its center. We
are given the hallucinatory effect of viewing one work through
another, as though a slip in time had opened between them.
And with these repetitions scattered throughout her oeuvre
comes the possibility of infinite regress, framings of framings
of framings, for not only do DeFeo's gestures occur synchroni-
cally across works, they also extend back into her past and
uncannily into her future. As DeFeo put it in 1975, "Painting
is an endless growth of continuing images," and one imagines
this endlessness extending into and through the surfaces of her
works, opening up portals between them, connecting disparate
points. When we begin thinking in this way, her work becomes
rife with the possibility to compress and invert cause and
effect, manifesting openings through which the work bubbles
up through itself.

As a postscript, we could remember that the ritual
object is above all allegorical, that it delivers us meaning as
both metaphor and metonym, that it stands within our world
as it simultaneously reflects upon it. Here, the tissue box
appears as a suffering body, and yet of course it is one of the
things the suffering body relies on, especially a body being
ravaged by lung cancer. It would prompt DeFeo to remark,
during a lecture at the University of California, Santa Cruz,
in 1989, that the works are "really quite prophetic in as much
as they, to me, looking at them in retrospect, look quite symbolic of the oncoming knowledge that I have a very, very serious illness, namely lung cancer. And as I look back on this
series of drawings, they almost seem to be kind of an internal
view of that knowledge which I hadn't really known about,
you know, objectively speaking, at the time."

She could not, of course, see her own death on the horizon at the time they were made, something her repeated return

to the body as a fragment, as a frail and partial thing, would
seem to prefigure. That said, she was not immune to a fascination with prophesy, a fascination that all ritualists share,
for they see in life a cycle, a circular movement that endlessly
returns to the beginning, where the order of things is less
important than the cycle of endless returns. The objects,
in this sense, do contain the intimate knowledge of her demise,
or, rather, the ritual object is also an object of prophesy,
an object that assumes meanings and implications that it could
not logically contain, that it, as a signifier, is meant to perform just this sort of work, telling the future as though it
were the past, because its future is both behind and in front
of it. For in it is staged the unconsciousness of the group,
an unconsciousness that exceeds the boundaries of any individual, an unconsciousness that presents itself as timeless or,
rather outside time, just as DeFeo had to set her paintings outside of time, outside of history, to create a space in which she
could work. Ritual objects more than accept such projections,
they produce them, they create a location for mythology to be
inserted into the repetitions of daily life, they contain the
promise that the sum is greater than the parts, and that the
common can achieve divinity. Most importantly, this achieve-
ment, this ascent, is realized step by step. DeFeo wrote in her
journal that, "there is no such thing as inanimate matter &
that there is God or Divinity in all matter & it is all living
energy." Spiritualism aside, we are reminded that each experience of any object is another moment in its circulation through
the world, a circulation that imbues it with meaning, which
adds to it, and that this circulation occurs directly through
us. If matter is living, it is us who lend it life, who animate
it with our own, and thus it is through these objects that we
in turn live, and it was this intertwining of fates that DeFeo
made palpable.

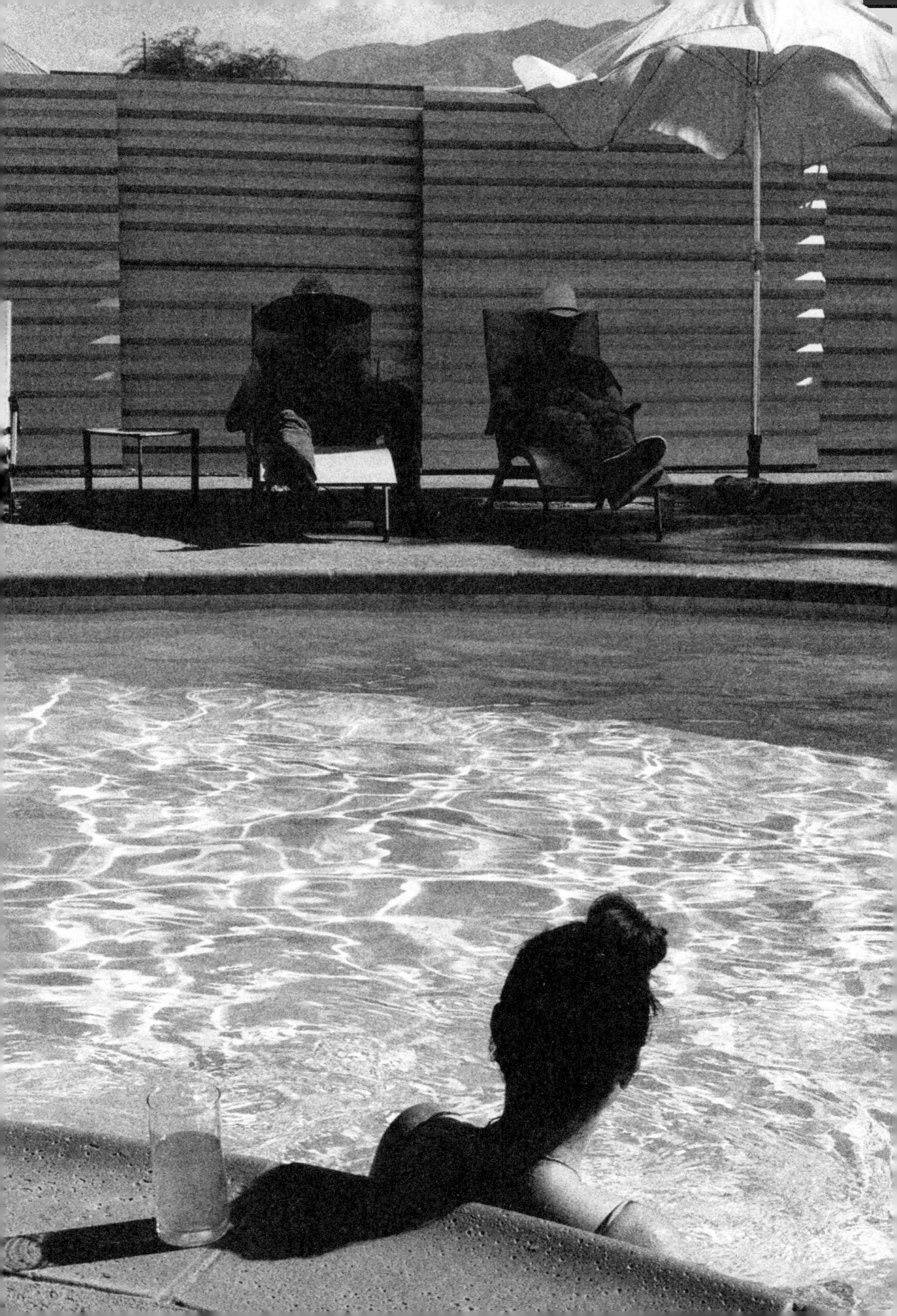

The Story of O:
Gesture in the Work of Laura Owens

First published in <u>Laura Owens</u>, Skira Rizzoli, New York 2015, p. 129-137.

... the eyes receive each others' reflections and impress
from there little images as in mirrors. Such an emana-
tion of beauty, flowing down through them into the
soul, is a kind of copulation at a distance.
—Achilles Tatius

We could begin with a mark: modest and momentary, one in a procession that seems to extend backward into the canvases indefinitely. Like ripples on water, each mirrors the last, sliding
easily between media: pixels merge into brushstrokes, gooey
expanses terminate in hard edges, screen prints transition into
gesso. A scribble made with a stylus and tablet is projected
onto a canvas, where it is traced by hand, taped out and filled
in with still more. Those that avoid the projector's lens experience similarly varied changes of state, some are exported as
stencils by a vinyl plotter that are then rubbed with charcoal,
yielding soft silvery black forms where hard pixels had previ-
ously sat, others are burnt into silkscreens or layered heavily
with impasto. Some might be photographed again, and set off
on still another sequence of transformations. During each phase
a material shift takes place, movements of the hand find their
way into the digital or industrial sphere, only to have that
trajectory reversed, a single slight movement of the hand rendered and re-rendered through an array of indexical media,

inscribed, cut out, piled up or covered over, each layering a
weaving together of disparate means. And while we suspect that
all this has transpired, that nothing here is simply what it
appears to be, the works are never explicit about what took
place; we simply sense the transformations that lay behind the
surface. Each discernable mark offers a fixed point between an
expanse of manifestations, from which the possibility for an
infinite number of other becomings extend. The phenomenological
immediacy of the work draws these layers forward; we see marks
inside or, more precisely, through other marks. Swooshing forms
are silhouetted, knocked out, and filled in by what lies beneath
them, a sequence of stenciling that reaches into the analog
and digital in equal measure, inflecting the former's concreteness with the latter's buoyancy, projecting false depths and
plastic thinness, as various moments of the painting's making
are laid bare and pressed up against the picture plane.

     This cadence extends throughout the paintings, marks
bounding from canvas to canvas, recalling how the words
"Pavement Karaoke" or rather, "P-A-V-E-M-E-N-T-K-A-R-A-O-K-E"
could be read across seven comparably massive canvases exhibited just a few months earlier in a pristine gallery space in
London's Soho neighborhood. Those too were crisscrossed with
swooshes and grids, bearing similar passages of thinness inter-
spersed with patches of viscous materiality. Here, a world away
in a lightly renovated warehouse in Los Angeles' grimy downtown, we have a similar sensation of reading across the works,
despite the absence of a phrase to drag us along their surfaces.
Instead, the repeating gestures are what is read, our eyes
following a cadence of blips and geometries into and out of the
canvases. Some of the accumulations of paint achieve a gelati-
nous protuberance that appears both cartoonish and bodily.
Others recall one of J. M. W. Turner's renderings of the sun
as a cake of white bulging off the canvas, but these paintings
offer much weightier passages, almost bowing under the heft
of their material. In some of the canvases, the colorful blobs
appear as if they were forced up through the playful imagery
that sits lightly on their surfaces, while in others the masses

appear as though they were plopped on top of the canvas like
a noxious garnish. In more than one painting, the goop seems to
dangle precariously, as if it could find its way to the floor
or onto a viewer's head if it were disturbed by a passing breeze.
But this unruliness never seems out of control, the blobs are
rigid, if appearing unstable, their placement precise despite
allusions to off-handedness, and they never engulf the canvas
as they do in the gravy paintings of Larry Poons or Susan
Rothenberg. Rather, they are contained in perfectly rounded
shapes, as crisp and hard as their contents are not.

But we should take a step back to where we first saw
the paintings, because this is where one always begins, at a distance, and from there we have the unmistakable sense that the
paintings are simply enlargements. Like the absent-minded drawings of a child giant, the pictures appear loose and monumental,
breezy renderings of sail boats, cats, flowers and so on, left
to tower over viewers, sometimes with massive newspaper personal
ads serving as a partial ground in another nod to the spaces
of domestic life. Rather than the familiarly brutish scale of
Richard Serra's dwarfing steel curves, we are left with a more
novel, playfully liberated sensation of smallness. Up close what
seemed simply oversized transforms into the phenomenological
oddity of multiple scales compressed together. We notice an individual touch executed at varied proportions, each at a remove,
none betraying a handmade authenticity. None of the marks seem
to have preceded the others; there is no hierarchy that is
apparent from their treatment. That is to say, these paintings
deny us a point of reference by which a mark might be evaluated. When confronted by deformations of scale, we usually have
our bodies to rely on for proportion, but here our bodies seem
out of synch, gestures of the hand appearing in a range of
scales, none of which seem as intuitive or as loose as their
shape would lead us to believe.

Just as scale refuses to resolve neatly, the question
of what constitutes an authentic or originary mark provides us
with little to go on, for no mark seems to wholly precede or
produce any other. The canvases are no more a play of original

and copy than they are simply a game of the small made large.
Instead, all of these oppositions are intertwined and confused.
The tone of painterly improvisation, what some call "hand," is
filtered through and imbedded within the digital and the industrial; who made the marks on the canvas is unclear and simultaneously irrelevant. Here, authorship is a far more complicated
proposition than simply being a question of the originator of
the mark, while not being locatable in one particular moment
or passage within the paintings, it also seems to be everywhere
present, diffused evenly through strata of disparate media.
In this sense, the authorial mark causes the various materials
and processes to flow together, reverberating throughout the
work, drawing distinct elements into a fleeting harmony.

And so, we confront moments where the messiness of paint
and the labor of screen-printing merge with the smooth scale-
lessness of the digital, as though the airbrushed foam sets of
Honey, I Shrunk the Kids were combined with the slippery anonymous surfaces of _Toy Story_. Even in the foam world we have
an innate sense of scale, our own reality maintained in its margins, but in the digital world we renounce our bodies, we simply
morph along with the scene, big to small and back again without
friction or pause. In the digital world, we lose the viscerality
of analog imaginings—more specifically, we loose how touch
and feel might extend into these universes of projection—rather
we are delivered wholly malleable abstractions, worlds where
proportion is fully elastic, where we are liberated from our
bodies. It is elating as much as it is alienating. Much art
incorporates one or the other of these effects, the haptic presentness of objects, or the fluid anomie of digitally morphing
imagery, but these paintings are not exclusively of one or
the other universe, managing to intertwine and conflate these
effects, making the distinctions between them irrelevant. From
them, marks and their varied manifestations blur analog and
digital procedures as they appear and reappear in painting
after painting in slightly altered forms and at varied scales.
Each acts as a singular expression when taken in on its own, but
in total, they evoke a disorienting semiotic and phenomenological

play, offering no singular point of resolution, other than the
elusive marks that pulse through them.

   We might recall seeing marks that behaved similarly in
earlier paintings, like one from 1997 that features a sequence of
primitive seagull-like forms ghosted by crude drop shadows on
a field of pure blue (<u>Untitled</u>, 1997). The seagulls are schematic,
two bubbly arcs in succession that lay dumbly on the painting's
surface. They have the same improbable roundness that the new
paintings feature, only more than a decade earlier, and compared
to the recent canvases, they have an air of coarse simplicity.
Yet a similar sense of disorienting scale is in evidence, the marks
seeming like doodles blown up huge, much as the painting's
blue ground evokes the sensation of total flatness and infinite
regress at the same time, the sky acting both as a monochromatic
surface and an expanse of unmodulated deep space. We could
think further back into Owen's practice, when this mark can be
found yet again in a sequence of small drawings from the mid-
1990s, or think of one of its more mature moments when this
sort of mark appeared in grand scale in 2011. This time the once
modest mark is smeared across nine huge canvases of identical
size, and within it a sea of others begin to appear, alluding
to fractal-like worlds within worlds, evoking a universe seen
through a microscope, curling brushstrokes filling the canvases
like microbes darting around in a purple petri dish. The mark
itself is now room-sized, and we are at the prequel to the
Pavement paintings, which took that massive mark and then fractured it, split it up, knocked through it with text, only to
have the gesture break up even further by being sold individu-
ally. It leads us to read the marks like a line of indecipherable
text, attuning ourselves to every detail as we might when
confronted with a foreign language that we have only a rudi-
mentary familiarity with, grabbing ahold of repeating sounds,
rhythms and cadences to guide us to some level of comprehension.
It is an automatic process and it is nearly impossible to resist
the impulse to search for some semblance of structure when
confronted with something methodically inscrutable. This
cadence is how the linearity of the massive purple smear could

later coexist with the fragmentation present in the Pavement
paintings. The text in the Pavement paintings will always imply
the sequence of others even without the mandate that they be
kept together. Regardless of whether or not they were shunted
to a multitude of far off places never to be hung together
again, they could remain whole in absentia. This fragmentation
is, of course, how the marks had always been treated, dispersed
to homes and institutions around the world like a scattered
jigsaw puzzle, but here the tension between the works' fragmentation and its continuity became all the more clear, bits of
the phrase circulating through the world, creating an ever
expanding and ever rearranging constellation with the potential
to return them to a linear procession hardwired into their surfaces. Now the paintings act like a thread connecting New York
City, London, Paris, Dubai, Aspen or wherever else the wealthy
hide their treasures. Each painting a portal between places,
each implying its absent brethren, who are held together by
a single gesture that can be read as a phrase as easily as the
text that ghosts it.

These reflections and repetitions articulate a gesture
that unfolds through strata of mediation, linking together
works, their sites of display, and the seemingly disparate layers that comprise them. With the slipping away of painterly
commonplaces such as the authentic or signature mark, different
concerns take their place. Forms function to draw moments of
production together, skewering the paintings into relations
with one another along an axis outlined by a series of internal
duplications and gestural cadences. This effect is native to the
digital and the possibility it offers of accumulating endless
layers at multiple resolutions, and the pinning together of its
infinite duplications in the virtual space of the screen. But
here, the expressive immediacy of the hand's gesture, the slippery world of the digital, and the furrowed histories of accumu-
lated décollage coexist in a single move, brought about in real
space, while rendered in masking layers manipulated by mouse
click and filled in later by a laborious accumulation of paint.
The canvases attest to a mark that extends across time and

276

through layers of mediation. A mark that occupies the work as a dull rumble, which links together rather than punctuates.

It is this model of gesture that Giorgio Agamben argued for, describing it as "a communication of communicability." For Agamben, the true gesture "has precisely nothing to say because what it shows is the being-in-language of human beings as pure mediality."[1] Here we could say that instead of asserting our "being-in-language" Owens is asserting our "being-in-aesthetics." We are constantly replaying, reusing, and transforming found materials (in language and in aesthetics alike), we quote and re-quote ourselves as we reiterate phrases and stories distorting them slightly each time, and this reuse and referentiality is not opposed to production, but is in actuality the core of production; it is through this that individuals and things are linked together, that new outcomes are produced, and on the surface of every discrete object is the evidence of a multitude that preceded it, whose marks are present on it like a sequence of runes; these points of connection draw the world along with the work wherever it may go. Thus, the location of the gesture is not simply in the act, in its manifestation in immediate and discrete terms, but rather it is in the space between manifestations or materializations, in the gaps through which the gesture passes unnoticed until it finds something to reverberate off of, resonating with what it is compatible with, and in so doing, draws a pathway through the world that is specific to it.

Owens displayed a very early sensitivity to the in-between, as in a 1997 painting showing two canvases hung obliquely in relation to one another, and it makes sense that the first engagement with the gaps between things would be an attempt to simply depict it. As Owens had recounted, "I'd been thinking about the relationship between the viewer's body when looking at paintings and walking past them or even being in-between them or seeing them in your periphery."[2] Two years later, this interest would present itself experientially in the pair of mirrored numbers paintings. Hung on opposite walls, it was impossible to see both at once, making the viewer the fulcrum between works, and the vessel of the works' transmission; it was through

the viewer and their movement, their pivoting, their attempts
to remember the specifics of the painting they were just looking at to compare it with the one they held in their view,
that draws the works into relation with one another. The scene
she had earlier only depicted is brought to life in the active
negotiation with the paintings as objects in space. In turning
between them, the paintings flicker into and out of perception,
alternating between a visual and a mnemonic experience, the
body of the viewer mediating their oscillation through its repositioning. That is to say, the physical movement of the viewer,
and their use of the memory of what they had just seen forms
the axis on which the pair of paintings establish meaning;
thus meaning is not located in the painting, but between the
paintings. As Owen's herself put it, the viewer "would be
between paintings … activat(ing) the whole space." The viewer
carries the work with them, and through the inhabitation of
the viewer, the work expands into the entire room. This simple
mnemonic prompt connects the canvases to one another as much
as it connects them to the world and people they are surrounded
by, and forms the basis for a gesture that extends indefinitely
as it dissipates through the bodies and the world they circu-
late within in the form of the new sensitivities they carry
with them. This chain of proximities distributes the gesture
of the work, sending its pulsations into an ever-expanding
field of relations.

But what does this sort of gesture mean to the history
of painting, which still relies on the authenticity of the mark
and its ability to express in a singular act? And we would
do well to consider that the mark is the residue of a gesture,
a snapshot of its passage, like a footprint or bullet hole,
different gestures leave different traces, both materially and
experientially. Owens puts it in terms of gender, asking " …
is it even possible for a woman artist to be the one who marks?
At the same time, in 2013, does anyone at all have this ability,
or is it an antiquated or sentimental idea? Isn't it interesting
that the male orgasm has a DNA imprint that will replicate
itself over and over again, reinforcing itself the way language

278

or naming might, but the female orgasm has no use, no mark,
no locatability? … I want to think about how it can be the
model for a new gesture."[4] To misunderstand Owens' definition
of this sort of mark as anti-authorial would be to position
the female as an absence, as lacking something her male counterpart could presume. Rather, this "female" gesture permeates
layers of mediation and reference, surging through boundaries
and calling forward the circumstances that surround it as it
diffuses through them. Rather than puncturing through, it
inhabits the layers it moves through causing them to resonate
with one another, and because of that, its scale and force are
far more expansive, leaving a multiplicity of markings in its
wake. We could say that for the masculine gesture, the mark
is its culmination, a singular impact that announces itself in
the explosive disturbance it makes, its energies dissipating
quickly. The gesture that Owen's posits favors connection over
finiteness; it locates meaning in connectivity, and pleasure
in cursivity.

It is just this notion of having no explicit use and
thus refusing instrumentality, while at the same time having
no "locatability" or no "ends," that so strongly resonates with
Agamben's notion of the potential of the gesture. He writes,
"… gesture breaks with the false alternatives between ends and
means … and presents means that, <u>as such</u>, evade the orbit of
mediality without becoming, for this reason, ends."[5] We have, in
Owens' painting, the proposition of a mark which neither finds
definition in a singular formal composition, nor as renouncing
composition for the open-endedness of process for its own sake.
Rather it is "the exhibition of mediality," a "purposiveness
without purpose," that extends through the works.[6]

Owens gives us neither the assertion of a singular and
expressive index of furious motion, nor its dismantling, the
latter being most familiar in painting of the postmodern period,
which perversely extended the Greenbergian model through
its ritualized parody, preserving it through acts of negation.
Owens' locates a third term adjacent to this binary, engaging
in an investigation of depth, the flatness of painting and

the grid, both in earnest and with a healthy dose of perversity. We see grids—that emblem of modernist resoluteness—defiled, punched through with arrays of willowy flowers and cartoonish scrawls rendered in pastels or the vulgarities of hot pinks and yellows, but still they offer the staid and stoic assertion of painterly flatness and the material rigor we had come to expect of them. Owens deploys these grids in paradoxically representational terms, giving them drop shadows, or transforming their somber geometries into gingham tablecloths or plant trellises. It is not that these are incompatible moves, rather they show the opposition between decorative flourish and formal seriousness is specious at best. She makes this abundantly clear at the beginning of her career, where, in one of her earliest paintings, a gingham motif and a hard edged grid are paired with a shallowly rendered shadow: illusionism, materialism, and the decorative smeared together in one deceptively spare composition. She does not hide the grid; each evocation of this modernist scaffolding stands to the fore of her canvases, operating as a signifying element while engaging in a provocative play with painterly depth and deductive structure. The result is a set of marks that refuse to fit neatly into any discourse about materialism and referentiality. In 2011, the grid paintings reappear in the faces of functioning clocks, the hands poking out from the canvas like hash marks, fragmented lines, and irregular crosses that constantly rearrange themselves. Then in 2012, the grid would become the scaffolding holding a series of paintings together, extending between the canvases which cling to it like a creeping vine. False depth shifts into actual depth and modernist rhetoric becomes domestic kitsch, like a sequence of Mondrians in drag, utopian functionalist form is brought into the vulgarities of the commonplace, contaminated by the improvisation and the "making do" that defines everyday life.

It was Judith Butler who, in the maelstrom of 80s identity politics, pointed out that even gender is something we try on, perform, and dispose of, an insight that was presaged in C.E. 8 by the story of Tiresias in Ovid's _Metamorphoses_, who as punishment was turned into a woman by the god Hera. After

spending eight years as a female, he would be called upon for
the expertise he acquired to settle a bet between Hera and Zeus
as to which sex derived more pleasure from copulation. To this,
he responded that while male pleasure was as narrow as it was
explosive, like a swiftly running stream, female pleasure was as
wide and deep as the sea. His answer displeased Hera, making
Zeus the winner of their bet, and as punishment Hera struck him
blind, as though he, in confessing this, had betrayed a secret
held in confidence. Blinding was unmistakably a sexual punishment, a second phallic smiting, a reminder of both the frailty
and limitations of the masculine. To ameliorate this act, Zeus
gave him divine insight, his vision no longer one that pierced
and separated, but one that connected things together, that
experienced the world as a sequence of trajectories rather than
an accumulation of finite things and impermeable surfaces; it
was a transformation from the divisive to the cursive. His was
now a vision attuned to fluidities.

What becomes literalized in this story is the arrival of
a kind of sight, one that follows the harmonies and reverbera-
tions between things, that sees a network of interrelations and
rearticulations rather than hard edges and discrete entities.
Owens' work inhabits this way of seeing, finding meaning in resonances, and redirecting our attentions to them. She draws the
grid of modernity into the territory of the backyard gardener,
the hobbyist, the domestic, appearing as plant trellises, newspaper personals, gingham table cloths, screen doors, and so on,
deflating its pomposity while embracing its formal utility. And
transforming the gestural mark into a slow rumble that permeates across works and time, emerging with renewed intensity in
unexpected forms. Owens succeeds in formulating a gestural mark
that is not exhausted in its expression or repetition, that is
not singular in its moment, but seems to gain momentum through
its reduplication and echoing, reverberating through the paintings, and the people and places they come into contact with. It
is the pleasure of connectivity, of things being in connection
with one another, rather than in the awe of the explosive, discrete, and finite. It acts as we do in life, at once inhabiting

the extant forms around us, mimicking and mirroring what has
come before, and adding our own momentum to them while also
using them for our own purposes, altering their trajectories in
a manner that finds specificity in repetition, in the collaging
together of the iterations of others, which are themselves borrowed, a sequence of endless duplications and recombinations
that build over time, finding agency in these acts while culti-
vating a sensitivity to the significance each pathway carves
through the world.

NOTES

1. Giorgio Agamben, <u>Means Without End: Notes on Politics</u>, trans. Vincenzo Binetti
and Cesare Casarino, University of Minnesota Press, Minneapolis 2000, p. 59.

2. "Laura Owens in Conversation with Scott Rothkopf," in <u>Laura Owens</u>, JRP|Ringier,
Kunsthalle Zurich 2006, p. 195.

3. Ibid., p. 197.

4. "Optical Drive: Sarah Lehrer-Graiwer Talks with Laura Owens" <u>Artforum</u>, March
2013, p. 236.

5. Agamben, <u>Means Without End,</u> p. 56.

6. Ibid., p. 57.

Lesson: Notes for an Introductory Lecture

First published in <u>Akademie X: Lessons in Art + Life</u>, Phaidon, London 2014, p. 14-27.

It all begins with basic materials: cellulose, lipids, proteins, plastics, our physical presence among other physical presences and the sensations those presences produce. The term "aesthetics" comes from the Greek <u>aisthētikos</u>, meaning to perceive, or "relating to perception by the senses"[1] ("perception" from the Latin <u>percipere</u>, meaning to "seize, understand"). Thus aesthetics is understanding that arises through the senses (from the Latin verb <u>sentire</u>, meaning to "feel") when bodies come into contact with one another. And so, aesthetic judgment is situated in the world of things, not concepts, and aesthetic meaning is the result of physical experience rather than the "reading" or "decoding" of the abstract, symbolic, or metaphorical. In short, aesthetics does not produce meaning in the manner language does.

Objects have no meaning in themselves, rather they are prompts for a field of possible meanings that are dependent on context. Meaning often implies something fixed, but in this instance, let's understand meaning as that which arises as the result of an object's exposure to a specific circumstance. That is, objects facilitate certain outcomes rather than contain certain meanings, and each interaction presents the possibility for a range of outcomes to arise that are not wholly predictable. These interactions accumulate over time, thus the meaning of an object is ever evolving. When we assume that objects simply contain meaning, this complex dynamic is obscured.

Aesthetics is a primary form of communication whose effects are material, manifest through the actions and behaviors it engenders. The form of an object dictates how we relate to it and to one another while around it, for example how we treat a person behind a desk differently from one across a table from us. These effects are established through repetition, and these systems become more complex when realized on a societal level where aesthetics serve to indicate an array of nuanced power relations. For example, when we are confronted with a traffic light, a police officer, or enter a library, our role within a network of power relations is communicated to us in an instant, and our behavior changes as a result. These changes are immediate and often automatic or unthought. We perform in radically different and often incongruous ways in different contexts, or to put it more precisely, we occupy different subject positions depending on the context and how we are being addressed. This is how aesthetics is political. It signals our role as members of the polis (the citizenry). It tells us how we are to expect to be treated and how we should treat others. This is what Jacques Rancière was referring to when he wrote of the "distribution of the sensible," as "the system of self-evident facts of sense perception that simultaneously discloses the existence of something in common, and the delimitations that define the respective parts and positions within it … determin[ing] those who have a part in the community of citizens."[2]

But what about art? The most precise thing one could say about art is that it is a discourse about aesthetics staged through aesthetics, and thus has the capacity to both examine and enact the production of aesthetic meaning. Therefore, art is capable of interrogating how aesthetics produces a distribution of the sensible, while also speculating on how this distribution might be transformed or expanded. Like philosophy, which seeks to know knowing, art seeks to perceive perceiving in its broadest sense. Thus, art must keep this process of perceiving open; it must endlessly defer an arrival at conclusive meaning to maintain its focus on how meaning is established.

One way that art holds aesthetic meaning at arm's length
is by making the familiar strange, placing meaning at the horizon, out of reach but still in sight. In so doing, art reflects
what it means to be in a world of aesthetics. It affirms that to
be human is to be within aesthetics, not simply a consumer of
aesthetic messages, but as an agent within a dynamic system of
aesthetic producers. Art requires circulation to keep its object
of inquiry present; stasis is its enemy, for its meaning is established through its exposure to a range of circumstances. This
transitory nature is what John Kelsey was pointing to when he
wrote, "The gallery is … an activated space where information,
bodies, and money are rapidly circulated, and where this power
of circulation is momentarily frozen in images and objects."[3]
If we fail to realize that the stasis of the exhibition space is
momentary, we will see in the exhibition hall what Theodor Adorno
punned into existence—the museum as mausoleum—and artworks
as memento mori.[4] The exhibition hall (whether a museum, kunsthalle, commercial gallery, etc.) is a distribution hub for the
work of art, expanding the circulation of artworks through the
actions and activities that take place in these contexts (schools
serving a similar function), and in so doing, they are also
producers of an artwork's meaning.

Objects are given meaning through use, and over time
certain uses become naturalized; what results is convention.
Through the accumulation of patterns of use, certain conventions
become standardized. Painting, for example, has developed a
certain set of base conventions (e.g. canvas, rectilinear form,
wall as support, portability). These conventions form the starting point for a dialogue, an agreement regarding the nature of
the communication that will be taking place. For example, if a
painting has a "conventional" relationship to the wall on which
it hangs, we would be acting in bad faith if we were to discuss
the paint on that wall as part of the work. In art, these
conventions designate what is inside and what is outside of
the work. The boundary between the work and its surroundings
is manifest through its adherence to convention.

Conventions arise from the patterns of behavior that objects encourage, and constitute a tacit agreement between entities engaged in communication. Conventions are thus reinforced over time even as they slowly change form; like a path worn through a meadow, day-to-day changes are often imperceptible. Convention is necessary, because in order to communicate we must begin with a point of reference, something that we hold between us collectively. But just as convention helps to make actions understandable by identifying them as significant, it also turns a blind eye to things whose significance is emergent or unexpected. Thus we often discount the context in which an artwork is shown and the significance of "secondary" materials, such as writing about the work, documentation, the artist's lecture, and so on. Such materials are the chief means by which an artwork enters the public sphere. This is why Dan Graham's comment that works of art only exist once they have been written about and photographed continues to resonate.[5] Graham's insight was to see these extensions of the work of art as an essential element of its existence in the world, for how a work lends itself to being photographed, or is available to written description, is central to how it is understood, especially to those who will never see it in person (who are in the majority). In this sense, works of art only exist as art through their circulation and distribution.

Each aesthetic production is a recombinatory process, a piecing together of fragments taken from elsewhere. Matter is never destroyed, it is simply recycled: the gold filling in your tooth was once at the center of a star. Likewise, all productions are dependent on the existence of previous productions (one could think of convention as the aggregate of this dependency). The anthropologist and semiotician Claude Lévi-Strauss proposed the <u>bricoleur</u> as the model aesthetic producer who "derives his poetry [<u>poesis</u>] from the fact that he does not confine himself to accomplishment and execution: he 'speaks' not only with things … but also through the medium of things … by the choices he makes between the limited possibilities."[6] In short, the <u>bricoleur</u> draws things from her/his surroundings to redirect their circulation through the world. Because they operate under clear constraints, they also present the possibility of alternative productions that could be conceived under those very same constraints. This is how bricolage objects are not only things, but also propositions of a certain ethics of production, indicative of an attitude toward making that privileges transparency and foregrounds interdependency. Thus bricolage is a potent tool for the disenfranchised, since it works against self-validating power by tinkering with established meaning, undermining the myth of its solidity by displaying our ability to repurpose and pervert it to alternate ends.

As Vilém Flusser defines it, communication is "a process by which a system is changed by another system in such a way that the sum of information is greater at the end of the process than at its beginning."[7] To communicate is to add; there is no communication that is subtractive. While all communication is materially indexed, we do not always know what to look for. Consider an example that Kenny Goldsmith offers in his book Uncreative Writing. When one writes an email, a mass of additional information is attached to the text by the email program. This text is the material trace of the network that distributes the text, and is usually invisible to both the sender and receiver.[8] In the act of sending, the message is produced, for it does not exist as an email prior to its being sent. Distribution is always concrete and integral to production. Even the internet, the collective fantasy of a dematerialized anomie, leaves ample physical residue around the world.[9] As Google says, "Visit where your computer has already been."

To this end, what would the pulsing electricity that transmits an email be without the computer or program to receive it? Is there really a clear boundary between these entities? And if not, how would we claim one as the message and the other as mute carrier? If this seems unanswerable, it might help simply to reverse the flow and work against convention. For example, let us place a digital image into a word-processing program (a computer program acts like a convention). When we open an image file in a word processor, we see a stream of symbols that make little sense. Without the proper interpretive conventions in place, the image is no longer an image, yet the file remains unchanged. And what if once we open the image file in a word processor, we treat it accordingly? What if we edit it and then try to open it within an image application? Small changes enacted within one program create large transformations within the context of another. When these two applications or conventions are read "against" one another, the logic of the image file is partially revealed. But what is this new form that exists between these applications, between modes of distribution? Is it a new possibility or a dead end?

The notion of critique or negation is a convention borrowed from philosophy; it is part of a language game. Only in a hypothetical world could one object negate or even be "about" another. This is why negation and critique make no sense in art or in the world of objects; they are conceptual and linguistic operations alone. For example, when Robert Rauschenberg erased Willem de Kooning's drawing, he did not negate it, he added to it, he placed marks on top of it. The original drawing is still present, both in the object's history and literally within the object itself. The drawing is more than what it was, not less. All activities are additive; this applies even to those actions that seem immaterial such as discussion, which can radically transform the meaning of an object.

No one managed to use the transformation that discourse can effect on aesthetic objects more dramatically than Marcel Duchamp. As Thierry de Duve observed, the readymade put on display the "pact that would unite the spectators of the future around some object, an object … bearing no other function than that of a pure signifier of the <u>pact itself</u>."[10] De Duve is describing the social contract of aesthetics, the agreement we tacitly make to accept a certain set of preconditions. The readymade displays the pact that initiates the social relations around an object and the behaviors that ensue. Duchamp showed that this agreement did not require a specific object (which is not to say that his objects were not specific); the object simply acts as a marker of an agreement, a fulcrum around which

a particular social organization forms, and meaning arises from
how this group makes use of that agreement. All aesthetics are
the result of a similar sort of pact, and art is where it is possible to lay that agreement bare.

This agreement constitutes the quality of the art object
that Rosalind Krauss termed "exhibitionality."[11] The term "exhibition" comes from the legal context, from the Latin _exhibere_,
literally to "hold out" before an authority. And so an exhibition
is a presentation to a sovereign power. Once this meant the
king, but now it implies the public, a term that capitalist demo-
cracies like to keep vague. Art is where this agreement is
consciously made, where individuals can step back and consider
the aesthetic agreements they engage in on a daily basis and
reimagine them. This social agreement is where the politics of
the art object lie, defined in the room, not somewhere else but
immediately in front of you. Thus the work of art exists in
the collective that is constituted through the artwork's existence as a point of reference.

This text, like all texts, conceals its collective nature.
While it may be written in a singular voice, it is an amalgam
of many entities. The voices of the editors, designers, printers,
binders, shippers, shop assistants who sold it to you or the web
page you ordered it from are all at work in the text, covered
over by inks and varnishes, cellophane and UPC codes. All of
these together constitute the meaning of this text. Yet we are
taught not to think of all the mediations through which it has
passed, changing along the way; we think instead of a single
individual addressing us. When we consider that we are actually
dealing with an object, an object with a history specific to
itself that is comprised by a multitude, we are allowed a possible opening into expansive worlds within worlds.

Some closing practicalities. Art school is an abstraction
of the art world, but the world it reflects is not necessarily
a contemporary one. Art schools are dispersed around the world
like alternate universes, microcosms of the best intentions, and
the most stubborn biases. … One must remember the art school
is an artificial scenario, a fantasy, and some are pleasant while

others are perversely hellish. Regardless of their construction, art schools reflect possibilities rather than facts. They contain a history of ideas and methodologies that are the product of their axioms; none are accurate, each is a fun house mirror, a distorted schema of the world. They provide a place from which to speculate on what the conditions of being an artist might be rather than a testament to what an artist necessarily is.

Remember that the conversation is always changing, and that there are many taking place simultaneously. If none are to your liking, you can easily invent a new one. Also, despite the amount of time wasted on discussing it, the market is not as powerful as some pretend. It does not think or make judgments. It is incapable of representing or communicating complexity. It is furtive, inconsistent and at best one circulation system among many. Those who discuss it with exuberant derision are most often its clergymen, giving it divine provenance and false solidity. The only rule is not to try to outthink it; the market is too stupid to outwit; treat it like the wind.

Speaking of clergymen, self-proclaimed populists who champion themselves as plainspoken "tell it like it is" warriors of art appreciation, are not to be trusted. Populism is a code for thinking that people are stupid; the populist critic uses this as an excuse to exercise self-validating authority. When artists are articulate about their work, the populist whines about elitism. Art requires a large investment of time and energy. Its discussion is complex and requires study and expertise. But just because the discussion of art is complex, it does not mean that it is elitist. Doctors are not elitist because they employ complex technical terminology. Art is one of the few disciplines where the claim is made that a complex discourse among its professionals makes its offerings elitist. The problem with this faux issue is that it conceals much more repressive and problematic aspects of art and aesthetics, mostly that access to the commons and to public discourse is almost exclusively mediated by large corporations and the supposedly inalienable right of free speech is often predicated on wealth. The populist critic is often the agent of such monopolies.

Approach one of these critics and suggest that the next time
they need medical treatment, you will act as their doctor.
If necessary, act as their doctor against their will.

Forgetting has its advantages. Get a Whitney Biennial
catalog from 20 years ago, do the same with a 20-year-old
auction catalog; how many artists do you recognize? Do the
same with _Artforum_, and pay attention to names in the ads, both
those of the artists and the galleries. Find out who had the
cover of _Artforum_ the most over its entire history. Have you
heard of him or her? Consider all the impending disappearances.

NOTES

1. The more common definition, "a set of principles concerned with the nature and appreciation of beauty, esp. in art," was adopted into English in the early 19th century, having been coined in Germany in the late 18th century as "concerned with beauty." This definition refers to the philosophical field of aesthetics. It is not germane to this discussion.

2. Jacques Ranciére, The Politics of Aesthetics, La fabrique éditions, Paris 2000, p. 12.

3. John Kelsey, "100%," in Rich Texts: Selected Writing for Art, eds. Daniel Birnbaum and Isabelle Graw, Sternberg Press, Berlin 2010, p. 19.

4. Theodor W. Adorno, "Valèry Proust Museum," Prisms, trans. Samuel and Shirley Weber, MIT Press, Cambridge 1967, p. 175.

5. Dan Graham, "My Works for Magazine Pages: 'A History of Conceptual Art,'" in Dan Graham, ed. Gary Dufour, exh. cat., Art Gallery of Western Australia, Perth 1985, p. 8-13.

6. Claude Lévi-Strauss, The Savage Mind, The University of Chicago Press, Chicago 1966, p. 21.

7. Vilém Flusser, "On the Theory of Communication," Writings, ed. Andreas Ströhl, trans. Erik Eisel, University of Minnesota Press, Minneapolis 2002, p. 8.

8. Kenneth Goldsmith, Uncreative Writing, Columbia University Press, New York 2011, p. 30.

9. See James Glanz, "Cloud Factories: Power, Pollution and the Internet," The New York Times, September 22, 2012.

10. Thierry de Duve, Pictorial Nominalism: On Marcel Duchamp's Passage from Painting to the Readymade, University of Minnesota Press, Minneapolis 1991, p. 115. Emphasis added.

11. Rosalind Krauss, "Photography's Discursive Spaces," The Originality of the Avant-Garde and Other Modernist Myths, MIT Press, Cambridge 1985, p. 131-150.

Toward an Aesthetics of Ethics

First published as "Introduction: Toward an Aesthetics of Ethics," in Ethics, ed. Walead Besthy, Documents of Contemporary Art, MIT Press/ Whitechapel Gallery, Cambridge and London 2015, p. 12-23.

> There are no static things. Everything is dynamic.
> —Lygia Clark, "Full Emptiness" (1960)[1]

It has become a commonplace observation that over the past 40 years artistic production has become increasingly reflexive about its relation to the social conditions that surround it, expanding into the complexities of the commons, and deploying increasingly open-ended and contingent conditions of reception. Such expansions are not only manifest under the umbrella of terms like "happenings," "institutional critique" or "relational aesthetics," but have also affected the way that the most conventionally realized and exhibited object-based practices are understood and enacted. Even painting, perhaps the most traditional of art objects, has been increasingly subjected to an analysis that incorporates systems of distribution and social relations in its assessments. For example, in his contribution to Wade Guyton's monograph Black Paintings (2011), the artist, critic, and gallerist John Kelsey observes that "[t]he gallery is no longer a theater of human activity or even passivity, but an activated space where information, bodies and money are rapidly circulated, and where this power of circulation is momentarily frozen in images and objects." He goes on to comment that Guyton's "canvases … are not so much finished, final things as they are a series of interrupted movements." David Joselit, in his essay "Painting Beside Itself," articulates a similar point, noting that artists such as Michael Krebber, Merlin Carpenter, and Jutta Koether "have developed practices in which painting sutures a virtual world of images onto an actual network composed of human actors, allowing neither aspect to eclipse the other."[2] Each of these statements would have seemed cynically perverse, if not absurd, some 20 years ago, but now they seem, if not obvious, then certainly not outlandish. Such a transformation reflects the culmination of the postmodernist war on aesthetic autonomy, marking the ascent of a dynamic and socially derived formalism that takes not only the significance of both the site of reception and mode of distribution of the work of art as a given, but recognizes this as integral to the meaning of the work itself.

ART AS PACT/ART AS SOCIAL CONTRACT

> ... artworks not only are products of given circumstances, they also contribute to the existence of these very circumstances.
> —Dorothea von Hantelmann, How to Do Things with Art[3]

Such a shift in contemporary art is not the subject of this volume, nor this introduction, but suffice it to say that this change is the result of numerous factors, not least of which is the radical transformation of the conditions of labor and production in the post-Fordist epoch, an era that saw the transition of western economies from secondary to tertiary, i.e. from industrially-based production to the ethereal world of finance capital, flexible workforces and the service industry (what has been variously described as "late capitalism" by the Marxist political theorist Fredric Jameson, "flexible accumulation" by the social theorist and political economist David Harvey, or as the third "Spirit of Capitalism" by economist Eve Chiapello and sociologist Luc Boltanski). If we think of the avant-gardes as a response to, and assimilation of, the effects of urbanization and industrialization in the 19th and early

20th century within aesthetic terms, the move toward both
socially constituted practices (i.e. those which have no specific
conventional art object as their focus) and the socially inflected understanding of conventional artistic forms should
come as no surprise, given the mass cultural changes that paral-
leled them. Numerous essays and books have addressed the social
dimensions of contemporary practice, yet despite this recently
emergent, widespread critical focus on the social parameters
of the work of art, the methodological implications—whether
they are from the perspective of production or that of the art
historian or critic—remain largely unexplored.

A full examination of this shift would require at least
a book length treatment, thus a more schematic outline will have
to suffice here. For provisional purposes the most significant
precedents for these recent developments both come from the
early 20th century: Constantin Brancusi's experimentations with
the interdependency of sculpture and its material support and
the eventual dissolution of the barrier between them, and Marcel
Duchamp's invention of the socially contingent work of art in
the form of the readymade; innovations that would quickly come
to define the trajectory of art of the 20th and 21st centuries.
The significance of the work of these artists is no revelation,
yet their reception is at this point incomplete, dominated by an
analysis that positions these works as a negation, refusal, or
critique of the conventions of art and artistic meaning, thereby
limiting the understanding of their importance for the contemporary moment. Rosalind Krauss, for example, describes Brancusi's
placement of the sculpture directly on the floor as a "reach[ing]
downward to absorb the pedestal into itself and away from
actual place,"[4] claiming it as a disassociation of the work of
art from its site of reception. Yet hindsight casts Brancusi's
gesture as a step toward sculpture's merging with its support,
confusing the distinction between the work and its frame,
and destabilizing rather than reifying the notion of aesthetic
autonomy. If it did manifest some form of aesthetic autonomy,
Brancusi's version only managed to hasten its exhaustion, his
work having become integral to a trajectory that has slowly

and steadily moved further into zones of interdependency and contingency, becoming a key precedent for the works of artists as ideologically and formally disparate as David Smith and Anthony Caro, whose work came to exclude any delineation between object and support; Minimalist practices exemplified by works like Robert Morris' landmark show of polyhedron forms at Green Gallery, New York, in 1964; or any number of Light and Space practices, where sculptural production was integrated with the architectural frame such that it could not exist without it; to numerous works of Michael Asher, where the institution itself—defined as a complex of social and material supports—is intertwined with, or "absorbed" into the work, just as much as the work is "absorbed" into its context. The works of contemporary artists such as Andrea Fraser and Merlin Carpenter draw this absorption of the context of art production to more extreme, and perhaps perverse, ends. These are but a few of many possible examples, and their diversity alone should indicate that this was not a transformation cloistered within a subgroup of 20th century art, but an integral element in the development of contemporary artistic discourse. Each of these endeavors shifted away from discreteness, refusing the possibility of separating the artwork from its context, precipitating a movement from the realization of the interdependency of object and support to the artwork's expansion into the social apparatus that surround it.

In tandem with Brancusi, Duchamp's readymades ushered in the understanding that the artwork was not only materially inextricable from its support (here realized as the social conditions that designated an object as an object of art), but further articulated its existence—and by extension, the existence of all aesthetics—as a form of social contract. Rather than initiating a slowly evolving discourse around the art object, the readymade marked a radical departure, defining the core of the work of art as an agreement located within a group that holds the artwork in common. Duchamp reduced the object at the heart of this agreement to a commonplace industrialized product, which in its initial deployment contained no aspiration for expressive or contemplative function. As a readymade, an object becomes the marker for the social contract, a node around which individuals congregate and transact, and it is this contract and those who are drawn together through it that give the work any possibility for artistic meaning. As the critic Thierry de Duve put it in his seminal treatment of Duchamp, <u>Pictorial Nominalism</u>,

> Duchamp ... reserved for himself the naked symbolic function, the speech act that would name art ... the pact that would unite the spectators of the future around some object, an object that added nothing to the constructed environment and did not improve on it but, quite the contrary, pulled away from it, bearing no other function than that of pure signifier, the pact itself.[5]

Following de Duve's line of thought, the work is not only dependent on the social constructs that surround it, but is literally constituted by those systems of relations. The "pact itself" then, is no insignificant matter. Rather than being an assertion of emptiness or aesthetic refusal, a "pulling away" as de Duve and others have argued, it is in fact an expansion of its boundaries into the dynamic and amorphous territories of the social sphere. Despite de Duve's notion that the readymade retreated from the world (an observation consistent with the dominant interpretation trafficked within the more theoretically fluent art-historical circles of the 1970s and 80s, derived from the writings of Peter Bürger, specifically his 1974 Theory of the Avant-Garde, which situated avant-garde practice as a prolonged negation of bourgeois art), recent art has used Duchamp's insight to unmistakably opposite effect, deploying the social conditions around the art object, or art event, to establish aesthetic meaning, rather than negate it. The pact that de Duve refers to, which establishes both the work of art and the community around it, is what the philosopher Jacques Rancière has described as the "distribution of the sensible," that "system of self-evident facts of sense perception that simultaneously discloses the existence of something in common and the delimitations that define the respective parts and positions within it ...

determin[ing] those who have a part in the community of citizens."[6]
Through the possibility of establishing or revising this network of inclusions and exclusions, art has the capacity to
restructure the social field, even if these relations are provisional or fleeting. As Dorothea von Hantelmann observes,

> Not only is social reality represented in artworks,
> but they also constitute it both concretely and categor-
> ically. "Concretely" here refers to processes that are
> initiated by the production and the existence of the
> artwork; "categorically" refers to categories that are
> intentionally or unintentionally reproduced in the
> process. Seen from this angle, the artwork is far from
> powerless; on the contrary—as an integral part of soci-
> ety—it has an inherent agency …[7]

The discussion of these impacts requires an excision of the
notion of critical or political art as negation—an analysis that
often dead-ends in melancholic ramblings and empty revelations
of social anomie—and the innovation of a new set of tools for
the evaluation of art's "agency," which is predicated on its connection to, rather than its distance from, the social world in
which it operates.

THE PROBLEM OF EVALUATIVE CRITERIA

> … the correct political tendency of a work extends also
> to its literary quality: because a political tendency
> which is correct comprises a literary tendency which is
> correct.
> —Walter Benjamin, "The Author as Producer" (1934)[8]

As art production bleeds into the dynamic world of the social,
reflecting its participation within open-ended circulatory
systems, the meaning and significance of the <u>work</u> of art is
increasingly difficult to discuss within the object-based
discourses of art history and criticism, which favor discrete,

easily delineated and predominantly static objects of investigation. Change over time is particularly difficult for such
discourses to describe, often resulting in an indeterminate and
vague terminology that dead-ends in buzzwords such as "interac-
tive," "contingent," or "open-ended," without producing much
clarity about the nature of the variables at work in each instance. In light of such shortcomings, the question arises as
to what criteria ought to be applied to works that make active
use of their dependence on systems of distribution and social
traffic. One strategy has been the application of activist,
public health or social work criteria to ascertain the efficacy
of the art object, thereby skirting the attendant problems of
instrumentalization, while also eschewing the line of critique
that dismisses art as elitist, bourgeois, or simply vacant décor
for the wealthy. The trouble is that social efficacy is in no
way the same as artistic efficacy; not only is the former much
easier to define in fixed terms, but in addition, a successful
social project can easily have little or no aesthetic value.
Yet often social efficacy becomes the primary justification for
a certain form of participatory political art, often applied
regardless of its actual ability to be viable within the public
sphere, thus failing both as art and as social work. As Rancière
points out, such practices " … generally take for granted
that the politics of art can be identified with a certain type
of efficacy. Art … is supposed to be political because … it is
wrested from its own specific realm and sites to be transformed
into a social practice."[9] The implications of this conflation
do not only affect the deployment and reception of activist or
socially-based art practices. The more detrimental effect is felt
when one examines the anemic concept of aesthetics and politics
it implies. When social efficacy is equated with the politics
of the art object, the political implications of aesthetics are
ignored (aesthetics here is taken to refer to the Greek origin
of the term, relating to the perceivable or sensate, rather than
the German Romantic understanding, relating to the beautiful).
Such sidestepping of the political complexities of aesthetics
ultimately imposes severe limitations on the discussion of an

artwork's life within a broader social context, and excises
it from any meaningful relationship to the history of art.

In Relational Aesthetics (1998), the curator Nicolas
Bourriaud identifies this problem, referring to exhibitions as
"arenas of exchange." Bourriaud proposes that works of art
"must be judged on the basis of aesthetic criteria … by analyz-
ing the coherence of its form, and then the symbolic value of
the 'world' it suggests to us, and of the image of human relations reflected by it." Despite Bourriaud's compelling methodological outline for an approach to aesthetic analysis that
incorporates human relations, he fails to demonstrate how such
an approach might actually be deployed in specific terms, leaving the proposition only partially realized. Since his text was
published in English in 2002, several thinkers, most notably
Claire Bishop and Grant Kester, have turned to this question.
Bishop, who became noted as Bourriaud's most robust critic,
similarly calls for the development of a critical apparatus
by which such socially constructed works might be analyzed in
her text "Antagonism and Relational Aesthetics," providing a
more comprehensive theoretical armature for what aesthetic
criteria might be brought to bear on such practices. She asks:

> how do we measure or compare these relationships?
> The quality of the relationships in "relational aesthet-
> ics" is never examined or called into question […] I
> sense that this question is [for Bourriaud] unnecessary;
> all relations that permit "dialogue" are automatically
> assumed to be democratic and therefore good. But what
> does "democracy" really mean in this context? If rela-
> tional art produces human relations, then the next logi-
> cal question to ask is what types of relations are being
> produced, for whom, and why?[10]

These queries as to the concrete political effects of the works
in aesthetic terms open up a territory that Bourriaud leaves
relatively untouched. What Bishop goes on to offer is the integration of a notion of the democratic proposed by Ernesto

Laclau and Chantal Mouffe with a version of Bürger's model of avant-gardist artistic critique, praising disjunctive or alienated experiences (such as those occurring in the work of Thomas Hirschhorn and Santiago Sierra) as reflecting the discord implicit in democracy, and leaving the affirmative dimension of social practice at best sidelined, if not dismissed out of hand. Kester, who has publicly taken issue with Bishop's formulations precisely for this reason, points to the dominance of post-structuralist theory, with its emphasis on distance, alienation, and critique as the reason for the lack of a developed discourse on socially-based practices. Yet Kester focuses primarily on practices that have far less visibility or prominence in the field than those analyzed by Bishop, implying that these concerns are at the periphery of art discourse and not a factor in mainstream artistic production. Each of these formidable contributions to the discussion develop the invaluable groundwork for a methodological approach to the social dynamics of art, yet surprisingly Bishop and Kester restrict their focus to works that overtly incorporate the viewer within them and make use of indeterminate, socially contingent sites of reception. By doing so they exclude the even more dramatic implications this understanding has for art production in general. Thus, despite the frequency with which socially derived practice is called up as a new paradigm for art that requires urgent attention, the theoretical inroads remain at an early stage, and those invested in understanding the broader methodological implications for the fields of art history and criticism as a whole remain relatively few in number.

WHY ETHICS?

> ... the rigid isolated object (work, novel, book) is of no use whatsoever. It must be inserted into the context of living social relations ...
> —Walter Benjamin, "The Author as Producer"[11]

All of this necessitates continued reflection on the specific
quality and nature of the social field the art object constructs,
and of which it is simultaneously a part, an endeavor to which
the discourse of ethics is particularly well suited. Here we
might be best served by turning to Bourriaud, who, despite his
emphasis on practices that include a participatory dimension,
neither limited himself to artists who exclusively produced
events nor eschewed traditional object making, instead describing artistic practices that were concerned with "learning to
inhabit the world in a better way," a notion that encapsulates
in lay terms what the discourse of ethics is chiefly designed to
discern, i.e. a description of a mode of inhabiting the world.
As the philosopher Alain Badiou writes, "ethics designates today
a principle that governs how we relate to what is going on, a
vague way of regulating our commentary on historical situations
(the ethics of human rights), technico-scientific situations
(medical ethics, bio-ethics), 'social' situations (the ethics of
being-together), media situations (the ethics of communication),
and so on."[12]

Thus the evaluation of the aesthetic condition of ethics
(the barometer by which we ascertain the value and quality of
interpersonal relations) has become one possibility, if not the
only possibility, for the discussion of the aesthetics of the
social field. As Kester notes,

> the relatively undeveloped status of reception theory in
> art history is particularly evident in research associ-
> ated with contemporary art practice. This is due in part
> to the tendency in much recent scholarship simply to
> import generic reception models taken from the tradi-
> tions of post-structuralist literary and critical theory
> into the analysis of contemporary visual art.[13]

Ethics provides one viable option that may offer a solution to
the blind spots in contemporary aesthetic theory. To clarify:
rather than an ethics of aesthetics, which despite being a worthy endeavor, has been undertaken numerous times before, and

further, invariably resolves itself in a discourse external to
that of art, the question examined here is, what might it mean
to speak of an "aesthetics of ethics"? That is, what is an aesthetics (again, from the Greek root pertaining to the perceptible,
the appearance of things) of social relations, and how do ethical relations create aesthetic form? This distinction is key to
understanding the spirit behind this volume and the specific
conditions it seeks to address.

ETHICS VERSUS MORALS

Before moving on to the question of what an aesthetics of ethics
actually is—the broad question that the texts within this volume collectively begin to address—it may be useful to distinguish
the term ethics from the term it is commonly associated with:
morals. Even in some scholarly contexts, the term ethics is conflated with morals, the latter of which I would provisionally
define as a fixed set of rules or laws that prescribe how one
ought to live one's life regardless of circumstance. Ethics,
in the philosophical sense developed by Aristotle, contains no
fixed parameters. Instead, ethics describes a dynamic system
in which the common good is maximized, this common good being
characterized as the living of a virtuous life. As Badiou
describes it, the "ethical principle [refers to] immediate action,
while morality is to concern reflexive action." He goes on to
state that "rather than link the word [ethics] to abstract categories (Man or Human, Right or Law, the Other …), it should be
referred back to particular situations,"[14] meaning that ethics
always refers to the particular rather than the abstract.
Ethics and morals are conceptually antithetical. For example,
while a moral claim would argue that to kill another human
being is wrong in all circumstances, ethics provides no absolute
rule, but rather establishes a basis for analysis that arises
from the circumstance itself. This is not to say that ethics
equates with relativism, but simply that there are no prima
facie criteria other than the maximization of the common good,
and that the common good is increased by acting in a virtuous

manner (thus, a killing that saves lives would not necessarily
be ethical, for the true ethicist would also maintain a belief in
the individual's right in the face of the many, and furthermore,
would not assert one or the other position without an evaluation
of the specific circumstance in question). In the context of a
situation, the ethical conditions of a particular event or site
are a means to describe the sort of interaction that is created
by that event or site. While moral criteria are always external
to the circumstances to which they are applied, the ethical
is immanent to the site of its deployment. A turn to ethics is
a turn to the affirmative question of art, not art as negation,
allegory or critique, but the description of an art that operates directly upon the world it is situated in; it is a definition of art that is not at all premised on representation. This
turn is parallel to Giorgio Agamben's assertion of an affirmative definition of life, in contrast to Michel Foucault's notion
of the power over life being defined in its denial or negation,
i.e. by death. Agamben situates life in the affirmative conditions of thought and of communicability, as he does in his text
"Form-of-Life" (1993) for example. Thus it is a notion of life
that is not governed by the juridical or repressive functions
of the state, but one constituted in affirmative terms as actions
rather than as a quality that is defined tacitly by external
prohibitions. Similarly, we could imagine a discourse on art
that does not define art simply as a reflection or revelation
of repressive forms, i.e. that defines art's efficacy in negative
terms, as the pointing out of "bad," or politically regressive
forms of aesthetics, but the establishment of new aesthetic
parameters for social relations.

The moral and the ethical are often practically at odds.
An individual who asserts a morally acceptable, i.e. normatively
correct or just, position can deploy unethical means to achieve
it. Within aesthetics, consider the use of propaganda: the message of propaganda may be morally "correct," seeking to promote
positive action, but may also be unethical, in that it subordi-
nates a viewer, addressing her or him in a coercive or threatening manner, or by appealing to fears or prejudices. This is

the paradox of political art that deploys propagandist forms. While such a work might call for freedom from repression, it deploys a mode of address that assumes self-validating authority nonetheless, a reification of the very powers it claims to usurp. In semiotic or representational terms, the message may align itself against power, but in practice use this very power to assert its position, in effect reifying that form of power. An aesthetics of ethics offers the possibility of distinguishing between means and ends by enacting a shift from a hermeneutic approach, which emphasizes decoding, to the study of the means by which that thing being examined comes into being and is circulated, in short, how the work creates conditions of reception, how it makes whatever its message is perceivable.

The central concern of an ethical analysis is not whether the work can be evaluated positively or negatively in ethical terms, but instead resides in the more complex question of the aesthetic manifestation of the ethical dimension of the work of art, i.e. its proposal of a modification to the social contract, with the artwork acting as the signification of this modification. So, if an artwork is understood as affecting or generating relations among viewers, how is this negotiation with the ethical dimensions of an artwork manifest in aesthetic terms (i.e. how are these aspects of its social existence manifest in the appearance of the work itself)? Even if it is participation-based, the core question is not whether an artwork initiates a successful social program (there is already a well developed discourse on social efficacy which has little bearing on the history of art), but what are the aesthetic implications of an action that modifies social relations. This would be the fundamental reason for asserting such an action within the frame of artistic practice rather than simply within the social field alone. We could turn to Duchamp for some clarity in this regard, for if art consists of a kind of social pact amounting to a collective decision to discuss something in a certain way (i.e. as art), ethics proposes how we could address those aesthetic implications in more than experiential or anecdotal terms. Ethics, then, is not a criterion by which one can justify a work; it is, rather, a methodology.

Much as the discourse related to apprehending "beauty" within
an artwork does not require it to be beautiful to be significant, but exists as a set of tools to approach the work's discussion, ethics can likewise function as a methodological approach
which can address the aesthetic conditions of an artwork in
light of the effects it produces on the social field of which it
is a part.

This is a more radical proposition than it might seem
initially; when one asks what the aesthetics of ethics are, one
redefines the condition of aesthetics, for if aesthetics chiefly
deals with the conditions of perception, negotiating what is
perceivable, knowable, or sensate (in Rancière's terminology:
the "distribution of the sensible"), a definition of artistic
practice that accepts its social foundations as a raw material
for its production radically expands the notion of what can
be made perceivable and seeable. We then might ask, if contemporary painting necessarily incorporates a consideration of the
broader social implications surrounding its making, such as
the various modes of distribution—i.e. the network of magazines,
dealers, critics, and so on, as Kelsey or Joselit have argued—
does it look markedly different from a painting which does
not arise from a consideration of these forces? We could easily
answer in the affirmative, but the more complex question is <u>how</u>
it looks different. Such an answer lies beyond the means of
contemporary critical discourse, and it is this question that
an aesthetics of ethics would allow us to answer.

NOTES

1 Lygia Clark, "O vazio-pleno," <u>Jornal do Brasil</u> (Rio de Janeiro), April 2, 1960, p. 5; trans. in <u>Lygia Clark</u>, Fundació Antoni Tàpies, Barcelona 1998, p. 111-113; translation revised.

2 David Joselit, "Painting Beside Itself," <u>October</u> 130, Fall 2009, p. 125-134.

3 Dorothea von Hantelmann, <u>How to Do Things with Art</u>, JRP|Ringier, Zurich 2010, p. 151.

4 Rosalind Krauss, "Sculpture in the Expanded Field," <u>October</u>, vol. 8, Spring 1979, p. 34.

5 Thierry de Duve, <u>Pictorial Nominalism: On Marcel Duchamp's Passage from Painting to the Readymade</u>, University of Minnesota Press, Minneapolis 1991, p. 115.

6 Jacques Rancière, "The Distribution of the Sensible: Politics and Aesthetics" (2000); trans. Gabriel Rockhill, in Rancière, <u>The Politics of Aesthetics</u>, Continuum, London and New York 2004, p. 12.

7 Dorothea von Hantelmann, <u>How to Do Things with Art</u>.

8 Walter Benjamin, "The Author as Producer" (1934); trans. Edmund Jephcott, in Walter Benjamin, <u>Reflections</u>, Harcourt Brace Jovanovich, New York 1978, p. 221.

9 Jacques Rancière, "Paradoxes of Political Art' (2005); in <u>Homeworks III: A Forum on Cultural Practices</u>, Ashkal Alwan, Beirut 2008, p. 44.

10 Claire Bishop, "Antagonism and Relational Aesthetics," <u>October</u>, no. 110, Fall 2004, p. 65.

11 Walter Benjamin, "The Author as Producer," p. 222.

12 Alain Badiou, <u>Ethics: An Essay on the Understanding of Evil</u> (1993), trans. Peter Hallward, Verso, London and New York, 2002, p. 2.

14 Grant Kester, in "Questionnaire on 'The Contemporary,'" ed. Hal Foster, et al., <u>October</u> 130, Fall 2009, p. 8.

14 Alain Badiou, <u>Ethics: An Essay on the Understanding of Evil</u>, p. 3.

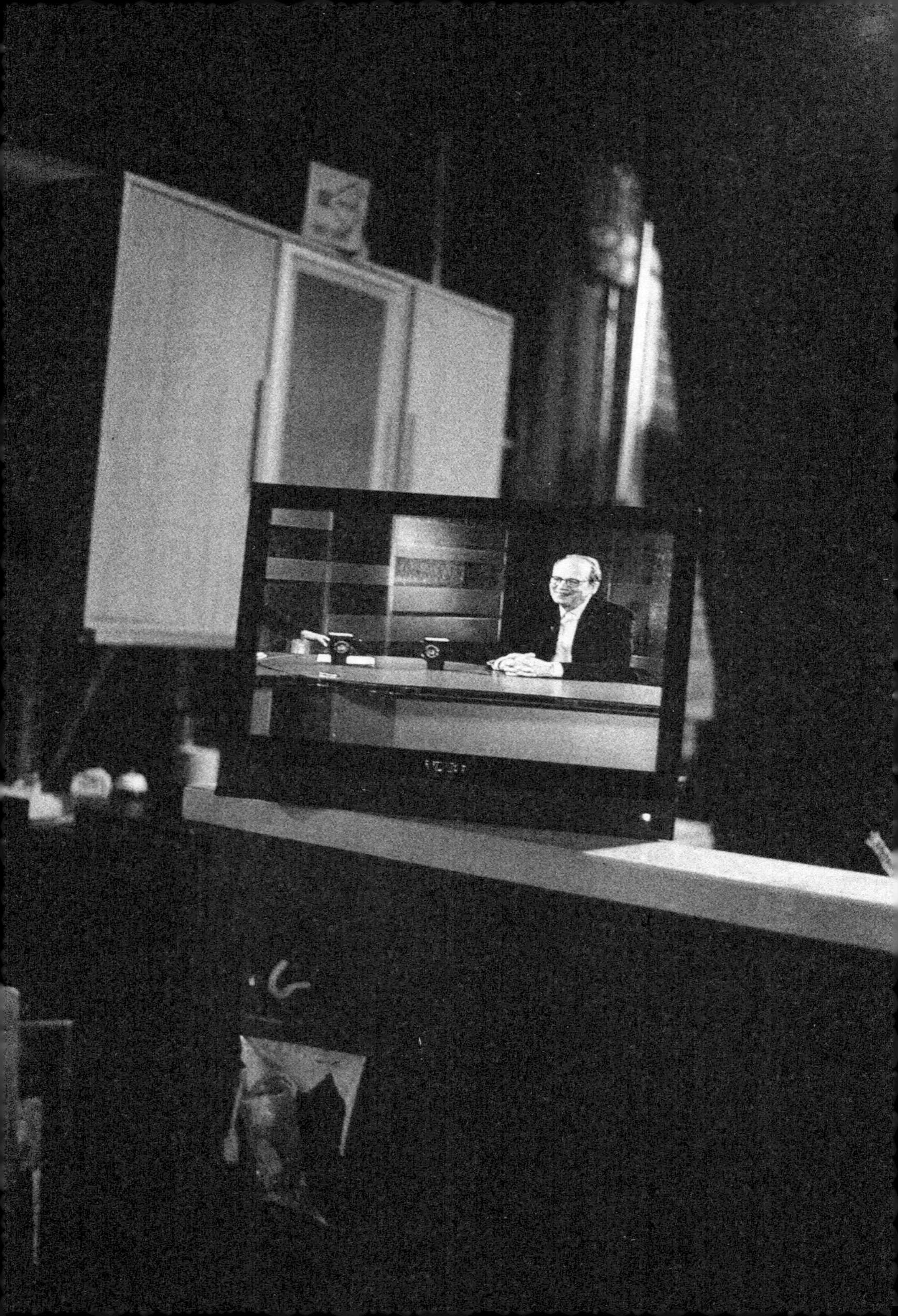

Morgan Fisher in conversation with Walead Beshty

First published in <u>Morgan Fisher: Conversations</u>, Aspen Art Press,
Aspen 2015, p. 23-40.

WALEAD BESHTY: With the series of drawings in your most recent
show at Galerie Buchholz [<u>Works on Paper: 1968-2008</u>, 2010],
I was thinking that by including a range of conventions for
pictorial drawing, they avoid asserting a universalized form of
depiction that is privileged over others. The one convention
they don't include is perspective, which we often think of as
being the most lifelike. So the drawings as a group denaturalize
perspective by showing alternatives to it. No single convention
claims a total experiential fidelity, but rather they complement
each other to offer a more complete understanding of visual
space. Isometric drawing shows a shape in space, as perspective
does, but unlike perspective, you can obtain the measurements
of the object by measuring the drawing.

MORGAN FISHER: Yes, exactly. My father, who was an architect,
taught me isometric drawing when I was a teenager. At the time,
its appeal was that it was so easy to use. Another of the conventions in that group of drawings is orthographic, in which
the depth disappears. It's as if you're looking directly at
the object and there's no sense of how one plane in the object is
farther away than another. I would want to make a distinction
between conventions in which the convention is evident in contrast to one such as perspective, which we tend not to notice is
a convention because it simulates the appearance of monocular

human vision, with vanishing points and with objects becoming
smaller as they approach the horizon. A classic illustration
of this is telephone poles. In perspective, telephone poles,
even though they're all the same height, seem to get shorter
and shorter and closer and closer together as they near the
horizon.

WB: In a regular pattern.

MF: Absolutely regular. We're so used to thinking of perspective
as being the same as human vision that we lose sight of the fact
that how we interpret the perspective of what we see produces
something that we no longer see as perspective. The classic way
to illustrate this difference is to compare a view of a landscape
with a photograph of it. Let's say you're looking at a view here
in Los Angeles. If it's a clear day, we can see the San Gabriel
Mountains with snow on them. If we took a photograph of that
same scene, we would be disappointed by how small the mountains
are. It's the fault, so to speak, of the camera, because a camera
exactly obeys the regime of monocular perspective. With human
vision, even though the mountains are in fact that small optically, our paying attention to them, our reading them as what's
important, makes them what they really are.

WB: Because you're isolating that object by concentrating on it.

MF: However it works, the way we interpret the scene, which in
fact is a perspective, overrules the regime that perspective
imposes, liberates the scene from it.

WB: It's a distinction between the cognitive and mechanical.
Because in curved space—the space of the eye—the viewer is
always the center, and the viewer's position distorts the scene.
As they move, so do the relations between things. But not
only that, the objects themselves change shape. There's also
stereopsis, which makes these distortions more extreme.

MF: Yes, which is something I don't have personal knowledge
of because I don't have stereopsis. I don't see with both eyes
simultaneously.

WB: What exactly does that mean? Does it mean that your brain
chooses one eye over the other?

MF: That's correct. That's exactly what it means.

WB: This relates to something I was thinking about <u>Phi Phenomenon</u>
[1968]. When you screened it at the Hammer Museum recently,
Thom [Andersen]'s comments about Jean-Louis Baudry and the
reduction of apparatus theory to being just about the projector
and the camera and ignoring the expanded condition of cinematic
reception really resonated with me in thinking about your
film. Of course, the audience, the man laughing, all the noises,
but also the room, the carpet, et cetera: this is all part of
the apparatus of cinema. The audience was activated by the way
that time plays out in the film. The film exploits the disparity
between the time of the clock and cinematic time, how these
temporalities are not in sync.

The audience, as a collective, also began to act like a
kind of clock. The audience punctuated time with coughs, laugh-
ter, or shuffling, just like the ticking clock or the whirring
projector. When the tension of the audience's silence was broken,
there would be this shift in the experience of duration. In
these moments, you become conscious of other bodies. That shifting between the perception mediated by this machine, and the
experience being mediated by who surrounds you, even something
as mundane as how comfortable your seat is, functioned to create these divergent senses of time that the film encapsulated.
The film brought all of this forward as part of the apparatus
of cinema.

Another dimension is the question of work, of labor,
because the time of the clock is really the time of work, of
the factory, and cinema and the factory have a special relationship. Most of your films have this sensation of the industrial

about them, of labor, and so often the films are being made in
some way as they are seen.

What seems so remarkable about that film, at least to
me in my experience of it, was this heightened sensitivity
that seemed to shift; I found myself caught between these temporalities, with none being absolute. I found myself bouncing
between a cinematic time, then a time of the audience, then of
the clock. I felt my perception of duration move around drasti-
cally. I realized that I couldn't experience these different
passages of time simultaneously, and I couldn't put them at
a distance; I was simply submerged in one or the other.

MF: One thing that ordinary movies attempt their absolute best
to do is to make us forget time or duration. Of course you
understand that the experience is taking place in time, but people who make commercial films don't want you to be conscious of
anything except what's going on in the world that they've con-
trived for you. That means that they try to make you unaware
of the time that it takes for them to tell you the story itself.
And Phi Phenomenon does something very different, which was
part of the idea, although I can't say that I fully articulated
it to myself at the time.

WB: What's so remarkable about it is that it's such a straight-
forward work, but it becomes extremely complicated when you
try to sort it out and think through what is actually happening.
Just knowing what the work is, you can't imagine how complicated the experience of it is. At least, I couldn't imagine. I knew
what the subject matter of the film was because I had seen it
as a video bootleg. I knew what I was in for—I knew about the
experience and I understood the title as well. And yet, at
the same time, there was something so deeply experiential and
ever-changing about viewing the film, even though the "event"
it was depicting never deviated from my expectation. I wasn't
ready for it to be that complex. In Picture and Sound Rushes
[1973] there's an exhaustion of options presented from a certain
set of possible combinations of sound and image.

In <u>Phi Phenomenon</u>, there isn't that kind of exhaustion of
possibilities, but rather an indeterminate number of modes of
thought, or types of experience, whose activation isn't directly
the result of what happens on screen.

MF: The film doesn't program them, yes.

WB: In a way this echoes the perspective question. Because in
the end it's about how these modes activate the viewer, how
seemingly innate things like time and vision are constructions.
And also about how different perspectival systems are incompatible with one another, as with the distinction that you were
making between Renaissance perspective and axonometric or isometric views, or the plan view. One slowly becomes conscious of
the information that has been omitted in each instance, and also
very aware of their deviation from our experience of the world.
And these systems support each other. So with these different
types of drawings being important for the construction of,
say, buildings, is the idea that there is not a true or authentic
rendering, but rather multiple renderings, each an abstraction
with its own conceits.

MF: Absolutely, but let's not call them "renderings," because in
pictorial drawing that term has a special meaning. The important
thing, as you say, is that they are all conventions, even if
we don't think of all of them as such. We readily think of the
orthographic and oblique and axonometric, which includes isometric, as conventions, because they look more or less strange,
not lifelike, but we don't think of perspective as one, even
though it is, because it more resembles the world as we see it.
When I started doing non-film work such as drawings and so
forth, I was attracted to the isometric because it involved far
fewer choices than were involved when working in perspective.
In perspective, in principle there are an infinite number of
points of view.
        Let's say you want to take a photograph of a building
and you want to photograph the front and a side and the top.

In principle, the number of different station points from which
you can take the picture is infinite. What this means, in effect,
is that you're making a compositional decision. It's the same
thing in perspectival drawing. Whereas with an isometric method
you can look at an object from one of eight possible viewpoints,
and eight is a lot fewer than an infinite number. With an
orthographic view, for any one face of an object—for example,
the facade of a building—there's only one view. That's even
fewer choices; in fact, there's no choice. So on the one hand you
have perspective, which, even though it's a convention, requires
a choice from an infinite number of possibilities, and on the
other you have conventions with a very narrow range of choices,
and in the most extreme case, no choice. Without my really being
conscious about it or thinking about where it came from, from
the very beginning my film work was very much concerned with
finding a way for the work to come into existence while circum-
venting what I would call composition. One of my very early
films, for example, reproduces the convention of copy photography, a special case of photography in which there is no choice
in the angle. It's a totally prescribed point of view, like
the orthographic. It's a non-interpretive or a non-expressive
convention. Later films, such as <u>Production Stills</u> [1970] and
<u>Standard Gauge</u> [1984], employ exactly the model of copy photo-
graphy. This requires the camera to look straight at what it's
photographing, so even <u>Picture and Sound Rushes</u> is a rough sort
of copy photograph, because the camera is pointed directly at
the wall. From the beginning there was this tendency to want to
avoid having to make compositional decisions with respect to
the angle of view. I don't know why this happened, but it was
obviously very important.

WB: All these various forms of perspectival drawing or rendering
depth or understanding the position of the objects in space:
they all require the existence of each other, a kind of transparency about the rules and conventions that are at play
in each one, that they are all complementary, that you switch
between them. They are all provisional in some sense.

314

MF: Strictly speaking, that is not the case, although in a general sort of way it is. An orthographic drawing and an oblique drawing of the same object are both correct, each in its own way, although the orthographic will be more complete than the oblique. But showing the same object in different conventions lets you visualize the object more completely and so understand it in a richer way. To the extent that this is so, different conventions are, as you say, complementary. An orthographic view is least lifelike. You see the same object from three predetermined views, and the three views together allow you, in principle, to visualize the object completely. What's missing in one view is in one or both of the other views. So in that one convention, the views are complementary. Together they represent the object. The curious thing is that perspective, the most lifelike convention, can show you only three sides of the object, supposing the object is a like a box. You can't see what is going on with the three other sides. You need another perspective to see them. But even then, the perspectives don't tell you what the dimensions of the object are. Perspectives aren't used that way, to give complete and precise knowledge of an object, as the orthographic does. The three views in the orthographic show you all six sides of the box, although you have to assemble the three into something you visualize rather than see directly, as you can a perspective. And the three views also show you the dimensions.

These other conventions—orthographic, oblique, isometric—are, I would say, more or less abstract. Not literally abstract, because each is still a picture, but it's a special kind of picture such that the congruence that we see between a perspectival drawing—in which the object is readily recognizable—and the object it depicts is absent from these other kinds of drawings; there's some kind of a gap or a distance. Even though these other conventions are equally pictures, they're so mediated by convention that there's a kind of rupture between the drawing of the object and the object itself. In perspective that's not true.

WB: Most of the information being conveyed is there to simply
establish the convention. They serve as an affirmation of a set
of rules for interpretation. This is part of what I was trying
to get at with the distinction between the way the human eye
sees the world, and how the optical lens sees the world. Despite
the assumed verisimilitude of an optical, lens-made picture and
the assumption that it's not abstract, it approaches abstraction
as it's modified to relate to this model of space, in this
instance, Renaissance perspectival form. It seems particularly
perverse that the most naturalized form of representation is
actually the one that's most abstract and dissimilar to how the
world functions; it gives us the least information about the
world around us.

MF: For me a problem with perspective is less a matter of its
being an abstraction than its being optically literal. But
you're certainly right, perspective has the least amount of
information of a useful kind; for example, the information
necessary to physically reproduce the object, exactly reproduce
it. It shows you what it looks like from that point of view,
but that's it.

WB: It makes me wonder if your work in painting and your work
in film both turn on this cleaving of convention from experience,
or turn on the idea that experience is not innate. And this
could extend to the ideological conditions of representation,
or ideological constraints of optical media. For example, one
that privileges a flat field, a rectilinear rather than a curved
space. It makes me wonder if this is an attempt at transparency,
an assertion of transparency about the production of representations, in the sense that decisions about focal length or
other decisions about how space is represented in a film are
often inaccessible to a viewer.

MF: I think that because what we tend to want from photographs
is the world as we see it, or the world as we think we see it,
photographers are inclined to work with the focal lengths that

fall within the range to produce that. Distortion gets in the
way. I understand that professional portrait photographers
tend to use lenses with a longer than normal focal length to
avoid the distortion that a normal lens produces when showing
an object close-up.

One way to think about your work is that it's trying to
interrogate or go beyond the idea of the image as something
that's contained within a flat rectangle. This is in your work
over and over again. There are the photographs that curve down
onto the floor or up onto the ceiling, or images that continue
across multiple panels.

For me it's very much about rejecting the model of the
window as a rectangular container, or frame, or just moving
beyond it. Acknowledging it, maybe, but then insisting that we
not accept it as the unspoken condition that governs a photographic event.

One of the reasons I'm interested in Tiepolo, for example, is because a lot of the paintings are not rectangular, in
fact they're very elaborate departures from the rectangular.
There's one in the Metropolitan where there's an irregular curve
on the top, which is duplicated on the bottom, but diagonally.
It's not mirror symmetrical, but rather diagonally symmetrical.
These are questions that I'm thinking about.

WB: It's tricky though, because I would accept the rectilinear
due to its ubiquity. The standard is arbitrary. It doesn't follow automatically from an idea of the photographic, the cinematic, or the optical. If one made a choice to make circular photographs, for example, it would be defined in opposition to the
rectilinear, and thus reaffirm the rectilinear as the default.
The issue seems to me to be how does one find a motivated reason
to break the convention, to find where it doesn't work, rather
than simply contradicting it for the sake of contradiction.

Rather than break conventions, I usually try to extend
their logic to the points where they conflict with one another
or fail to perform the task they are designed for. In this
sense, in my work, the conventions produce the results and

I just try to follow them. The darkroom machinery is all designed
to project cyan, magenta, and yellow light based on those three
filters in color photography, so it made sense to me to start
there. And to use a rule that accepted the starting points that
are implicit within the technology associated with photography.
The curling comes from the tooth of the paper, how it is mad and
transported on rolls. How it curls dictates the forms, because
the paper is allowed to fall or drape onto itself.

The paper acts as its own negative: it is both the thing
being depicted and also the thing registering the depiction.
As the paper moves due to environmental conditions such as the
HVAC system of the particular place that I'm printing, the
vibrations in the floor, things like that, misregistrations
between exposures arise, which cause the color banding. I think
of the managerial aspects of the medium as a generative force,
rather than a force to fight against. There's a certain level
where practices can organize themselves as opposed to some form
of dominance. To that end, the question is how much does being
opposed to some form of dominant structure …

MF: Just reinforce it?

WB: Yes. And how can one stage something that's outside of an
established vocabulary? I don't think it's possible to exist
outside of such operations. One is always implicated within the
systems in which one is working, and I think that is positive.
Concealing is the problem, pretending to exist outside of something (outside of the market, or outside of power dynamics)
that is abhorrent to me. The option, or the way through that
problem, for me, was to follow the rules better than they're
usually followed, if that makes sense.

For example, there's an unrealized project that I conceived of for the Wexner Center for the Arts. Peter Eisenman's
design for the Wexner's building is based on the intersection
between two grids—representing the city grid of Columbus and
the Olmsted Brothers' plan for Ohio State University—which
are displaced from one another by 12.25 degrees. There are no

right angles in the building because it's only the intersection
between those grids that allow walls to meet.

MF: The building aggressively limits how exhibitions and works
can be presented.

WB: That was intentional. Eisenman was quoted as saying that
the building was a challenge to artists, and the building operates more like an art object in that it proposes a relation
between aesthetics and form, but for the most part ignores the
conditions of use. When it comes to use, it is extremely conventional; in terms of appearance, it is quite aggressive.

As an artist, you can't win if you fight a building like
that. But one can pervert the building by extending its logic,
by being a false friend to its conceptual conceits. In a building that size it's impossible to build an actual 12.25-degree
angle. Construction contractors cannot build to that tolerance.
In fact, the angles in the building vary between 11 and 14
degrees, or so I was told. So instead of trying to outdo the
building, or just plopping something down without considering
the context, I proposed to the Wexner to bring in artisans who
are used to working within tolerances of .25 degrees and have
them refinish the exhibition space they offered me. In the process, the walls would be sanded down to adhere more exactly to
Eisenman's design. The walls were by then covered by ten years
of paint. Looking at their archival photos, I saw that they
had used a wide variety of colors over the years, so I think the
result would have been quite compelling, a kind of color-coded
history of the museum brought about by being more strict about
the concept behind the building.

Thinking about that is similar to how I think about the
idea of photography, or those conventions or rules that are embedded within systems of representation or rendering. To follow
a set of rules to the point where they start generating their
own outcomes is a way to bring them forward without the dramatic
performance of revelation, of pulling back the curtain. Letting
things come into view, rather than thrusting them into view.

MF: I think it was important for Eisenman to be able to say that
there was a reason for the building to be this way that's not
arbitrary. And that interests me because this is something I've
talked a lot about in relation to my own work. To me, the arbitrary was always a sign of the compositional, so in my work I
try to have nonarbitrary reasons for things to be as they are.
But on the other hand, in the case of the Wexner I would say
that the results of Eisenman's embrace of there being reasons
produces a building that is very interesting, yet hostile to its
intended purpose. So in other words, there's a kind of tension.
The non-compositional or the nonarbitrary doesn't necessarily
produce an interesting result. And of course, architecture has
to meet the criterion of function.

WB: Yes, it does. But it's also the premise of architecture as
critique—an idea so central to Eisenman's project—that is the
work's shortcoming. It is always set up against some outside
thing, while the other question, the more important one, is what
the building does propose as a positive option. You can say that
all buildings are built with right angles, on grid systems, and
that this is some sort of ideological constraint. So what? It's
also convenient for a number of reasons. But to assert an alternative plan is to open up other options, and then the question
isn't about what the building isn't doing, but what it is doing.

MF: Going back to your work, one way that we tend to think of
a photograph is to look through the surface to what it depicts.
But this is not how we relate to your photographs. In your
work, we don't look through the surface at an image that we see
behind it. We look at the surface of the photograph as much as
we look at the image. Or sometimes we look <u>only</u> at the surface
because the image, to the extent that we see one, is in the plane
of the surface. And at the same time, the physical surfaces
themselves are not flat, not framed as windows.

WB: You make me think of your adopting the model of the copy
photograph. I think I was struggling with something similar,

in that conventional perspectival space implies the possibility
of an infinite extension of the perspectival lines, and thus
the extension of the grid, which implies order and control,
to all that surrounds it. In actuality, this ordering that the
eye can offer is really limited to a sphere around the viewer,
around the point from which one is looking. It doesn't extend
indefinitely, but curves into itself in a more hermetic, provisional way.

The initial impulse behind the photograms was to take
the image plane and bend it. By bending the picture plane—
whether through folding or crumpling or curling—it wouldn't
be able to speak of anything outside its own parameters. It
would be clear about its boundaries, and also clear that it was
a specific thing, contained only on the surface specific to it.
At the time, I was very interested in the idea of an anisotropic
image—something that Erwin Panofsky refers to in _Perspective
as Symbolic Form_. In such an image, the picture plane is irregular in every direction and there's not a fixed plane of vision
or point from which a scene is being apprehended; rather it's
all a construction of these materials coming into contact with
reference to the surfaces. Contingency and provisionality,
rather than universality and homogeneity.

MF: This brings us back to the gap between the homogeneity and
boundedness of perspectival space and the perceptual experience
of lived space. Perspective only rules, so to speak, within the
border of the picture. It's impossible to extrapolate the scene
beyond what it actually shows us, unless of course we know
the scene and so know what lies outside the picture's borders.

In the case of a photograph, even though it enacts the
model of monocular perspective, we customarily understand it
as extracted from the larger world. If we don't actually know
what lies outside the frame, we can extrapolate, if only crudely.
And even if we can't, at least we know the world continues beyond
the image. But in a perspective painting or drawing, that
extrapolation isn't possible, and the image doesn't tell us that
the world continues beyond its perimeter. It's not a piece of

the larger world; it's a construction that does not necessarily
imply anything beyond its limits.

WB: Panofsky was also arguing that the reason you would have
a space that was non-curved, or rectilinear, is so that it had
the potential to be expanded, to extend in every direction, to
expand the optic domain, to claim the world could be surveyed
and brought under control.

It was very much because of Panofsky that I started
making the photograms. The question that occurred to me was
how do you make a photograph that is anisotropic, that doesn't
tacitly propose an expansive logic, but rather is provisional,
that presents itself as an object in the world as much as a
rendering of it? In other words, how would one make a photograph that was non-pictorial, or not abstract, while still
being photographic. That's where the idea of bending the picture plane came in.

MF: Do you think of those photographs as being pictures?

WB: Not in the standard sense, no.

MF: I think that's an interesting idea, that there can be a
photograph that's not a picture. Because to me the almost automatic condition of a photograph is that we read it as a picture.
Even if it's an abstract image, we read it as a picture of an
abstract image.

WB: I would also reject the term "abstraction" for my work.

MF: So they're photographs, but they're not pictures and they're
not abstract. Do you think abstraction in photography is
possible?

WB: Well, I would say that pictures are always abstractions. They
are presented as some sort of re-formation of the world, a kind
of diagram of it that uses a set of operations to isolate certain

322

aspects and discard others. So a picture is diagrammatic, and
diagrams are abstractions. Photography is designed to produce
pictures, but I don't think it is inherently pictorial. In
other words, you could call something a photograph that is not
pictorial.

As for what is an abstraction, and what is not, it
depends on information in most cases. If one doesn't know where
an image comes from, what it is abstracted from, then it is not
an abstraction. An abstraction only works in relation to some
other object, something to be "abstracted from." There's no such
thing as an abstraction on its own. To say something is abstract
without saying what it is an abstraction of is meaningless.

MF: This is to insist on the root of the word, that it is something
drawn from something. So that abstraction, inevitably, refers
back to something to which it has a connection of some kind,
even though it no longer directly inscribes that connection.

WB: Abstractions are always a filtration of information into
another form, distinct from the original, which is often more
portable than the thing it is abstracted from: like a landscape
painting, because you can't take the landscape with you; or a
blueprint, because you can't transport the whole building with
you. Or an abstract of a text. I would say this becomes ambiguous in art, and thus in art the term is misused because for
some reason it has been difficult to discuss art's instrumental
function.

MF: So what you're describing is a code. It just has to do with
knowledge, knowledge of the code.

WB: Yes, I think where abstraction becomes expressive is when
the absence of the key, or thing it is modeling, is willful.
Then the interiority of the maker is offered as the key. I would
always use the term "non-figurative," or "concrete," to describe
my work, rather than abstract.

MF: Really?

WB: Yes, it seems more clear because the term is so often misused.
Abstraction also implies that something is missing, that the
thing is "about" some other thing. I think that is problematic.

MF: As you suggest, abstraction has several meanings. I place
the highest value on a certain understanding of abstraction,
and to try to get to it I want to make a distinction between
other understandings of the word and the one that is important
to me. As you suggest, one meaning of the word is simplification.
That's how I take your saying that a diagram is an abstraction.
Yes, a diagram is certainly a simplification, but I can't go
along with the idea that a diagram is a form of abstraction
as such, at least not in the sense that I want to use the word.
Charles Sanders Peirce puts the diagram under the heading
of the icon, which means there is a resemblance of some kind to
something else. Perhaps that something else is the thing you
say that abstraction implies is missing. The London subway
doesn't literally look like the map that is familiar, but the
relations of connection are correct, so it's a diagram. It
simplifies—in fact distorts—the relative locations in space
of the different lines of the subway system while accurately
representing certain facts about it. For me a diagram is a representation, even if it seems, so to speak, abstract, that is,
simplified. But simplification is not abstraction in the sense
that is important to me. Another example of abstraction as simplification (abstraction in the not useful sense) is the series
of etchings that Pablo Picasso did of the bull. The topical
accuracy of the bull vanishes, but even at the end it's still a
picture of a bull, recognizable as such, even without our seeing
the series of simplifying steps that got us there. To me the
necessary condition of abstraction is that there is no referent.
What we are looking at does not refer to something that already
exists in the world, does not transcribe that already existing
thing, whether it is a scene in front of us, a scene that we
imagine, an interior mental state, and so on.

WB: I agree with your description of how I am using the term,
except that I would add that for me an abstraction has a certain
richness in that it can posit a complex logic through which
to comprehend the world, while accruing other qualities that
do not refer back to the object from which it is abstracted.
Peirce's model places a lot of emphasis on the viewer, or inter-
pretant, if I remember his terminology correctly, so to me his
classification system speaks more about how much information
a viewer might have about how a certain sign has arisen or been
assigned meaning, than a quality of that sign itself. Where you
use the term "abstraction," I prefer the term "materialist," or
"concrete." This seems to me a way to describe an object, which
does not imply that it is a reduction, transformation, or sche-
matization of some other object, which does not require a referent to have meaning, but rather its meaning arises out of it
and the immediate conditions of viewership it produces. In other
words, it presents itself as another object in the world, and
does not ask for one to imagine or project some other thing in
its place.

MF: With Peirce, an index can be an index without our knowing
it, which means we don't know how to read it. It's still an
index, even if it's opaque to the viewer. Icons are different
because they are created intentionally, not automatically the
way an index is. If the maker of the icon—whether it is an
image, a diagram, or the third subdivision, which no one talks
about, a metaphor—finds that people don't understand the icon,
the maker has to take responsibility and will likely revise the
icon. What strikes me about icons is that they can be extremely
simple, seemingly abstract, and yet still readily understood as
icons, as referring to something else. But perhaps such instances
are specific to certain cultures. What one culture can instantly
read as an icon is, to those who are not members of that culture,
an abstraction. I would say it's a kind of coding: once you
understand how it's an icon to that culture you say, "Oh, yes,
of course, it's obvious." The meaning I want for "abstraction"
is precisely that it is without a referent. Here's a painting.

It's not a picture of anything. We do not, so to speak, recognize
it. And yet we want to find meaning in it, since the work is
offered to us as intentional, as having meaning. As Yve-Alain
Bois has taught us, the way to get to the meaning of an abstract painting is by dealing with the concrete material object.
In any case, as you suggest, dealing with abstraction of this
kind absolutely rules out projection, as if we are looking at
an inkblot: "I see this or that," or "It reminds me of this or
that." To me it's less about conditions of viewership than about
paying attention to the object, but maybe those things are
closer to each other or merge into each other more than I would
have thought.

WB: I'm curious about the relationship between works such as the
Pendant Pair Paintings [2007], which have no representational
dimension and operate phenomenologically, for lack of a better
term, and the most recent series of works derived from the book-
let Exterior and Interior Color Beauty? Or, for that matter,
the self-portrait paintings? These works seem to operate quite
differently with regard to their points of reference. I wonder
how your notion of abstraction works in tandem with some
of the autobiographical points of reference within your work.
Perhaps it's not autobiographical per se, but it does point
to your life. Standard Gauge referred directly to your experiences, so for a long time you've made works that refer to your
life. Do you think of it as incidental, as in you just happen
to be around so you act in your films or use material from your
life in your works? Could a pure abstraction, a kind of total
fulfillment of the category of abstraction that did not refer
outside of itself, still have these references to the life of
the artist?

MF: For me abstraction is the ideal. I wish I knew why I felt
so strongly about this. It's a hugely powerful model, a model
with a moral dimension. In itself it is guaranteed to avoid the
pitfalls and inadequacies of representation and its problems—
illustration, iconography. But abstraction is extremely

difficult, in fact maybe impossible. A lot of my work expresses
the wish to be abstract through its resemblance to historical
models of abstraction—for example, the monochrome—but very
little of it actually is. The Pendant Pair Paintings aren't
directly representational in that they are not pictures, as pendant pairs were historically, but they allude to, refer to, a
model from art history as well as to the color wheel, something
that we know existed before I made the work. Whether we want
to call these allusions or references matters less than the fact
that both the pendant pair and the color wheel preexisted the
making of the work.

The paintings derived from Exterior and Interior Color
Beauty are enlarged copies of color chips. We can think of them
as hard-edged relatives of Claes Oldenburg's soft enlargements.
At first glance they could be abstract, but they're not; they're
copies. Similarly, the self-portraits look abstract but they're
not; they're representational, albeit in a very attenuated way.
That work reflected my love of the monochrome as the most radical trope of modernism, but the question was how to work with
the monochrome without repeating it. The answer was to have
the size and shape mean something, which meant the paintings
weren't abstract any more, but at least they gave you a new way
to think about the monochrome, so at least they are not a simple
repetition of it. And maybe they also give us a new way to
think about representation, in that they are not pictures but
are still representational, if in an oblique way.

I try to get away from the work's referring to my life.
For example, there are the paintings whose source is architecture, but nonetheless there is that strain—though I would like
to think that it's mediated, distanced, such that its claim is
not its biographical origin but rather the form of the work
that the biographical origin makes possible. In Standard Gauge,
autobiography was only the device to organize the pieces of
film, which to me were the film's subject.

The short answer to your question about whether pure
abstraction could still allude to the life of the artist—what a
romantic phrase—is no, and I hope that doesn't disappoint you.

Beyond that, we have to face whether pure abstraction is in
fact even possible. I used to think it was, and I think it was
how I was taught art history that told me this. The work was
described as abstract, and I accepted it as abstract without
thinking about it. But I have thought about this question in
relation to my own work, even in the paintings that I think
are the most abstract. For example, with the Back and Forth
Paintings, there is not a referent in the usual sense—they're
not pictures of something—but the procedures I followed in
making them come forward as their subject. They are about how
I made them, and how I made them is there to see. The procedure
was extremely simple: reflection in the horizontal and the vertical. Transformation by reflection already existed as a model
in the world, so the paintings are referential, if indirectly.
Ultimately, the subject is the wish to make work that is not
compositional. The paintings refer to that model, of which I
had prior knowledge, but that doesn't make them autobiography
in the sense that Standard Gauge is. Abstraction, real abstraction, is still an ideal for me, but I have to wonder if I will
ever achieve it.

WB: It's interesting, because from this perspective it seems as
though autobiography can become part of a materialist approach,
perhaps even an abstract approach. in the sense that you use
the term. I say this because it treats the life of the artist,
the experiences of the artist, as an extension of the work,
a kind of implicit condition of production intertwined with the
thing itself. This is different from the way personal reference
usually occurs in art, where the work of art is presented as
some sort of extension of the person, in other words, where
the artist legitimates the work through a claim for emotional
authenticity and the form's ability to convey those emotions.
Here it is the total opposite: the autobiographical is called
forth by the materialist procedures. It's compelling to me
because it allows a kind of emotional and more radically
narrative content to coexist with a materialist tradition,
one exemplified for me in the tradition of the monochrome,

or avant-garde film. For example, I find <u>Standard Gauge</u> to be
a really moving film, and yet this emotional dimension is linked
to a kind of radical materialist transparency. The most arresting aspect is that the autobiographical arises from an unexpected
place, and thus it is able to reach the viewer without tacitly
exalting the experience of the artist as somehow more special or
more valuable than the viewer's. This is the ethic that I see
in all of the work, a kind of generosity that gives the viewers
space to rediscover things. I think of your definition of
abstraction being like this, a thing that presents itself fully,
that doesn't conceal, and that offers the viewer a form of rea-
ligned sensitivity to the world around them.

MF: Thank you very much!

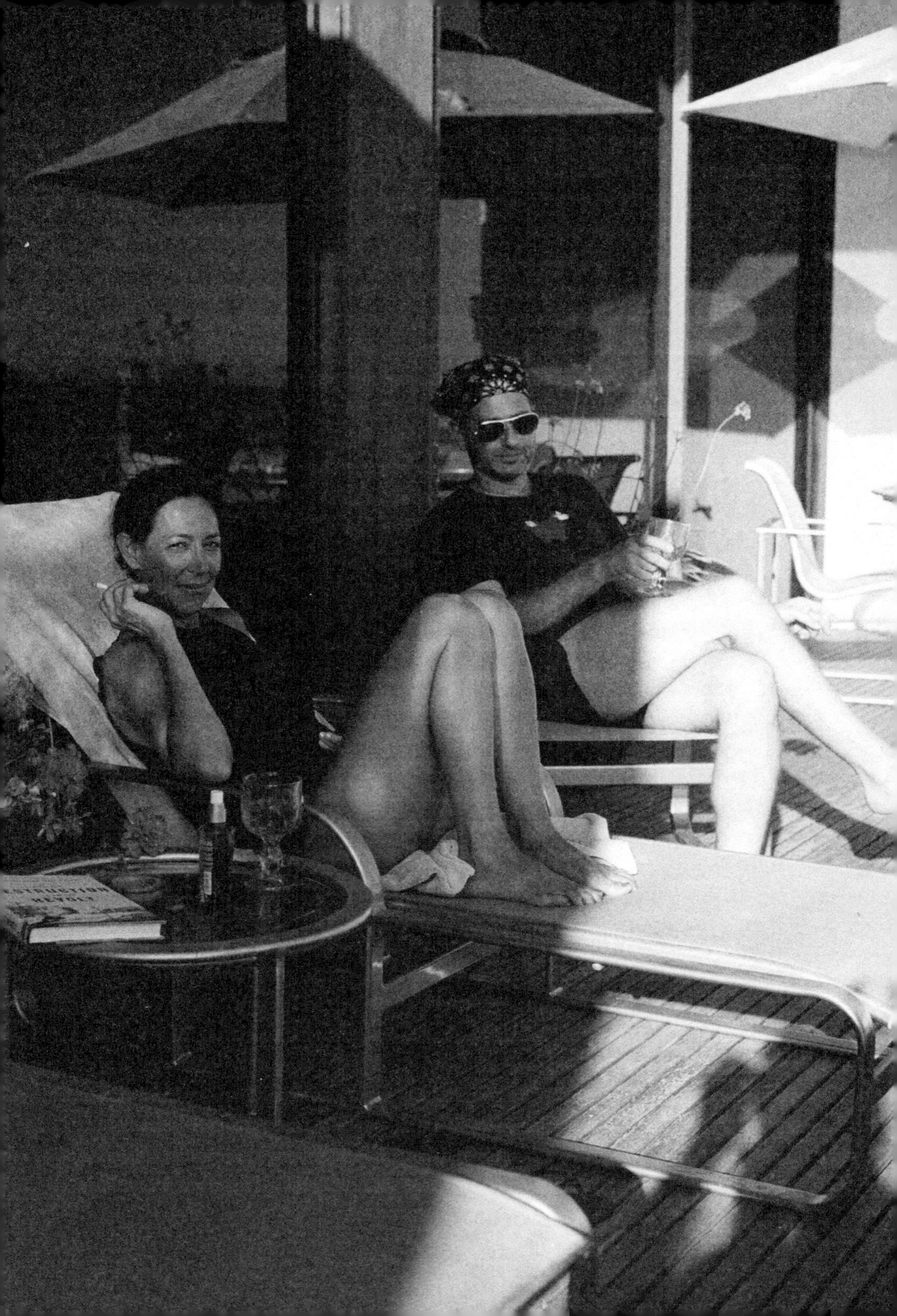

Acknowledgments
Walead Beshty

When one writes, one is on borrowed time. To write one must
recognize that the act that makes a text exist is not the writer's, but that of the reader. From their generosity a text
becomes animate, and their decision to welcome an alien voice
in good faith is an anonymous form of kindness. I did not earn
that trust, and should the writing convey the presumption
that I have, it is mere pantomime. I do not depend on writing
for my livelihood so it is not justified by necessity, nor does
the act come by the way of a natural talent that obliges me
in its cultivation. I have not toiled in academia, accruing the
commensurate accolades, nor have I offered the practice my daily
devotion. At best I've muddled through, guided by a desire to
participate in a conversation that I have not earned a place
within. Along the way, generous and patient individuals supported
my attempts to string together ideas on a page, coaxing them
to cohere. In that sense, the texts are the material manifestation of a web of unquantifiable and unacknowleged generosities.
What follows is a partial accounting of the debt that is owed.

So I will begin with the volume at hand (or in hand),
and the support of Lionel Bovier, his faith in this project, and
his untiring efforts to bring it to fruition is both flattering
and humbling. Our friendship began with his thoughtful guidance
as an editor, and grew with each of our collaborations. The books
we have done together first and foremost are the product of one

of my most treasured friendships. Albeit in a different manner,
writing brought me another of my dearest friends, George Baker,
to whom I owe a two-fold debt, not only for his personally
touching and intellectually clarifying introduction, but also
for years of friendship and impassioned discussion. George and
I met because I picked a fight with him in print (in a text published in this volume), a childish way to try to instigate a dialog with a writer and thinker whom I admired greatly. A similar
selfish desire lies at the heart of all of my writing, a desire
to speak back to those who made my intellectual world, who
inserted ideas into a mind that would be grey and fallow without them. My earliest attempts at this dialog were the equivalent of hurling little stones from the sidelines. The kindest
and most generous of my targets struck up a dialog afterward,
but none has been as formative a relationship as the one I
have had with George, and I can't thank him enough for seeing
my provocation for what it was, nor could I repay his partner
Silvia, both for her friendship and for encouraging him in
that interpretation. I realize now this was a pattern developed
between me and my father, who flinched a bit at open affection,
but would show his love by engaging fully in open-ended and
serious discussions with a six-year-old. As a child, I had no
idea I was not an intellectual equal, and he never bothered to
point this out to me even at my most petulent. The ecstacy of
impassioned discussion, the urge to pry open the world and the
presumption that I was allowed to do so, came to me through him.

I also owe a debt to my friend and studio manager John
Ryan Moore, who has now been with me for nearly a decade, and
suffered through multiple readings, and rereadings of everything
I've ever published. To Bryne Rasmussen-Smith, who provided
invaluable support and patience in seeing this through to completion, and similarly subjected herself to my work without
complaint. Their efforts exceed any possibility for remuneration.
I would also like to thank the artists and estates who trusted
me to care for their work in print, Morgan Fisher, Annette Kelm,
Luisa Lambri, Leah Levy (of The Jay DeFeo Trust), Sharon Lockhart,
Laura Owens, and Kelley Walker. Their decision to trust in me

was, and continues to be, deeply touching. I would also like to
thank all the editors and commissioners who supported my work
over the years, particularly those three of whom each simultaneously and independently commissioned my first texts, Jack
Bankowsky, Gil Blank, and Clemens Krümmel (and John Miller for
recommending me to Clemens). I leaned heavily on my friend
Bob Nickas also, who kindly read through drafts of my earliest
texts, which I was (rightly) too embarrassed to share with anyone else, and whose work gave me a model of art writing to
which I will always aspire. In addition, I would like to thank
the other editors and supporters who approached me to write,
or suffered through the process of editing, Zoe Crosher, Eli
Diner, Philipp Ekardt, Ian Farr, Bettina Funke, Craig Garrett,
Isabelle Graw, Tim Griffin, Jens Hoffmann, Alex Klein, Pablo
Lafuente, Thomas Lawson, Don McMahon, Lucy Mitchell-Innes,
Rebecca Morrill, Deidre O'Dwyer, Silke Otto-Knapp, João Ribas,
André Rottmann, Elizabeth Schambelan, Harold Silverman, Urs
Stahel, Isabel Venero, Eva Wilson, Matthew Witkovsky, and Brian
Kuan Wood. Also those who took the time to encourage and
inspire me whether by a momentary yet memorable vote of confi-
dence, or long term support, Alexander Alberro, Michael Asher,
Lewis Baltz, Christopher Bedford, Nicolas Bourriaud, François
Chantala, Laurie Dahlberg, Stan Douglas, Noam Elcott, Janine
Foeller, Andrea Fraser, Jarrett Gregory, Jane Hait, Suzanne
Hudson, Corey Keller, Alex Kitnick, John Knight, Jennifer Loh,
Roxana Marcoci, Molly Nesbit, Catherine Opie, Jacob Proctor,
Erica Redling, Shaun Regen, Eva Respini, Miljohn Ruperto,
Eric Schwab, Stephen Shore, Jason E. Smith, James Welling,
and Christopher Wood, among so many others.

Finally, those who I admired from afar, some of whom
I was lucky enough to later come to know: the critics who first
filled me with the desire to make art, Benjamin H.D. Buchloh,
Rosalind Krauss, Craig Owens, and the artists who inspired me
to write, Andrea Fraser, Dan Graham, Seth Price, Martha Rosler,
Allan Sekula, and Frances Stark.

POSITIONS 11
Walead Beshty

This book is the eleventh in the "Positions" series, dedicated to artists' writings published in French or/and English.

Series Editors: Lionel Bovier and Xavier Douroux
Associate Series Editors: Christophe Cherix and Fabrice Stroun

In the same series:

Liam Gillick, <u>Proxemics. Selected Writings (1988-2006)</u>
English, ISBN 978-3-905701-01-2

Dan Graham, <u>Nuggets. New and Old Writing on Art, Architecture, and Culture</u>
English, ISBN 978-3-03764-198-9

Susan Hiller, <u>The Provisional Texture of Reality. Selected Talks and Texts (1977-2007)</u>
English, ISBN: 978-3-905829-56-3

Mike Kelley, <u>Interviews, Conversations, and Chit-Chat (1986-2004)</u>
English, ISBN 978-3-905701-00-5

Thomas Lawson, <u>Mining for Gold. Selected Writings (1976-2002)</u>
English, ISBN 978-2-940271-22-1

John Miller, <u>The Price Club. Selected Writings (1977-1998)</u>
English, ISBN 978-2-940271-05-4

John Miller, <u>The Ruin of Exchange, And Other Writings on Art</u>
English, ISBN 978-3-03764-194-1

Yvonne Rainer, <u>Une femme qui… Écrits, entretiens, essais critiques</u>
French, ISBN 978-2-84066-262-4 (Les presses du réel)

David Robbins, <u>The Velvet Grind. Selected Essays, Interviews, Satires (1983-2005)</u>
English, ISBN 978-3-905701-02-9

Special edition:

Robert Morris, <u>Bemerkungen zur Skulptur. Zwölf Texte</u>
German, ISBN: 978-3-03764-128-6

Editor
Lionel Bovier

Editorial Coordination
Bryne Rasmussen-Smith

Editing and Proofreading
Clare Manchester

Design Concept
Gilles Gavillet & Cornel Windlin

Design
Nicolas Eigenheer & Vera Kaspar

Typeface
Number Two, Martha Stutteregger, Vienna

Cover
Armin Linke, Milan (www.arminlinke.com)

Printing and Binding
Présence Graphique, Monts (Indre-et-Loire)

Photo Credits
All images used to illustrate this book stem from Walead Beshty's
Industrial Portraits (2007-) and Art Handling (2009-) series.

ISBN: 978-3-03764-442-3

Printed in Europe

PUBLISHED BY

JRP|Ringier
Limmatstrasse 270
CH-8005 Zurich
T +41 (0) 43 311 27 50
F +41 (0) 43 311 27 51
E info@jrp-ringier.com
www.jrp-ringier.com

DISTRIBUTION

JRP|Ringier books are available internationally at selected bookstores
and from the following distribution partners:

Switzerland
AVA Verlagsauslieferung AG, Centralweg 16, CH-8910 Affoltern a.A.,
verlagsservice@ava.ch, www.ava.ch

France
Les presses du réel, 35 rue Colson, F-21000 Dijon,
info@lespressesdureel.com, www.lespressesdureel.com

Germany and Austria
Vice Versa Distribution, Immanuelkirchstrasse 12, D-10405 Berlin,
info@vice-versa-distribution.com, www.vice-versa-distribution.com

UK and other European countries
Cornerhouse Publications, HOME, 2 Tony Wilson Place, UK-Manchester M15 4FN,
publications@cornerhouse.org, www.cornerhousepublications.org/books

USA, Canada, Asia, and Australia
ARTBOOK|D.A.P., 155 Sixth Avenue, 2nd Floor, USA-New York, NY 10013,
orders@dapinc.com, www.artbook.com

For a list of our partner bookshops or for any general questions,
please contact JRP|Ringier directly at info@jrp-ringier.com,
or visit our homepage www.jrp-ringier.com for further information
about our program.